Welcome to...
Personal Computers

3RD EDITION

By Kris Jamsa

MIS:
PRESS

A Subsidiary of
Henry Holt and Co., Inc.

First Edition—1995

Printed in the United States of America.

Library of Congress Cataloging-in-Publication Data

Jamsa, Kris A.
    Welcome to— personal computers / Kris Jamsa. — 3rd ed.
        p.   cm.
    ISBN 1-55828-421-4
    1. Microcomputers.   I. Title.
QA76.5.J32   1995
004.165—dc20   95-9412
                                                                                 CIP

10 9 8 7 6 5 4 3 2 1

Associate Publisher: *Paul Farrell*

Managing Editor: *Cary Sullivan*   Production Editor: *Anne Alessi*
Development Editor: *Judy Brief*   Technical Editor: *Phil Schmauder*
Copy Edit Manager: *Shari Chappell*   Copy Editor: *Winifred Davis*

Table of Contents

LESSON 6: Getting to Know Your Monitor   61

LESSON 7: Getting to Know Your Printer   75

LESSON 8: Getting to Know Your Disk 91

LESSON 9: Of Mice and Men 111

LESSON 38: PC Do's and Don'ts   341

LESSON 42: Commonly Asked Questions   379

Introduction

By virtue of the fact that you picked up this book, you either want to learn about personal computers, or someone else thinks you need to. In either case, you picked up the right book.

If you are like most people, just the thought of learning about computers is scary. You probably already have enough stress in your life without worrying about computers. Relax. By following the lessons in this book, you will find that learning to use a personal computer (we'll call them PCs) is quite easy. Our goal isn't to turn you into a computer scientist. Instead, we'll first make you comfortable with the PC, and then we'll make you productive. Each lesson is short, written to take only 10 or 15 minutes of your time. As you read, feel free to skip around. Although the book's lessons build upon a previous lesson's topic, you may have a need to understand modems or printers to help you complete a purchase. You can jump to those lessons as you need them.

Who Should Read This Book?

If you just bought a PC, are thinking about buying one, or your boss just put one on your desk, this book is for you. In just a few minutes you'll get to know the PC, what makes it work, and more importantly, what it can do for you. We'll talk about the problems that users who don't read this book encounter, and the ways you can avoid them. If you are thinking about buying your own PC or new software programs, this book contains buyer's guides you should follow to save time and money.

Before You Get Started

There's no rule that says learning about PCs can't be fun. Just as you can watch a lot of videos without knowing how to program your VCR, you don't have to be a programmer to put your PC to work. Take a few minutes and review Lesson 1. You will be amazed at just how fast you learn.

If you need specifics on what you'll learn, quickly review the following list. If some of the terms are new, don't worry, you'll learn about each of them in the lessons that make up this book:

- ❖ Understand the pieces that make up your computer and how to connect them together! Setting up a computer is very easy!
- ❖ Understand software (computer programs), how they work, how to use them, and tricks you can use to get started faster.
- ❖ Examine buyer's guides for software, modems, printers, memory, disks, tapes, and even multimedia software and hardware.
- ❖ Learn the current trends and ways to keep your expensive investment from becoming obsolete.
- ❖ Understand what DOS is and why you need it.
- ❖ Learn step by step procedures you can follow when your hardware or software doesn't work.
- ❖ Learn how to feel at home with your computer so it can help you accomplish your tasks at hand!
- ❖ ... and much, much more!

Lesson 1: Getting to Know Your Computer

Everyone is understandably nervous when they decide to learn how to use a computer. After all, computers are very powerful devices, involved in almost every part of our lives. Most new cars, television sets, and microwave ovens use a computer. Luckily, you don't have to be a computer programmer to watch your TV—you just have to know a few basics.

As you will find, once you learn a few fundamentals about the personal computer (we'll call it a *PC* for short), you'll replace your computer fears with confidence. Remember, just as you don't need to be an auto mechanic to drive your car, you don't need to be a scientist to put your computer to work.

This lesson introduces you to the PC. You'll learn about the computer's three major parts: the *system unit*, *monitor*, and *keyboard*, and the differences between computers such as the IBM PC and the Macintosh. You'll also learn what is meant by *hardware* and *software*, and lastly, we will take a look at a computer buyer's guide.

The PC's Three Major Parts

Regardless of the computer type, all PCs consist of three major parts: a system unit (sometimes called the *chassis*), a monitor, and a keyboard. Figure 1.1 shows these three parts for three different types of IBM PC compatible computers.

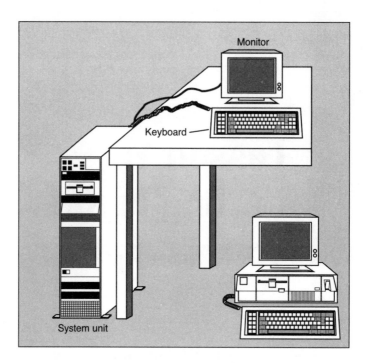

FIGURE 1.1 The system unit, monitor, and keyboard for two types of IBM-PC compatible computers.

Figure 1.1 illustrates a desktop computer and a tower-based computer that sits underneath or next to your desk. Both computer types perform the same function. Experienced users who often add new hardware to their computers find the tower-based computer convenient because the system unit is easy to access. In addition, tower-based computers free up considerable space on your desk. However, if you use a tower-based computer, you must place it in a safe location where it will not be accidentally knocked over and is out of the path of your vacuum. As you will learn, your vacuum can generate an electronic (static) flux that can damage the information stored on your computer's disk. If you use a desktop computer, keep it away from your telephone and electronic pencil sharpener for similar reasons.

Although this book's discussion focuses on IBM compatible personal computers, many of the concepts we'll discuss relate to other computer types such as an Apple II or Macintosh. Figure 1.2 illustrates the three primary computer parts for these two types of computers. Figure 1.3 illustrates a laptop, sometimes called a *notebook computer*. As you can see, the laptop combines the monitor, keyboard, and system unit into one case.

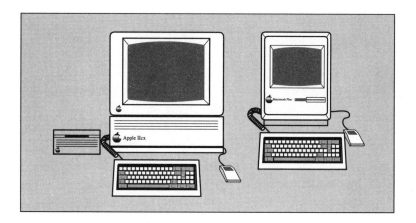

FIGURE 1.2 The system unit, monitor, and keyboard for an Apple II and Macintosh computer.

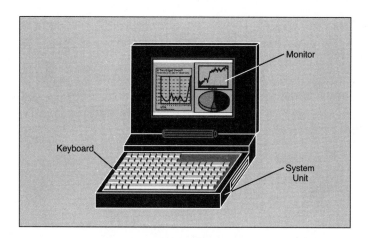

FIGURE 1.3 The system unit, monitor, and keyboard for a laptop computer.

Understanding the System Unit

A computer, like your television or stereo, contains powerful electronics. Most of these electronics reside within the system unit. The computer's powerful *central processing unit* (its electronic brain, or *CPU* for short) as well as the computer's memory reside within the system unit. When users talk about 486 and Pentium computers, they are actually talking about your computer's CPU. Each CPU has a unique name (number) that corresponds to its power and speed. The Pentium, for example, is newer and faster than a 486. Likewise, most system units hold one or more floppy or hard disk drives that you will use to store information from one computer session to the next.

Most new users do not have a need to open the computer's system unit. In fact, because the computer's internal electronics are easily damaged, you should only open the system unit when you need to add new hardware. Also, should you ever need to open the system unit, make sure you first unplug it.

In Lesson 3 you will learn how to set up a PC. At that time, you will learn how to connect the cables from the keyboard and monitor to the system unit. In Lesson 10 you will learn the steps you must follow to add new hardware to your system unit.

Understanding Your Monitor

The computer's monitor (or screen) lets you view the information you type, as well as the computer's response to your information. Think of the monitor as a small television set. Like a TV, the monitor can display information in black and white or in color. Most inexpensive laptop computers, for example, use black and white (monochrome) screens. As shown in Figure 1.4, your monitor has its own on/off switch as well as control knobs that let you adjust the screen's brightness and sharpness. Lesson 6 examines PC monitors in detail.

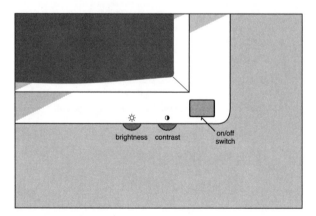

FIGURE 1.4 The computer's monitor has its own on/off switch and picture controls.

Understanding Your Keyboard

The keyboard lets you type information into the computer. The information might direct the computer to perform a specific command, or it may be a letter or report you are creating using a word processor. As you'll learn in Lesson 5, typing at your computer's keyboard is much easier than using a typewriter. If you mistype a word or letter, you can quickly correct your mistake and continue. If you have not typed before, or if you want to improve your typing speed, you can buy a software typing tutorial that runs on your computer. After only a few lessons, you'll be amazed how your typing skills increase.

Other Hardware Devices

Although the monitor lets you view information, you will normally need to print copies of your reports, letters, and other key information. As you will learn in Lesson 7, you can attach a printer to your system unit as shown in Figure 1.5.

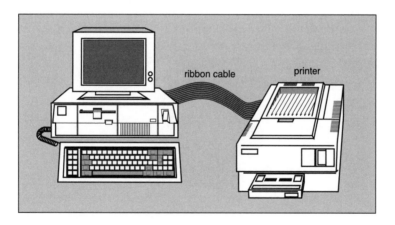

FIGURE 1.5 Like a keyboard and monitor, the printer attaches to the system unit.

Today, PCs come with a small hand-held device called a *mouse*, as shown in Figure 1.6. Using a mouse, many software programs let you quickly choose menu options, move throughout a large report or other document, or perform one of many program specific functions. To use your mouse, you slide the handheld device across your desktop. As you move your mouse, a small arrow-like pointer moves across your computer screen. To select a menu option using your mouse, for example, you aim your mouse at the option and then click the select button on your mouse. Like other hardware devices, you attach a mouse to the system unit. Lesson 9 looks at the mouse in detail.

FIGURE 1.6 A mouse lets you quickly perform a wide variety of program specific functions.

Because you may use your laptop computer in cramped quarters, such as an airplane, there may be times when using a mouse becomes difficult or impossible.

As shown in Figure 1.7, many laptop computers provide a built-in track ball that performs the same function as a mouse. However, as you will learn in Lesson 9, you can connect a standard mouse to most laptop computers when you are working at a desk.

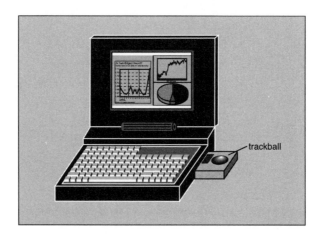

FIGURE 1.7 Laptop computers often use a trackball instead of a mouse.

Hardware and Software Work Together

To this point, this lesson's discussion has focused on your computer's hardware, its physical components such as the system unit, keyboard, cables, and nuts and bolts. Hardware, however, is only half the picture. To perform useful work, you use the computer's hardware to run software (software is computer programs). Lesson 2 discusses many common software programs including word processors, spreadsheets, and even computer games. Depending on the task you want the computer to perform, you will run a specific program. For example, to create a letter or report you would run a word processing program. Likewise, to track your bills and check book, you would run a personal accounting program, such as Quicken or Microsoft Money. For now, simply understand that software directs your computer to perform a specific task.

The PC Versus the Macintosh

Although the term PC was intended to abbreviate the words personal computer, over the years, PC has come to mean an IBM PC or PC compatible. A *compatible* PC is a PC that runs the same software programs as an IBM. Many people refer to compatibles as *clones*. Computer magazines are filled with advertisements of companies selling PC compatibles.

Apple Computer's Macintosh is not IBM compatible. In general, software programs written to run on the IBM PC will not run on the Macintosh and vice versa. Which computer is better? The one that best suits your needs.

If you use a PC or Macintosh at work, you'll probably want the same at home. Likewise, if you are buying a computer for a student who uses Apple II computers at school, a similar Apple may be your best choice.

In general, after you read Lesson 2, decide on the type of software you want to use. Next, buy a computer that supports the software. As it turns out, a newer system built by Apple and IBM called the *PowerPC* is capable of running Mac and IBM-PC software. If you work in an office that exchanges files between Mac and PC users, you may find the PowerPC is more cost-effective than purchasing both a Mac and a PC.

Damaging Your Computer's Hardware

For the most part, if you treat your computer's hardware with the same care as you would treat a television or stereo set, you will not damage your computer. By turning your computer equipment on and off, you cannot damage your equipment. However, as you'll learn, you can damage the information stored on your disk by turning your computer off at the wrong times. As a general rule, never turn off your computer while you have a software program running. By following this rule you will not damage your equipment or lose information stored on your disk.

Your PC Buyer's Guide

If you have not already bought your PC, please put off doing so until you have finished reading this book. Many of this book's lessons include buyer's guides to specific pieces of hardware.

Your first trip to the computer store can be very intimidating. There are many computer types, hardware options, and even more software programs. Unless you have a basic idea of the capabilities you need, the salesman must guess.

To start, make a list of the basic software programs you want, such as a word processor or spreadsheet. A salesman can explain the features that different programs provide. If possible, attend a PC user group meeting and discuss the software recommendations with experienced users. Take your time making your software selections. The cost of your various software programs can quickly add up to surpass your hardware costs.

Also, you probably don't want to purchase all your software at once. Every software program takes time to learn. Trying to learn too many programs too fast is a very frustrating experience.

Before you buy your hardware or software, take time to review several computer magazines to be sure the prices you have been given are fairly close to those listed in the magazines. In most cases, the mail order companies have lower prices. Initially, however, you may want to pay the extra cost for the support a local dealer can provide you.

Remember, many of the lessons in this book include buyer's guides for specific hardware. Use these guides as you select your system unit, monitor, printer, disk drives, and so on.

Lastly, compare the warranties and support options each dealership offers. Many local dealerships offer classes that can help you get up and running faster. In fact, you may find it very helpful to take an introductory class or two before you purchase your computer.

A Word on Extended Warranties

When you shop for a computer at a large computer store, one of your buying options is whether or not you want to purchase an extended warranty. Most computers come with a standard warranty which will cover the entire computer for 30 to 90 days.

The extended warranty increases the coverage to a year or more. As it turns out, if a computer is going to fail (quit working), the computer will probably do so within the first few days after you bring it home. If you only use your PC once in a while at home and you have access to an experienced user who can diagnose simple hardware errors, you probably don't need to have an extended warranty.

However, if your computer is an integral part of your business and you can't quickly diagnose and repair hardware errors on your own, you can consider the extended warranty as an insurance policy. Hopefully, you will never need to use the extended warranty, however, if you experience hardware errors, your extended warranty may give you preferential treatment at the computer store.

Computer Checklist

❖ Do you have a computer at work or school with which you need to be compatible?

❖ What software programs do you need?

– Word processor

– Spreadsheet

– Database

– Desktop

– Desktop Publishing

– Games

– Others

❖ What is the hardware warranty?

❖ What is the technical support policy?

❖ What training is available?

❖ What capabilities do you need today?

❖ What capabilities do you want in the future?

Putting It All Together

Although a personal computer is a very powerful device, you don't have to be a computer expert to effectively use the PC. The PC combines hardware (the computer's physical parts) with software (computer programs) to accomplish specific tasks.

Computers that can run the same programs are called *compatibles*. Because the IBM PC and the Apple Macintosh are not compatible, you cannot run software written for one on the other. Compatible computers can look very different. As shown in this lesson, an IBM PC compatible can be a desktop, laptop, or even a tower-based computer.

PCs have three primary parts: the system unit that contains most of the PC's electronics, the keyboard, and a monitor. Most users connect a printer and possibly a mouse to their computer.

Purchasing a PC represents a large investment. Take your time to carefully identify your hardware and software needs.

Glossary

clone or compatible
A computer that can freely exchange software (and possibly hardware parts) with another computer.

extended warranty
A warranty sold to you by a computer store that extends the basic warranty provided with your computer.

hardware
The computer's physical parts, such as the system unit, keyboard, monitor, as well as the cables that connect them.

PC   A personal computer.

software   Computer programs written to perform specific
                          tasks, such as a word processor or spreadsheet.

Lesson 2:
Using Software to Put Your Computer to Work

In Lesson 1 you learned that software consists of computer programs that tell your computer's hardware to perform a specific task, such as creating letters and reports using a word processor. Without software, your computer's hardware can do nothing. This lesson takes a look at several of the most common software programs in use today. The discussion should help you answer the question "What do I want my computer to do?"

Understanding Application Software

Software that helps you perform a specific task, such as word processing, accounting, or information management (a database) is *application software*. This section introduces you to several common application programs.

Creating Letters and Documents Using a Word Processor

The most commonly used application program is a *word processor* that lets you create letters, office memos, or professional quality reports. Using a word processor, you can type in your document and print one or more copies. If you need to make changes to the document, the word processor lets you quickly add, move, or delete text. Figure 2.1 illustrates how your screen might appear if you created a letter using a popular word processor.

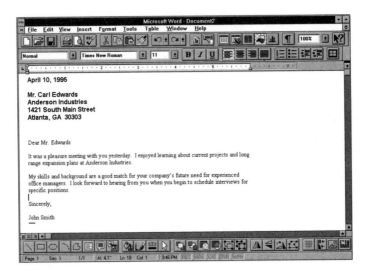

FIGURE 2.1 Creating a letter using a word processor.

Word processors let you format your document, using different character sizes and fonts. Figure 2.2 illustrates a printed word processing document.

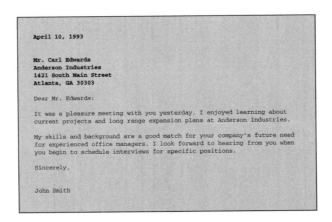

FIGURE 2.2 A printed word processing document.

In addition to letting you create, change, and print documents, most word processors provide a spell checker that examines your document for misspelled words. If a word is misspelled, the spell checker provides a list of possible corrections. Figure 2.3 for example, illustrates a spell checker's detection of a misspelled word and the possible list of alternatives.

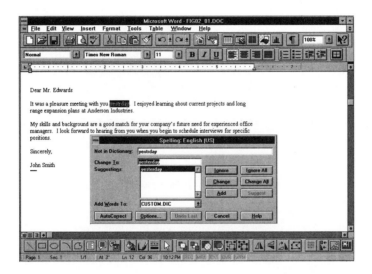

FIGURE 2.3 Spell checking a word processing document.

In addition to the spell checker many word processors can check your document's grammar, analyzing your sentences and helping you correct errors such as missing commas or other incorrect punctuation. By combining a spell and grammar checker, you can feel confident about the quality of your document. As shown in Figure 2.4, many word processors allow you to combine text and graphics (pictures) within your documents.

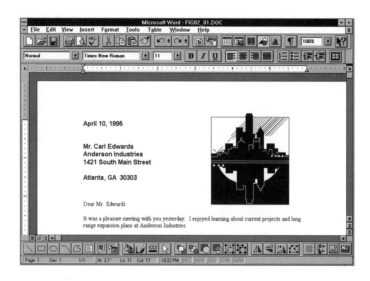

FIGURE 2.4 Combining text and graphics in a word processing document.

There are many different word processing programs available, whose capabilities and costs differ. Table 2.1 lists several of the most popular word processing programs.

TABLE 2.1 COMMON WORD PROCESSING PROGRAMS.

Software Name	Company Name
Word for Windows	Microsoft Corporation
WordPerfect for Windows	WordPerfect Corporation
Ami Pro for Windows	Lotus Corporation
WordPerfect for DOS	WordPerfect Corporation

Simplifying Accounting Operations Using a Spreadsheet

A spreadsheet program is software that displays on your screen an electronic version of an accountant's worksheet as shown.

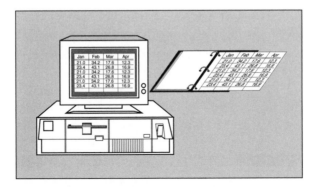

Using a spreadsheet, you can put aside your electronic calculator or adding machine. The spreadsheet software lets you quickly add rows or columns of values. Figure 2.5 illustrates how a spreadsheet program used for tracking your monthly expenses might appear on your screen.

FIGURE 2.5 Spreadsheet programs provide electronic worksheets.

Using a spreadsheet you can quickly balance your checkbook, manage your household budget, or even track your favorite stocks. Unlike a paper worksheet whose size is fixed, many electronic spreadsheets let you work with over a million values!

Many businesses use spreadsheets to perform "What if" calculations. Because a spreadsheet program can quickly perform complex calculations that may use thousands of values, an analyst can determine what the result would be, if they changed one or more values, such as product cost, or sales commission.

In addition to displaying values in their numeric form, many spreadsheet programs can display data using meaningful graphs, which let you quickly note important trends. Figure 2.6 illustrates two graphs for the previous budget information.

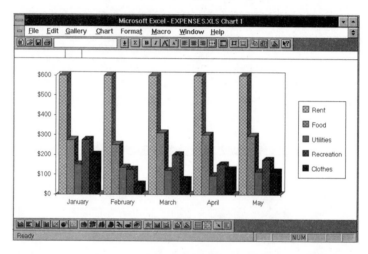

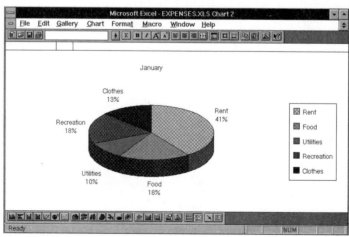

FIGURE 2.6 Using meaningful graphs to display data, spreadsheets let you quickly note important trends.

As was the case with word processors, there are many spreadsheet programs with different capabilities and costs. Table 2.2 lists several of the more popular spreadsheet packages.

TABLE 2.2 COMMON SPREADSHEET PROGRAMS.

Software Name	Company Name
Excel for Windows	Microsoft Corporation
Lotus 1-2-3 for Windows	Lotus Corporation
Quatro Pro for Windows	Borland International

Organizing Information Using a Database

Almost everyone keeps lists of one type or another, possibly a list of your relatives' birth dates, or detailed customer information. A *database* is a collection of information. A database program is software that helps you store, organize, and later retrieve information. Your database can be as simple as a mailing list of possible clients as shown in Figure 2.7 or it can be complex, containing many pieces of information (called fields of the database) as shown in Figure 2.8.

First Name	Initial	Last Name	Address	City	State	Zip Code
John	A	Anderson	1521 S. Maple St.	Las Vegas	NV	89119
Robert	J	Wilson	6791 W. Imperial Ave	Troy	NY	12180
Paul		Miller	3265 E. 15th Street	Berkeley	CA	94710
David	P	Workman	4813 Jeronimo	Irvine	CA	92714
Sam	W	Black	315 South Wilson Blvd	Wheeling	IL	60098
Gregg	C	Brown	P.O. Box 623	Jefferson	SD	57030
Ted	F	Simpson	4592 N. Cricket Ave	San Diego	CA	92121
Lance	O	Freeman	1 Cambridge Pkwy	Cambridge	MA	2142
Peter	A	Newman	8650 Vineyard Ave	St. Louis	MO	63130
Michael	G	Foster	P.O. Box 465	Richardson	TX	75001
Jerry	S	Ross	6723 S. Jones	Peabody	MA	1960

Table: Clients — Record: 1

FIGURE 2.7 A simple mailing list database.

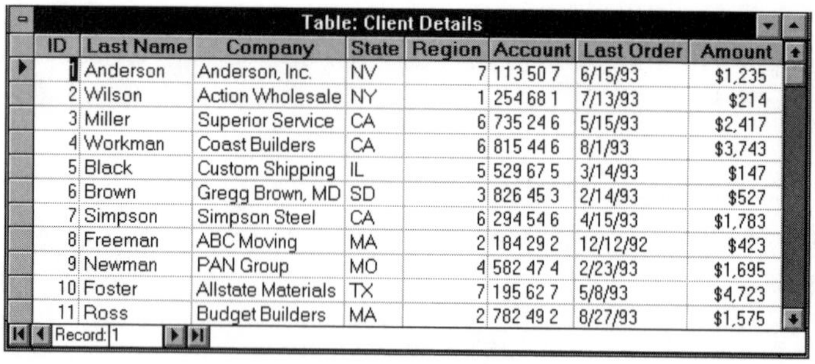

Table: Client Details							
ID	Last Name	Company	State	Region	Account	Last Order	Amount
1	Anderson	Anderson, Inc.	NV	7	113 50 7	6/15/93	$1,235
2	Wilson	Action Wholesale	NY	1	254 68 1	7/13/93	$214
3	Miller	Superior Service	CA	6	735 24 6	5/15/93	$2,417
4	Workman	Coast Builders	CA	6	815 44 6	8/1/93	$3,743
5	Black	Custom Shipping	IL	5	529 67 5	3/14/93	$147
6	Brown	Gregg Brown, MD	SD	3	826 45 3	2/14/93	$527
7	Simpson	Simpson Steel	CA	6	294 54 6	4/15/93	$1,783
8	Freeman	ABC Moving	MA	2	184 29 2	12/12/92	$423
9	Newman	PAN Group	MO	4	582 47 4	2/23/93	$1,695
10	Foster	Allstate Materials	TX	7	195 62 7	5/8/93	$4,723
11	Ross	Budget Builders	MA	2	782 49 2	8/27/93	$1,575

Record: 1

FIGURE 2.8 A database can contain many pieces of information called *fields*.

Using a database program, you can sort the information on a specific field, such as by name or zip code, or you can extract database entries that meet specific criteria. For example, a real estate agent might want to know the addresses of homes on the market, in a specific neighborhood, that have at least 3 bedrooms, a garage, and are under $125,000. Table 2.3 lists several of the most commonly used database programs.

TABLE 2.3 COMMON DATABASE PROGRAMS.

Software Name	Company Name
Access	Microsoft Corporation
FoxPro	Microsoft Corporation
dBASE IV	Borland International
Paradox	Borland International
Dataflex	Data Access Corporation

Publishing Newsletters and Professional Quality Reports

The PC's capabilities have changed people's quality expectations for reports and newsletters. In the past, companies often sent their documents out for typesetting, an expensive and time-consuming process. Desktop publishing software, however, gives users the ability to create (publish) professional quality newsletters and reports using the PC that sits right on their desk. This book, for example, was created using PC-based desktop publishing! By creating these documents them-selves, businesses not only save typesetting costs, they can easily add or change text and graphics at any time. Figure 2.9 illustrates a sample document produced via desktop publishing.

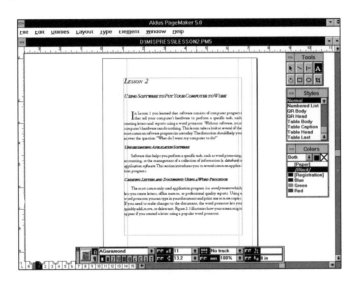

FIGURE 2.9 Desktop publishing software lets you create professional quality documents.

Desktop publishing software is very powerful, and as such, more difficult to use than a word processor. If you are new to computers, you'll want to get com-fortable with a word processor before you jump into desktop publishing. Table 2.4 lists several desktop publishing programs.

TABLE 2.4 COMMON DESKTOP PUBLISHING PROGRAMS.

Software Name	Company Name
Ventura	Corel Systems
Pagemaker	Aldus Corporation
QuarkXpress	Quark
PFS: First Publisher	Software Publishing Corp.
Publish It!	Timeworks

Pictures for Slides, Newsletters, and Presentations

Whether you are producing a company report, a newsletter, or a slide presentation, a picture is worth a thousand words. Graphics software lets you create your own pictures and use or change one or more of the images that accompany the software. In fact, graphics software has become so popular, software companies sell disks containing pictures for almost every profession. Figure 2.10 illustrates several such images, which are called *clip art*.

FIGURE 2.10 Samples of pictures available on clip art disks.

Clip art is so named because you can quickly clip it into your newsletter, slides, or other documents. Using your word processor, for example, you can place clip art images into a letter or report. Figure 2.11 shows how a graphics program might appear on your screen.

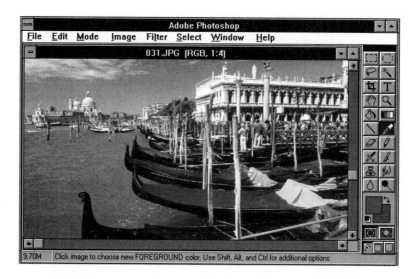

FIGURE 2.11 The screen appearance of a graphics program.

Table 2.5 lists several commonly used graphics programs.

TABLE 2.5 COMMON GRAPHICS PROGRAMS.

Software Name	Company Name
Harvard Graphics	Software Publishing Corp.
Animator	Autodesk
Draw Perfect	WordPerfect Corporation
CorelDraw	Corel Systems
PowerPoint	Microsoft Corporation

Computer-Aided Design

Because of its ability to respond to changes, many engineers and draftsmen have begun using *computer-aided design* (or *CAD*) software to draw buildings, boats, or even the arrangement of furniture in an office. Rather than having to draw—and later redraw—an object on paper by hand, the user draws the object using the computer screen and a mouse. Figure 2.12 illustrates the use of a CAD program. After the designer draws the image, the CAD software lets the designer change the object's size, rotate the object for viewing from a different perspective, or even merge the object with other objects to complete a design.

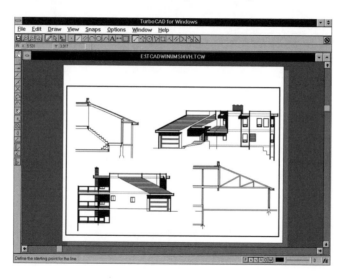

FIGURE 2.12 The screen appearance of a CAD program.

Table 2.6 lists several commonly used CAD programs.

TABLE 2.6 COMMON CAD PROGRAMS.

Software Name	Company Name
Autocad	Autodesk
Generic CADD	GenericSoftware
DesignCad 3-D	American Small Business Corporation

Educational Software

From typing tutorials to foreign language instruction to algebra, the number of educational programs available for the PC is endless. If you are planning to buy a computer to help a student, you'll probably want to buy the same computer type the student is using at school. If you already own a PC and the student is using an Apple at school, find out the name of the programs the school is using. You can probably purchase many of the same programs for the PC.

Whether you are interested in learning more about computers or about flight instruction, you can probably find software to help you. Just ask your computer dealer for a list of the available software.

Computer Games

If "all work and no play made Jack a dull boy," Jack didn't own a PC. Over the past ten years, computer games have emerged for users of all ages—from simple video games for kids to very realistic games such as Flight Simulator, which gives you the feel of flying an airplane. Be aware, computer games can be very addictive. You probably don't want to install games on office computers.

On-Line Services and Bulletin Boards

Lesson 19 discusses how a hardware device called a *modem* lets two computers exchange information over a phone line. By joining a service such as Compu-Serve or Prodigy (you pay a monthly fee, plus long distance charges) you can use your computer to shop, make flight reservations, get information about stocks, get up-to-date world news or weather information, or exchange messages with other users around the world.

If you have computer questions to which you can't find the answers, almost every city has a local computer bulletin board you can access using a modem. Other users who access the bulletin board can read your questions and offer solutions.

NOTE

Accessing bulletin boards or on-line services using a modem is no different from making a phone call. If you are calling a local number, there is no charge. If you are calling long distance, the phone company bills you the normal amount for a long distance call.

Lesson 30 introduces the Internet, today's information highway. Using the Internet, you can exchange electronic mail and files with users around the world. Likewise, Lesson 34 introduces the graphics-based World Wide Web which lets you access the Internet by pointing and clicking your mouse through hypertext documents. Millions of users access the Internet each day. In the future, most key software programs will provide support for the Internet.

Personal Information Management

Computers are quickly becoming a business person's right hand, storing such information as phone numbers, appointments, schedules, project deadlines, and other personal information. *Personal information management* (or *PIM*) software helps you manage the information you need on a daily basis. Figure 2.13 illustrates a simple appointment calendar that lets you schedule your day. By consolidating meeting dates, phone numbers, addresses, and other information you use regularly, PIM software has become very popular.

FIGURE 2.13 Scheduling daily appointments.

Multimedia Software

Multimedia is the combination of text, graphics, sound, and video to present information in a more meaningful way. The 1990s is destined to become the decade of multimedia programs that let your computer display video while generating sounds. Using multimedia, programs can teach a foreign language, generate the sounds of a jungle, or even let the user experience the sounds of the jungle. Multimedia programs are a very powerful teaching tool. Figure 2.14 illustrates a multimedia program by *Microsoft* called Cinemania that lets users watch and hear clips from their favorite movies.

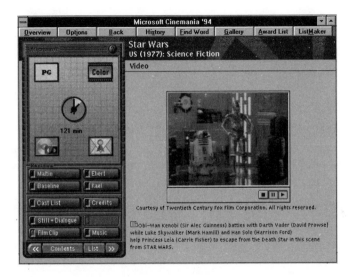

FIGURE 2.14 Watching video within a multimedia program.

Financial Management Software

One of the most popular uses of software in the past few years has been household financial management. Many software programs have emerged that help you balance your checkbook, determine your budget, and even track your tax deductions. Using financial management software you can generate and print your own checks, produce budget reports, or even pay bills electronically using a modem. Figure 2.15 illustrates an electronic check that you can fill in and print using one financial software package.

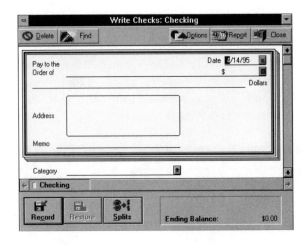

FIGURE 2.15 Preparing an electronic check.

Table 2.7 lists several popular financial management software programs.

TABLE 2.7 POPULAR FINANCIAL MANAGEMENT SOFTWARE.

Software Name	Company
Quicken	Intuit
Microsoft Money	Microsoft Corporation
Managing Your Money	MECA Software

Each year on April 15, millions of Americans rush to complete their taxes. Today, many computer users quickly and accurately complete their taxes using a tax program such as Turbo Tax. Using a tax program, users can not only complete their taxes, they can send their tax forms to the IRS electronically. In the future, most tax returns will be completed electronically in this way. Figure 2.16, for example, illustrates a software program for completing income taxes.

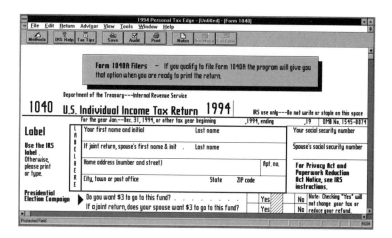

FIGURE 2.16 A software program for completing income taxes.

Electronic Mail

Users whose PCs are connected to a network or who use their modems to dial into on-line services such as Prodigy, AOL, or CompuServe often exchange electronic messages, or e-mail. Using e-mail software, you can send messages or files to one or more users. Likewise, users can use their e-mail software to read messages they receive from other users. Figure 2.17 illustrates an e-mail software program.

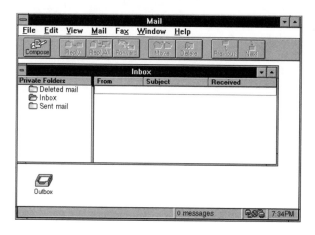

FIGURE 2.17 E-mail software lets users send and receive electronic messages.

Most users have little choice over the e-mail software they use. Normally, their network administrator chooses the e-mail program for use by all network users.

Fax Software

As the number of home offices as well as the number of users who travel with their PCs grows, the ability for users to send and receive faxes has become a must. Using fax software and a modem, users can send and receive faxes. After the fax software receives an incoming fax, the user can view the fax on screen, print the fax, or save the fax to a file on disk. Figure 2.18, for example, shows how an incoming fax might appear on a user's screen.

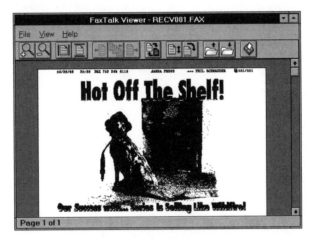

FIGURE 2.18 Fax software lets users send and receive faxes.

One shortcoming of using fax software and your PC as opposed to a fax machine is that you cannot send a paper fax, such as a contract you have just signed. However, if you have a scanner, you can scan a document to produce an electronic file that you can then send using your fax software.

Shell Software

A *shell* is a program that lets you run other programs. In many cases, a shell program displays a menu from which you can easily run other programs such as a word processor, spreadsheet, or your financial manager. The advantage of using a shell program is that you don't need to remember different commands to run your programs. Instead, you simply select the program you want from a menu. As you learn DOS, your computer's disk operating system provides a shell from which you can run programs. Figure 2.19 illustrates a menu of different programs you can select using the DOS shell.

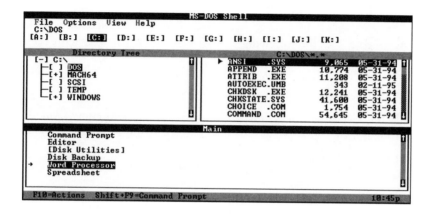

FIGURE 2.19 **Running programs using a shell.**

Software Suites

A *software* suite is a collection of programs that software companies bundle together to provide users with the key software they need such as a word processor, spreadsheet, database, and even a graphics program. By bundling the software into a single package, software companies ensure that users purchase and use more of their products. End users benefit from software suites because they pay significantly less for the software suite than they would for the individual software programs. Table 2.8 lists several different office suites.

TABLE 2.8 POPULAR SOFTWARE SUITES.

Software Suite	Company
Microsoft Office	Microsoft Corporation
SmartSuite	Lotus Corporation
Perfect Office	Novell Inc.

Software Buyer's Guide

As you have seen, the number of software programs is almost limitless. As discussed in Lesson 1, your software costs can quickly exceed the cost of your computer. Take the time to research a software program before you buy it. As was the case for purchasing hardware, check several computer magazines to compare the software cost. Use the following checklist guide to help you with your software purchases:

* List the capabilities the software must perform.
* Is the software compatible with your existing computer, monitor, and printer?
* Does the software require additional hardware such as more memory or a mouse?
* Does your computer support multimedia software? (See Lesson 23.)
* Is the software compatible with your version of DOS or Windows? (See Lesson 12.)
* What size floppy disk do you need for the software? (See Lesson 8.)
* Does the manufacturer provide technical support?
* Does the retailer provide training? Are books about the software available?
* What is the policy on returns? Most companies only allow returns for defective disks.

Putting It All Together

Software is the computer program that tells your computer's hardware what to do. If you want your computer to perform a specific task, you need to first run the corresponding software. In Lesson 37 you'll learn how to install newly purchased software on your computer so you can use it.

Glossary

application software   A computer program that performs a specific task such as word processing.

CAD

An abbreviation for computer-aided design. CAD software helps engineers and drafters create and change complex designs using a computer screen and mouse.

clip art

Pictures and other graphic images you can place unchanged in a report, newsletter or other document.

database

An organized collection of information.

database software

A computer program that helps you store, sort, print, and retrieve information.

desktop publishing

The creation and printing of professional quality reports and newsletters using a personal computer.

e-mail

An acronym for electronic mail. E-mail is a message sent from one computer user to another across a computer network.

field

An entry within a database record, such as an employee's name.

multimedia

The combination of text, sound, and video to present information in a meaningful way.

PIM

An abbreviation for personal information management. PIM software lets you organize the essential information you use to manage your appointments, schedules, and so on.

software suite

A collection of two or more key software programs such as a word processor, spreadsheet, and a database bundled together and sold as a single product.

spreadsheet

A computer program that automates an accountant's worksheet letting you track budgets, or other values, and perform "What If" forecasting.

word processor

A computer program that helps you create, change, format, and print documents such as letters, memos or reports.

Lesson 3:
Putting a PC
Together

When you purchase a PC, the computer normally arrives in several different boxes. One of the boxes normally contains an inventory sheet you should carefully check off to insure that all the parts are present. In this lesson you will learn how to connect your monitor, keyboard, and printer to your system unit. As you will find, setting up a computer is actually quite easy if you follow the steps presented in this lesson.

Selecting a Proper Work Area

One of the keys to your enjoyment and computer productivity is setting up a comfortable work area for your computer. To begin, your work space should be well lit. If you are working near a window, make sure light through the window won't cause glare that makes your monitor difficult to read. If you are using a desktop for your work area, make sure you leave adequate space for writing, as well as for pens, staplers, and other desktop items.

You must plug in your computer's system unit, monitor, and printer. Make sure your work area is close to a wall outlet. Do not plug your computer equipment into a power strip. Instead, purchase a surge suppressor into which you plug your equipment. Figure 3.1 illustrates several common surge suppressor types. Not only does the surge suppressor protect your computer equipment from possible electrical surges on the power lines, it helps you organize your electrical cables.

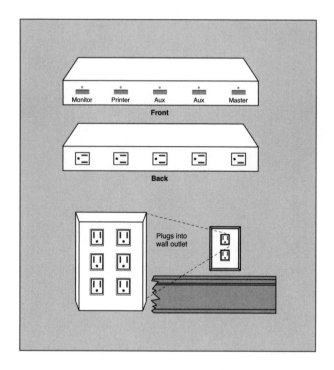

FIGURE 3.1 Protect your computer equipment with a surge suppressor.

Surge suppressors vary in price from $9.95 to $125.95. The more expensive suppressors provide power switches you can use individually to turn your equipment on and off. Regardless of the suppressor type you choose, make sure it has an Underwriters Laboratory (UL) approval. In addition, some surge suppressors provide surge protection for modem cables that you connect from you PC to your telephone wall outlet. If you use your computer with a modem, you should purchase a surge suppressor into which you can plug your modem's telephone cables.

Most users eventually spend hours at their computer. Make sure you have a comfortable chair that provides back support and adjusts to a height at which you can comfortably use your keyboard.

As you will learn in later lessons, your computer stores information on disk by magnetizing the information to the disk's surface. You should keep your disks away from electronic devices such as a pencil sharpener, or even an older phone.

Lastly, include space for the cables that connect your printer, mouse, and keyboard to your system unit.

Work Space Checklist

❖ Is your work space well lit and free from glare?

❖ Is your work space near a grounded power outlet?

❖ Are you using a surge suppressor?

❖ Does your work space provide room for writing and other paper work?

❖ Does your work space provide room for your desktop items such as a phone or pens and pencils?

❖ Is your keyboard height comfortable for long periods of typing?

❖ Does your chair provide adequate support and adjust to a comfortable height?

Connecting Your Computer

As you unpack your computer, you will probably want to save the boxes and styrofoam packing in case you ever need to move the system. To begin, start with your computer's system unit. Regardless of whether you are using a desktop or tower PC, if you examine the back of the system unit, you will find several connectors (often called *ports*) to which you attach your printer and monitor, as shown in Figure 3.2.

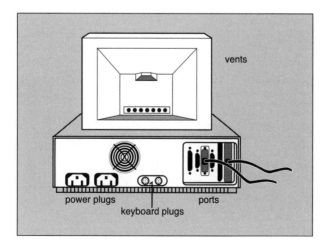

FIGURE 3.2 Your system unit contains ports to which you attach your printer and monitor.

Next, connect your monitor cable to the corresponding port on the back of your system unit. Depending on your monitor type, the connector has 9 or 15 pins as shown in Figure 3.3.

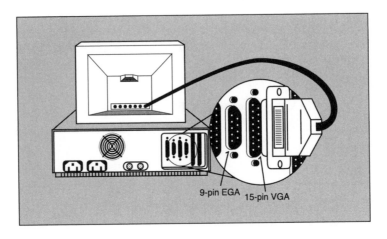

FIGURE 3.3 Depending on your monitor type, its cable connects to a 9- or 15-pin port.

Perform this same step, connecting your printer cable to the system unit. As shown in Figure 3.4, you must match your printer cable to the correct port connector.

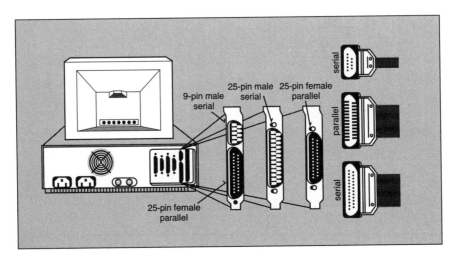

FIGURE 3.4 Depending on your printer type, the printer cable connects to a parallel or serial port.

Next, locate the keyboard plug on your system unit. The plug normally appears near the center of the back of the system unit as shown in Figure 3.5. Note that you must align the pins in the cable to match the plug's holes.

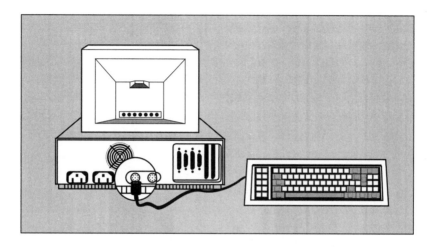

FIGURE 3.5 Insert the keyboard cable into the system plug.

Next, match the mouse connector cable to a system unit port and connect it.

Depending on your mouse type, you connect the mouse to a 9-pin serial port or to a special circular mouse port as shown in Figure 3.6.

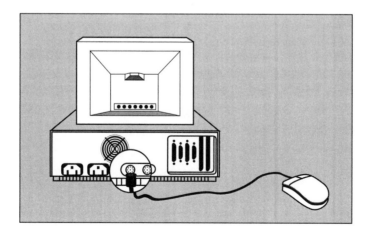

FIGURE 3.6 Connecting your mouse to your computer.

After you connect your mouse, plug in your system unit, monitor, and printer. As discussed, to protect your investment, you should plug your computer into a surge suppressor as opposed to directly into a wall outlet.

Connecting a Laptop

If you are using a laptop computer, you may need to open a small cover on the back of your computer to reveal the ports as shown in Figure 3.7.

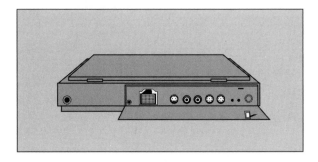

FIGURE 3.7 Ports on a laptop computer.

Using the ports shown in Figure 3.4 as your guide, you can locate your laptop computer's serial and parallel ports. Using these ports you can connect a mouse or printer to your computer.

Putting It All Together

Before you can feel comfortable working with your computer, you need to be comfortable at the work space you have set aside. Make sure your work space is well lit and has enough room for you to perform paperwork and other activities.

To set up your computer, perform the following steps:

❖ Connect your monitor cable to a 9- or 15-pin port on the system unit.

❖ Connect your printer to a parallel or serial port on the system unit.

❖ Align and connect the keyboard cable to the system unit.

❖ Connect your mouse to your system unit.

❖ Plug in your system unit, monitor, and printer, ideally into a surge suppressor.

Glossary

expansion slots	Slots within your computer's chassis into which you can insert a card such as a modem.
port	A connector on the back of your system unit to which you attach a printer, monitor, or other hardware device.
surge suppressor	A hardware device that sits between your wall plug and computer equipment that protects the equipment from damaging electrical bursts.
work space	The area you set aside at which you will work with the computer or perform other work-related tasks.

Lesson 4:
Turning On
Your Computer

In Lesson 3 you learned how to connect your computer's keyboard, monitor, and printer to the system unit. This lesson discusses the steps you should follow when you turn on your computer. In addition, you will learn a few trouble-shooting techniques you can use if your computer does not start.

Turning on Your Equipment

Your computer's system unit, monitor, and printer each have their own on and off switch. To start your computer, you must turn on each of these devices. The order in which you turn on the devices does not matter.

When you turn on your computer's system unit, the computer begins running a built-in diagnostic program that tests the system unit's internal parts. We refer to this test as the computer's *power-on self-test* (sometimes abbreviated as *POST*). As they execute this test, most computers display a count of the computer's working memory on the screen display as shown in Figure 4.1. Lesson 16 discusses computer memory in detail.

Should the system unit locate a hardware problem during the self-test, the computer may display an error message on the monitor describing the error.

Should your monitor display such an error message, write down the message to help the computer technician in locating and correcting the hardware problem.

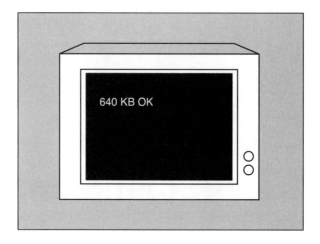

640 KB OK

FIGURE 4.1 Most computers display a count of their internal memory during the power-on self-test.

If your computer successfully passes its power-on self-test, it will next try to load and run a special software program called the operating system (DOS is the operating system used by most PCs). Before the computer can start the operating system, DOS must be present on your computer's disk. Many times, the computer retailer installs DOS on your computer for you. If DOS is present, your monitor may display a message telling you that DOS is starting and then possibly a message similar to the following that prompts you to type in the current date

```
Current date is Fri 09-30-1995
Enter new date (mm-dd-yy):
```

or your monitor may display characters similar to the following, which is called the *DOS prompt:*

```
C:\>
```

Lastly, your monitor might display the DOS shell shown in Figure 4.2, or Microsoft Windows 3.1 shown in Figure 4.3.

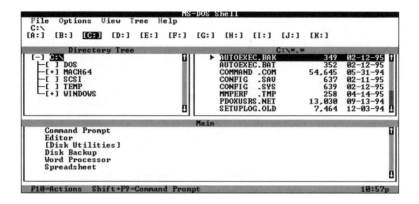

FIGURE 4.2 The DOS shell user interface.

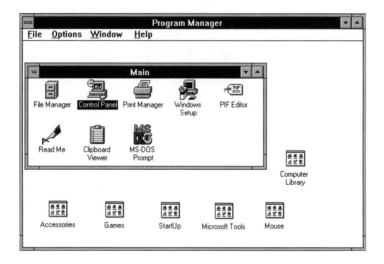

FIGURE 4.3 Microsoft Windows user interface.

If a monitor displays a screen similar to any of these, your computer has successfully loaded DOS. Lesson 15 discusses getting started with DOS.

If your monitor displays the message

```
Non-System disk or disk error
Replace and press any key when ready
```

47

and your computer has a hard disk, open your floppy disk drive and remove the floppy disk as shown in Figure 4.4. Next, press any key on your keyboard to start DOS. If you are using an older floppy-disk based system, place your DOS floppy disk in the drive and press any key to continue. If your monitor displays an error message that states no operating system was found, you need to install DOS on your computer. To install DOS, refer to the user manual that accompanied your computer, or to an introductory book on DOS.

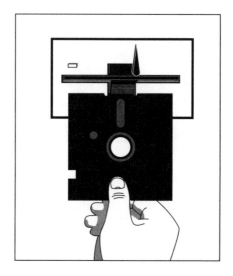

FIGURE 4.4 Remove a floppy disk from the drive before starting your computer.

Troubleshooting the Computer Startup

If your computer does not start DOS, and does not display an error message stating that no operating system was found, follow these troubleshooting steps to identify and possibly correct the problem.

❖ Are your system unit, monitor, and printer plugged into working wall outlets? Are your system unit, monitor, and printer each turned on?

❖ Are your monitor, keyboard, and printer connected to the system unit?

❖ Is your monitor's intensity adjusted so that you can read any text the monitor displays?

❖ Can you hear the system unit's internal fan? If not, your system unit's power supply may be bad and requires servicing.

❖ Did your computer display a count of its working memory? If not, your computer may be failing its built-in self-test and requires servicing.

❖ Did your computer illuminate the small light on your floppy disk drive? If not, your computer may be failing its built-in self-test and requires servicing.

Putting It All Together

Starting your computer isn't much more difficult than turning on your TV. If your system unit, monitor, and printer are plugged in, you simply turn each one on. The order in which you turn on the devices does not matter.

Each time you turn on your system unit, the computer runs a built-in diagnostic program that tests many of its internal parts. Should the computer experience an error during this testing, it may display an error message that you can provide to your service representative to help isolate the problem.

If the computer successfully passes its self-test, it tries to run a special program called the operating system. DOS is the most commonly used PC operating system. Once your computer successfully runs DOS, you can then run other programs. Most computer retailers install DOS for you. If DOS has not been installed on your computer, you must do so.

Glossary

DOS	An abbreviation for disk operating system. DOS is the most commonly used PC operating system.
operating system	A special software program your computer runs when it first starts. The operating system, in turn, lets you use devices such as your printer, store information on disk, and run other programs.
POST	An abbreviation for power-on self-test, the built-in diagnostic test that the system unit runs each time you turn on your computer.
system disk	A disk containing the operating system software.

Lesson 5:
Getting to Know
Your Keyboard

Whether you plan to use your personal computer for word processing, to run a spreadsheet program, or for running computer games, you will spend considerable time typing at the computer's keyboard. If you don't type, or if you hated your high school typing class, relax. Typing at the computer's keyboard is much easier than using a typewriter. As you will learn, the computer lets you quickly correct mistakes.

In this lesson you will examine the most common PC keyboards, noting the keys you use most often as you work with different application programs.

Common Keyboard Layouts

Figure 5.1 illustrates the most commonly used keyboard, the 101-key extended keyboard.

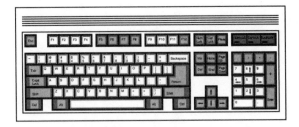

FIGURE 5.1 The 101-key extended keyboard is the most commonly used keyboard.

FIGURE 5.2 The 83-key keyboard provided with the original IBM PC.

The extended keyboard provides keys not found on the 83-key keyboard that accompanied the original IBM PC as shown in Figure 5.2 as well as the 84-key keyboard provided with the IBM PC AT shown in Figure 5.3.

If you are using or plan to buy a laptop computer, your keyboard will be more condensed due to the laptop's size constraints, appearing similar to the keyboard shown in Figure 5.4.

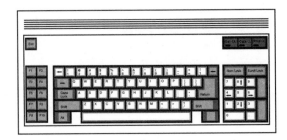

FIGURE 5.3 The 84-key keyboard provided with the IBM PC AT.

FIGURE 5.4 Laptop computer keyboards are more compressed, while providing the same functions as larger keyboards.

Although each of these keyboard types has a different number of keys and a slightly different key layout, all the keyboards have four major sections: the *standard typewriter keys, function keys, cursor movement keys,* and the *numeric key pad.*

Ergonomic Keyboards

As users spend more and more time at the keyboard, many users complain of sore wrists. To help reduce wrist strain, keyboard manufacturers have recently introduced *ergonomic keyboards* similar to that shown in Figure 5.5.

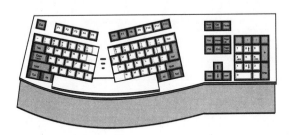

FIGURE 5.5 An ergonomic keyboard.

As you can see, the ergonomic keyboard's design moves your hands to reduce strain on your wrists. If you don't think the new keyboard design is for you, you should consider a wrist pad which elevates your wrists as shown in Figure 5.6. By elevating your wrists, the keyboard pads reduce strain on your wrists.

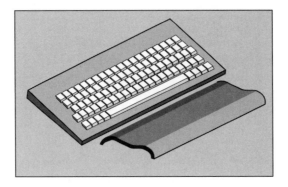

FIGURE 5.6 A wrist pad.

Standard Typewriter Keys

Your keyboard contains a set of keys that closely resembles the keys found on a typewriter. These keys are often called *QWERTY* keys because of the key positions for the letters Q through Y as shown in Figure 5.7.

FIGURE 5.7 The keyboard's standard typewriter key position is often called *QWERTY*.

As you type, the computer displays the corresponding letters on your monitor. Should you mistype a word, you can use the key labeled Backspace to erase the letter that appears before the flashing cursor. For example, if you mistype the word "today" as "today," you can press the **Backspace** key twice, erasing the letters *a* and *y*, so you can retype the letters in the correct order.

As briefly discussed in Lesson 1, there are several very good typing tutorial programs you can run using your computer that quickly improve your typing speed.

Function Keys

Depending on your keyboard type, you will find a set of keys labeled F1 through F10 or F1 through F15 as shown in Figure 5.8.

FIGURE 5.8 The task each function key performs depends on the program you are currently using.

The letter *F* indicates that these keys are special function keys, which, depending on the program you are currently running, may direct the program to perform a specific task when pressed. For example, a word processing program may print your document when you press the **F1** function key. Likewise, a spreadsheet program may display a graph of the current data values when you press **F1**.

Most software programs let you use one or more function keys. Unfortunately, not all programs use the same function keys for the same function.

Numeric Keypad

Your keyboard provides you with two ways to type numbers. First, you can use the row of numeric keys that correspond to the standard typewriter keys previously shown. Second, if you are familiar with a 10-key adding machine, you can use the keyboard's numeric keypad located at the far right side of the keyboard as shown in Figure 5.9. If you must type many numbers into a spreadsheet or as input to a different program, you may find that using the numeric keypad is very convenient.

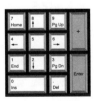

FIGURE 5.9 The numeric keypad resembles a 10-key adding machine.

Most keyboards have a small light with the label *NumLock*. When the keyboard illuminates this light, pressing one of the numeric keypad keys results in the corresponding number. If the **NumLock** light is not lit, the numeric keypad keys perform cursor movement discussed next.

Locate the keyboard key labeled NumLock. The NumLock key works as a *toggle*. The first time you press the key it may illuminate the **NumLock** light selecting the numeric keys. The second time you press the key it may select the cursor movement keys, turning off the **NumLock** light.

Cursor Movement Keys

As you create letters or reports using a word processor, you often move throughout your document adding and changing text. As discussed earlier, when you type the computer displays the corresponding letters at the current cursor location. Your keyboard's cursor positioning keys (the keys labeled with arrows) let you move the cursor right, left, up or down as you need. The keys labeled PgUp and PgDn let you quickly move through your document several lines at a time.

Depending on the program you're running, the cursor movement that occurs when you press the *Home* and *End* keys will differ. Some programs move the cursor to the start of the document when you press *Home*, while others move to the start of the current line. Likewise, pressing the *End* key may move the cursor to the end of the document, or possibly to the end of the current line.

Depending on your keyboard type, you may have a separate set of cursor movement keys, or you may need to press the *NumLock* key to toggle between the numeric and cursor movement keys as just discussed. Figure 5.10 illustrates the cursor movement keys.

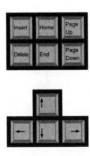

FIGURE 5.10 The cursor movement keys let you move the cursor through a word processing document or across the rows and columns in a spreadsheet.

Special Purpose Keys

You have already learned that pressing the **Backspace** key erases the character that appears immediately to the left of the cursor. This section examines several other commonly used keys. Take time to locate each key we discuss on the keyboard.

Enter Key

When you type on a typewriter, pressing the carriage return key advances you to the start of the next line. In a similar way your keyboard's **Enter** key moves the cursor to the start of the next line. Depending on your keyboard type, the Enter key may be labeled as Enter, Return, or it may have a long left-pointing arrow. As you type commands at your keyboard, you press **Enter** to indicate the end of the command.

Esc Key

Esc is an abbreviation for escape. As you work with different software, you may at first choose a menu option that you later decide you don't want to perform. Most software programs define the Esc key as a cancel key. If, for example, a program displays a menu of options, and you select the wrong option for the task you need to perform, pressing **Esc** may return you to the menu once again.

Caps Lock Key

Unless you hold down the left or right shift keys when you type a letter, your keyboard types lowercase letters such as *abc*. If you need to type in a list of names or other information that must appear in uppercase letters, you can either hold down a Shift key while you type each letter, or you can press the **CapsLock** key. CapsLock works as a toggle. The first time you press **CapsLock** your keyboard types letters in uppercase (pressing a **Shift** key results in lowercase). The second time you press **CapsLock** returns you to lowercase letters. Most keyboards have a small light labeled CapsLock. When you select **CapsLock**, your keyboard illuminates this light.

Tab Key

The Tab key is a cursor-positioning key that advances the cursor to the next tab stop (a column position within your 80-column screen). The Tab key is useful for indenting text or creating a table with several columns. Depending on the software that you're running, the tab stop locations may differ. Most word processing programs let you customize the locations of your tab stops to meet your specific needs. The Tab key either contains the label *Tab*, or possibly a left-facing arrow key above a right-facing arrow.

Ins Key

Ins is an abbreviation for insert. As you add or change text within a document using your word processor, there are times you want to insert the text on a line above existing text, and times you want to overwrite existing text with new text (called *overstriking*). The Ins key works as a toggle, letting you choose between insert and overstrike mode. When you type text in Insert mode, your word processor slides text appearing to the right of the cursor further right as you type, making room for the new text. When you type in Overstrike mode, the word processor overwrites the text at the cursor position with the new text.

Understanding Keyboard Combinations

A *keyboard combination* is a collection of one or more keys that you hold down at the same time. For example, to type the name Smith, you would hold down the **Shift** key and then type the letter S. Just as many software programs assign unique meanings to the function keys, many define specific keyboard combinations.

Most keyboard combinations use either the Ctrl or Alt keys. *Ctrl* is an abbreviation for control and *Alt* for alternate. Most books and magazines represent keyboard combinations by separating the keys with a plus sign (+) or hyphen (-). For example, to perform the Ctrl-C keyboard combination, you would first hold down the **Ctrl** key and then type C. The meaning of a keyboard combination depends on the program that you're running. A word processor may use the Ctrl-F2 keyboard combination to invoke its spell checker, whereas a spreadsheet program may use the same key combination to print the current worksheet.

For now, simply remember that if you must perform a specific keyboard combination, hold down each of the keys in the specified order.

Keyboard Buyer's Guide

In some cases, you may not have a choice over the keyboard you purchase (a laptop computer does not let you select a different keyboard). If you can select your keyboard, use the following checklist as a guide.

❖ Do you have a keyboard at work or elsewhere whose key positions you are already familiar with? It's very frustrating when the Shift or Ctrl keys aren't where you expect them to be.

❖ Are the keys responsive? Many keyboards feel spongy and may decrease your speed.

❖ Does the key layout meet your needs? Depending on how you use the keyboard, you may want to separate numeric and cursor movement keys.

❖ Does the keyboard reduce strain on your wrists? Would a keyboard pad help reduce wrist strain?

Putting It All Together

Regardless of which programs you run with your computer, you spend a considerable amount of time typing at the keyboard. Regardless of the keyboard type, PC keyboards consist of four major sections: the standard typewriter keys, function keys, the numeric keypad, and cursor movement keys.

Glossary

cursor movement keys	The set of keys that let you move the cursor up, down, right, or left throughout your document.
ergonomic keyboard	A keyboard specifically designed to reduce physical strain on your hands and wrists.
function key	A key labeled F1 through F15 to which a software program can associate a specific function such as printing or spell checking the current document.
keyboard combination	Two or more keys depressed at the same time. For example, to press the Ctrl-C keyboard combination, you would hold down the Ctrl key and type C.
keyboard pad	A small sponge-like pad that you place in front of your keyboard to elevate your wrists and reduce wrist strain.

numeric keypad

The set of number keys at the far right of the keyboard that resembles a 10-key adding machine.

overstriking

A keystroke that replaces or overwrites the character that immediately follows the cursor.

QWERTY

A keyboard layout for which the top row of letters begin with the letters Q through Y.

toggle key

A key, that when pressed, turns a function such as CapsLock or NumLock on or off based on the function's current setting.

Lesson 6:
Getting to Know
Your Monitor

Lesson 5 introduced you to the keyboard, the device you use to get information into the computer. This lesson examines the computer's monitor that lets you view the information you type as well as a program's response to the information. As you will learn, there are many types of monitors, with different picture quality and color capabilities.

Monitors are often confusing to new users because we refer to them with short names such as *CGA*, *EGA*, *VGA*, and *SuperVGA*. Don't let these names intimidate you. By the end of this lesson you will understand the capabilities each of these monitor types provide, as well as how to select the monitor type that best suits your needs.

Color Versus Black and White

When the IBM PC first released in 1981, there was a significant cost difference between color and black and white (often called *monochrome* because they only display a single [mono] color [chromatic]). As a result, older personal computers may have monochrome monitors attached.

Because of the long periods users spend at the computer, most new software programs make extensive use of color to help focus the user's attention and make the screen's appearance more desirable. If you have not yet purchased your monitor, don't save money by purchasing a monochrome monitor. In most cases, you won't be pleased with the screen appearance and you will eventually want to upgrade to color. Most programs today are written to make extensive use of colors. In fact, many programs can display up to 16 million different colors at one time! However, as you will learn later in this lesson, if you are shopping for a laptop computer, you will find a significant cost difference between color and monochrome monitors.

Displaying Text and Graphics

Monitors display information in one of two ways (called *modes*): as text or as graphics. In text mode, the monitor displays letters, numbers, and punctuation symbols. Figure 6.1 shows a letter prepared by a word processor in text mode. In graphics mode, the monitor can display both text and pictures, as shown in Figure 6.2.

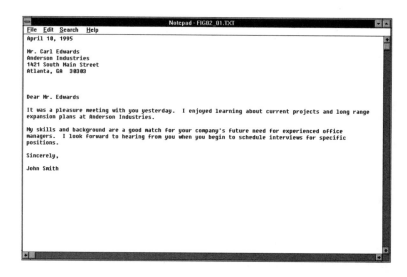

FIGURE 6.1 In text mode, the monitor displays letters, numbers, and punctuation symbols.

FIGURE 6.2 In graphics mode, the monitor can display a combination of text and graphics.

Today, most application programs make programs easier to use by displaying graphic symbols (called *icons*) on the screen that are easy to understand and remember. As you will learn, the monitor's resolution (and that of your video adapter card which resides within your computer chassis) control the sharpness of the image your screen displays.

Understanding Picture Sharpness

As shown in Figure 6.3, text mode monitors typically display 25 rows of text, each of which can contain 80 characters. As you will learn, newer monitors have the ability to display 43 or 50 lines of text depending on the monitor type.

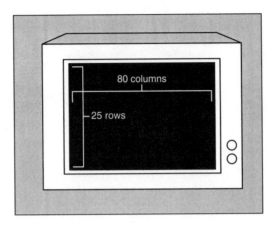

FIGURE 6.3 In text mode, most monitors display 25 rows of text. Each row can hold 80 characters.

In graphics mode, monitors don't display information using row and column character positions, but rather, they divide the screen into small dot positions called pixels (for picture elements). By turning different pixels on and off, or by assigning different color values to pixels, your monitor displays a graphics image. The number of pixels your monitor can display defines the monitor's *resolution*. Figure 6.4 illustrates two monitors, one with 320 x 200 (64,000 pixels) and a second with 1280 x 1024 (1,310,720 pixels).

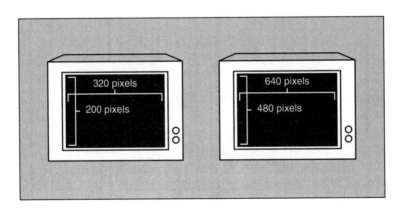

FIGURE 6.4 The number of pixels a monitor can use to represent an image controls the sharpness of the image.

The more pixels the monitor can use to display an image, the sharper the image appears. Figure 6.5 shows two graphic images. The first image is represented using 320 x 200 resolution, and the second using 1280 x 1024.

FIGURE 6.5 The same graphic image represented by two different screen resolutions. Note the blurriness in the second image.

In a similar way, Figure 6.6 illustrates the high-quality image you can display using 1280 x 1024 graphics mode.

FIGURE 6.6 Displaying a high-resolution graphics image.

Your Monitor Requires a System Unit Adapter (a Video Card)

For simplicity, the discussion presented in this lesson has implied that the monitor provides the different text and graphic capabilities. Actually, the monitor provides only half the picture. As you learned in Lesson 2, you must attach the monitor to a port at the back of the system unit. This port is the computer's *video adapter*, an electronic circuit board inside the computer that provides the actual text and graphic capabilities. When you buy a monitor, you must be sure that the monitor works (is compatible) with the video adapter. When we use terms such as CGA, EGA, or VGA, we are actually referring to the video adapter inside the system unit. The following section discusses the most commonly used video adapter types. Pay attention to each—the number of colors each adapter can display as well as the resolution.

Monochrome Display Adapter (MDA)

As discussed, many of the original IBM PCs did not use color monitors. The monochrome adapter displays text in one color. Depending on your monitor type, the text appears as white, green, or amber. Older, monochrome display adapters do not support graphics. If you try to run a program that uses graphics with an older monochrome display adapter, the program will not work.

Hercules Graphics Card (HGC)

To provide basic one-color graphics support for monochrome monitors, many users bought and installed a video adapter created by a company named *Hercules*. Using this adapter, monochrome monitors could display black and white graphics with 720 x 348 resolution.

Color Graphics Adapter (CGA)

The CGA was the first color adapter available for the PC. Using the CGA, users could display text and graphics. In text mode, the CGA supports sixteen foreground and eight background colors. In graphics mode, the CGA provides two resolutions: 320 x 200 with four available colors, or 640 x 200 with two colors. Using these two resolutions, users can choose between available colors and picture sharpness.

Enhanced Graphics Adapter (EGA)

In 1985, the enhanced graphics adapter improved text and graphics display quality. In text mode the EGA can display 25 rows of 80 columns or 43 rows of 80 columns. In graphics mode, the EGA supports the two CGA resolutions and provides a 640 x 350 sixteen color mode.

Multi-Color Graphics Array

When IBM released its PS/2 model 25 and 30 computers, they introduced an adapter called the MCGA. The MCGA provides all the capabilities of the CGA and adds two graphics resolutions: a 640 x 480 two-color mode and a 320 x 200 256-color mode.

Video Graphics Array (VGA)

The most common video adapter sold today is the VGA. In text mode, the VGA lets you display up to 50 rows of 80 characters. In graphics mode, the VGA provides a 640 x 480 sixteen-color mode as well as a 320 x 200, 256-color mode.

Table 6.1 summarizes the video adapter capabilities.

TABLE 6.1 VIDEO ADAPTER CAPABILITIES.

ADAPTER	TEXT MODE	GRAPHICS MODE
MDA	25 x 80	No graphics capability
HGA	25 x 80	720 x 348 monochrome
CGA	25 x 80 color	640 x 200 two color, 320 x 200 four-color
EGA	25 x 80 color, 43 x 80 color	CGA modes, 640 x 350 sixteen-color

TABLE 6.1 CONTINUED.

MCGA	25 x 80 color	CGA modes, 640 x 480 two-color, 320 x 200 256-color
VGA	25 x 80 color, 50 x 80 color	CGA and EGA modes, 640 x 480 sixteen-color, 320 x 200 256-color
SuperVGA	25 x 80 color, 50 x 80 color	CGA, EGA, and VGA modes, 1024 x 768 256-color

The video capabilities listed in Table 6.1 define video standards supported by the industry. In addition to these video display modes, you can purchase video cards that support graphics resolutions of 1280 x 1024 and display up to sixteen million different colors at one time!

Understanding 8-bit, 16-bit, and 24-bit Colors

As you have learned, your computer's video card controls the number of colors your screen displays. Video cards are described as 8-bit, 16-bit, or 24-bit based on the number of colors they support. For example, to represent 256 different colors, a video card uses 8 bits for each pixel. In a similar way, a 16-bit video card is capable of displaying 65,536 (64Kb) different colors. Using 24 bits for each pixel, a video card can represent over 4 million different colors! Today, most video cards support 24-bit video. However, if you are shopping for notebook computers, you may find that most (affordable) color notebook computers only support 8-bit color (or 256 colors).

Using a Graphics Accelerator Card

If you are using Microsoft Windows or another graphical program, you can improve your system performance tremendously by using a graphics accelerator card. In general, a graphics accelerator card is a high performance video card you place into one of your computer's expansion slots. The cards typically contain their own processor chips that can perform specialized graphics operations very quickly. In addition, some graphics cards bypass the normal bus (wires) used to communicate with the CPU and use instead, a very fast local bus that the computer normally reserves for data transfers between the CPU and memory. By using the high speed local bus, these video cards provide maximum performance. Before you purchase a local bus video card, however, you need to insure that your system will support it. If you use Windows on a regular basis, adding memory and using a video accelerator card are the two fastest ways to improve your system performance.

Measuring Your Monitor

When you shop for a monitor, you will find 14-, 15-, 17-, 19-, and even 21-inch monitors. As shown in Figure 6.7, a monitor's size corresponds to the diagonal length of the monitor's screen. Before you purchase a large monitor, make sure you know the size of the entire monitor (the monitor's *footprint*). Although the thought of a 21-inch screen may be inviting, the monitor itself may consume your entire desktop.

FIGURE 6.7 **A monitor's width is measured diagonally.**

If you plan to spend many hours in front of your computer, purchase a large monitor, such as a 15- or 17-inch display. Also, as shown in Figure 6. 8, many monitors provide a location to which you can attach multimedia speakers.

By attaching the speakers to your monitor in this way, you clear off space on your desktop.

FIGURE 6.8 Attaching speakers to a monitor.

Interlaced and Non-Interlaced Monitors

As discussed, newer video boards now support up to sixteen million colors and resolutions of 1280 by 1024. To represent sixteen million different colors, each pixel requires 24 bits (3 bytes) of data. To avoid flicker, your monitor normally refreshes (redraws its contents) around 70 times per second. To keep up with the tremendous amount of information that must be redrawn for over one million pixels, some monitors cheat and only redraw every other line on each pass. These monitors, called interlaced monitors, often advertise fast operations and high resolutions. However, because they really don't refresh the entire screen with each refresh operation, *interlaced* monitors do not have as sharp a picture as their non-interlaced counterparts. If a sharp screen is important to you, do not save money by purchasing an interlaced monitor. As you shop for monitors, ask your salesman if the monitor is interlaced or noninterlaced. Remember, you want to purchase a noninterlaced monitor.

Understanding Dot Pitch

When you shop for monitors, a term you may encounter is *dot pitch*. Computer screens display colors by combining three small dots that illuminate as red, green, and blue. As shown in Figure 6.9, dot pitch is the distance (along a slope) between two successive pixels of the same color. The smaller a monitor's dot pitch, the sharper the resulting image. Dot pitches less than or equal to 0.25 are excellent. A larger dot pitch may result in a coarse or ragged image display. As you price monitors, make sure you compare each monitor's dot pitch. If you plan to spend several hours a day in front of your monitor, purchase a monitor with a smaller dot pitch.

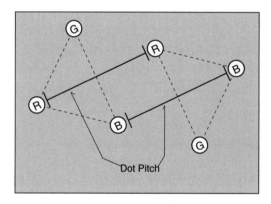

FIGURE 6.9 Dot pitch controls monitor sharpness.

Understanding Video Memory

As you have learned, a video card directs a monitor to display an image based on the contents of the card's video memory. As you shop for video cards, you will find that you can buy video cards with different amounts of memory. For example, you might find one card that contains 1Mb of video and a second, more expensive card that contains 4Mb!

Your video card's memory controls the number of colors the card will support at different screen resolutions. For example, in 256-color mode, the video card uses 1 byte to represent each pixel color. If the video card is in 640x480 resolution, the card needs to store 307,200 bytes. Likewise, in 256-color mode at 1280 x 1024 resolution, the card needs 1,310,720 bytes. As you have learned, to display 16 million colors, the card must track 3 bytes for each pixel. In 1280 x 640 mode, the video card would require 3,932,160 bytes. As you can see, the more memory a video card contains, the more colors the card can display at higher resolutions. As you shop, you will find that the more memory your video card contains, the higher the card's cost.

Video Buyer's Guide

As you have seen, there are many video adapters and monitors to choose from. Most newer computers come with the VGA and a compatible monitor. Be aware that some companies sell you the VGA card and a high-resolution monochrome monitor. If you want color, make sure you buy a color monitor.

If you are using programs that display graphics, better resolution improves the image appearance. If you are using programs that run in text mode, you may find that a better adapter and monitor can reduce your eye strain. Use the following list as your guide when you buy your video adapter and monitor:

- ❖ Do you need graphics capabilities? If so, what resolution?
- ❖ Do you have—or plan to buy—software that requires a specific adapter type?
- ❖ Do you need color?
- ❖ What is the monitor's dot pitch?
- ❖ Is the monitor non-interlaced?
- ❖ What is the monitor's refresh rate?
- ❖ Does the adapter card use a local video bus?
- ❖ Does your computer support local bus video?
- ❖ What size monitor do you require?
- ❖ Will the monitor selected work with the adapter card?
- ❖ How many hours a day do you expect to spend in front of the monitor?
- ❖ How much video memory do you require? In other words, how many colors do you need to display at high resolutions?

Putting It All Together

Just as your keyboard is an input device that lets you put information into the computer, your monitor is an output device that lets you display information. Monitors attach to a video adapter card at the back of your system unit. Working together, the video adapter and monitor display information in text or graphics mode. In text mode, the monitor displays letters, numbers, and punctuation symbols. In graphics mode, the monitor can combine text and pictures. Depending on your monitor and adapter type, the amount of text, the number of colors, and the quality of the image the monitor can display will differ.

Glossary

CRT	An abbreviation for cathode ray tube, a term often used for the screen display.
dot pitch	The distance, in millimeters between a monitor's successive red, green, or blue phosphors.
graphics mode	A video display mode in which the monitor can display both text and pictures.
icon	A graphic image that represents an object such as a program or printer.
interlaced monitor	A video monitor that displays images by refreshing every other line of the monitor's display with each vertical refresh operation.
LCD	An abbreviation for liquid crystal display, the monitor type used by many laptop and portable computers.
local bus video	A video card that communicates directly with the CPU using the fast (local) bus normally used by the CPU to access the computer's electronic memory.
multi-sync monitor	A monitor capable of recognizing multiple electronic signals such as those used by a VGA or EGA.

pixel

A picture element or dot that the monitor can turn on or off, or display in a unique color, which, when combined with other pixels, creates a graphics image.

refresh rate

The speed at which a monitor updates (refreshes) the red, green, and blue phosphors that create a screen image. The faster the refresh rate, the less monitors flicker.

resolution

The number of pixels the monitor can use to display an image. The higher the resolution, the sharper the image quality.

RGB

An abbreviation for the colors Red, Green, and Blue. The MCGA and CGA create additional colors by combining different combinations of red, green, and blue.

text mode

A video display mode in which the monitor displays letters, numbers, and punctuation symbols.

VDT

An abbreviation for video display terminal, a term often used for the screen display.

video adapter

An electronic circuit board within the system unit to which you attach the monitor that controls the text and graphics capabilities.

Lesson 7: Getting to Know Your Printer

Whether you use the computer for word processing, to track your budget with a spreadsheet, or just for recreation, you will eventually need to print information on paper. This lesson discusses the various printer types as well as the steps you need to perform in order to use the printer. Like most hardware devices, printers come in different types, with different costs and capabilities. By the end of this lesson you should be able to determine the best printer for your needs.

Understanding Different Printer Types

When the IBM PC was first released in 1981, the most common printer types were *impact printers* that produce their output by pressing a print head against an ink ribbon, transferring the ink to the paper. Recently, price reductions have made laser and ink jet printers very popular.

One of the terms most often used to describe a printer's capabilities is *letter quality*. In general, letter quality output matches the quality and appearance of text produced by a typewriter. As we examine the various printer types, note which printers provide letter quality. Also note the speed at which each printer prints.

As discussed in Lesson 3, you attach your printer cable to a printer port on the back of your system unit. Depending on your printer type, you use either a parallel or a serial port as discussed in Lesson 10.

Impact Printers

The two most common impact printers are the *dot matrix* and *daisy wheel*. Both of these printers use a print head to strike an ink ribbon against paper. Just as you must periodically change a typewriter's ribbon, the same is true for the ribbon in an impact printer. Because impact printers are mechanical, they are much slower and much noisier than non-impact printers. Today, impact printers are commonly used to print multipart forms.

Dot Matrix Printers

The dot matrix is the most common impact printer. The printer is so named because its print head fills a matrix of dots (rows and columns of dots) to form a character. The number of pins is typically 9 or 24. Figure 7.1 illustrates how a dot matrix printer might form different letters. As you can see, the more pins the print head contains, the better the print quality. Dot matrix printers do not produce letter quality output. If you examine the output of a dot matrix printer closely, you can see the individual dots that make up each letter.

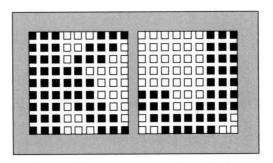

FIGURE 7.1 Representing letters using a dot matrix.

Most dot matrix printers use tractor feed paper that the printer pulls past its print head as shown in Figure 7.2. The edges of tractor feed paper contain small holes that match sprockets on the printer's tractor feed which allow the printer to grip and pull the paper. After a page prints, you can simply remove the perforated paper's edges that contain the tracks (called *bursting* the paper).

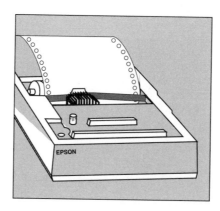

FIGURE 7.2 Tractor feed printers pull special paper past the print head.

Because of their mechanical nature, dot matrix printers are much slower than a laser printer. Typically, a dot matrix printer may print 150 to 300 characters per second.

Daisy Wheel Printers

A daisy wheel printer is very similar to a typewriter in that it uses unique keys to create each letter, number, or symbol. Figure 7.3 illustrates a partial daisy wheel. As the printer prints, it spins the daisy wheel to select the correct letter. Because the daisy wheel printer uses a key similar to a typewriter, the daisy wheel produces letter quality print. Unfortunately, because spinning the daisy wheel for each letter is a slow mechanical process, the daisy wheel printer is slow, printing 10 to 75 characters per second. A daisy wheel printer might use a tractor feed, or single sheet feed similar to a typewriter.

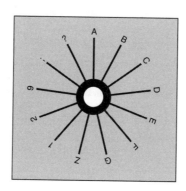

FIGURE 7.3 A possible key arrangement on a daisy wheel printer.

Non-Impact Printers

Over the past few years, non-impact printers such as the *laser* and *ink jet* printers have become very affordable and very popular. Such printers are much faster and quieter than impact printers and provide higher quality output with support for many different font sizes and styles.

Laser Printer

A laser printer, which looks like a small copying machine actually works in a similar way. The laser printer transfers a fine black powder called *toner* to paper. The laser printer contains a roller, that when magnetized, attracts the toner. Using a small laser, the printer magnetizes the roller at specific locations that match the page to be printed. As the roller passes over the paper, it transfers the toner. The printer then heats the toner causing it to attach permanently to the paper. Figure 7.4 illustrates a laser printer.

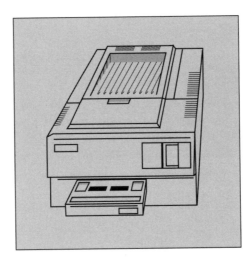

FIGURE 7.4 A laser printer looks and behaves like a small copy machine.

Laser printers do not use tractor feed paper. Instead, they use single sheets of paper, just like a copy machine. A typical laser printer has a sheet feeder that holds several hundred sheets of paper. Because the laser printer is not mechanical, it is the fastest and quietest printer, able to print between 6 and 20 pages per minute.

Just as you must periodically change printer ribbon, you must periodically change the laser printer's toner cartridge. Most cartridges last between three and five thousand pages. A replacement cartridge costs around $100. Figure 7.5 illustrates a laser printer toner cartridge.

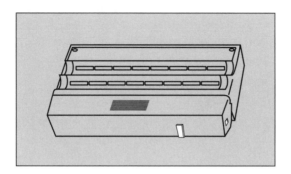

FIGURE 7.5 A laser printer toner cartridge.

Although its resolution is much sharper than a dot matrix printer, the laser printer still represents characters as a collection of dots. However, in the case of a laser printer, the number of dots used is typically 300 to 600 dots per inch, more than enough to produce letter quality output. In addition to printing on paper, most laser printers let you print on transparencies that you can then use with an overhead projector as shown in Figure 7.6. If you purchase transparencies for use with a laser printer, make sure the transparencies are laser printer certified. Otherwise, the laser printer may melt the plastic overhead sheet, possibly damaging the printer.

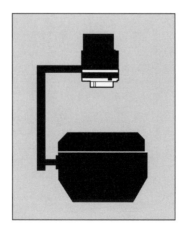

FIGURE 7.6 Displaying a transparency with an overhead projector.

Ink Jet Printer

In terms of price and capability, the ink jet printer lies between the dot matrix and laser printer. Figure 7.7 illustrates an ink jet printer. The ink jet printer creates letters by spraying ink through holes in a matrix, in a manner of a dot matrix. Because the ink jet printer does not use a mechanical head, it is quieter than an impact printer. Ink jet printers print between 120 and 240 characters per second.

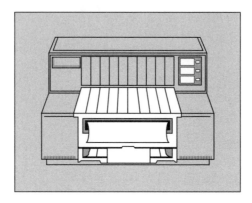

FIGURE 7.7 An ink jet printer creates letters by spraying ink through a matrix.

The ink jet printer uses small containers of ink you must replace about every 1,000 pages. The ink containers cost $15 to $20. Although most printers use black ink, you can buy the ink in different colors. Figure 7.8 illustrates an ink jet printer cartridge.

FIGURE 7.8 An ink jet printer cartridge.

Changing Printers

In most cases, the printer cable that connects a dot matrix printer can also be used to connect a laser printer. Should you change the printer attached to your computer to a different type, you may need to inform your application programs of the change by running a corresponding setup program. Most application programs, such as your word processor, use special software for each printer type. For information on changing the printer type, refer to the documentation that accompanied your program.

Fonts and Typefaces

Typewriters print characters in one or two sizes: *pica* and *elite*. Most dot matrix printers provide the ability to print characters as bold, italic, or compressed (increasing the number of characters per line from 80 to 132). If you are using a desktop publishing program you want the ability to change the size and shape of characters. A typeface consists of characters of a very specific type. Within each typeface, a character can have different sizes and styles. A font defines a specific character size and style. Figure 7.9 illustrates two different fonts.

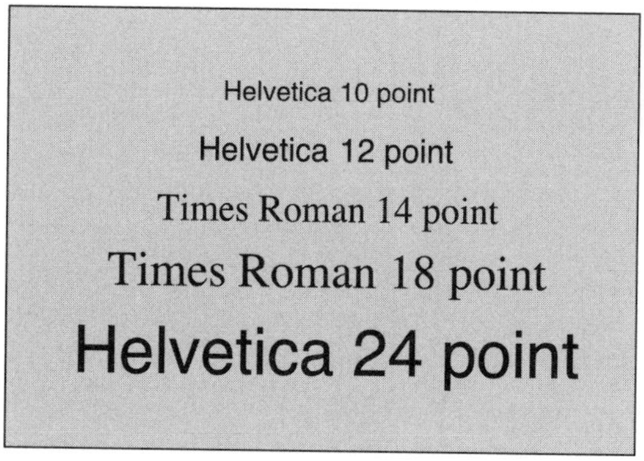

Helvetica 10 point

Helvetica 12 point

Times Roman 14 point

Times Roman 18 point

Helvetica 24 point

FIGURE 7.9 A font defines a character's size and style.

Most laser printers provide only a few basic fonts. As shown in Figure 7.10, however, depending on the printer type, you may be able to buy small *font cartridges* that insert into openings in the printer. When the font cartridges are present, the printer can use the fonts that they define. In addition, many software programs provide a set of fonts on disk (called *soft fonts*) that the program can load into your printer's memory as it needs the fonts. In addition, many programs let you buy and add other soft fonts as you require.

FIGURE 7.10 Inserting a font cartridge into a laser printer.

The point to remember is that, unless a font exists within your printer, a font cartridge, or as a soft font on disk, your printer cannot print the font.

Printing Graphics

If you are using a word processor, you may want to print documents that contain graphics (pictures). Likewise, if you are using a spreadsheet, you may want to print copies of pie charts or bar graphs of your data. Except for daisy wheel printers, all the printer types discussed in this lesson can print graphics. However, when you buy a software program that produces graphics, check the software documentation to make sure it supports your printer.

Understanding Printer Resolution

In Lesson 6 you learned that screen resolution describes the number of pixels on your screen that can be used to display an image. In a similar way, *printer resolution* describes the number of dots the printer can use to display an image on a printed page. Most laser printers use a resolution of 300 *dots per inch* (*DPI*). Some newer printers support 600 DPI. The larger the printer resolution, the sharper the printer can display graphics images. Many books, for example, are printed at 2540 DPI. When you shop for a printer, make sure you know the printer's resolution.

Understanding PostScript

As you examine printers, you will encounter many laser printers that support PostScript. In general, PostScript is a programming language for printers. Using PostScript, you (or the programs you run) can specify instructions the printer is to perform. PostScript printers allow you to create interesting images such as those shown in Figure 7.11.

A Subsidiary of
Henry Holt and Co., Inc.

FIGURE 7.11 Printing images using PostScript.

If you are shopping for laser printers, try to find one that supports PostScript. As the number of applications you use increases, you will find that many take advantage of PostScript.

Many graphics programs, such as Adobe Illustrator, let you store the images you create in a file that uses PostScript format. In most cases, you can print PostScript files on a wide variety of printers. Think of PostScript as a universal printer language. By representing graphics using PostScript (the universal language), the graphics programs insure that the images you create will print on your printer as well as the printer at a prepress shop.

Common Printer Operations

If you examine the printer closely, you will find a set of buttons, two of which may be labeled *On-Line* and *Form Feed* as shown in Figure 7.12. In addition, the printer may contain some small lights that indicate its current status. When the printer is ready to receive information from the computer, the printer illuminates the **On-Line** button. Normally, the only time this light is off is when the printer runs out of paper, or if you press **On-line** to temporarily suspend printer operations. The On-line button works as a *toggle*. The first time you press the button, the printer goes off-line, preventing the computer from sending more information to the printer. The second time you press **On-line**, it places the printer back on-line with the printer back on line with the computer, resuming normal printer operations.

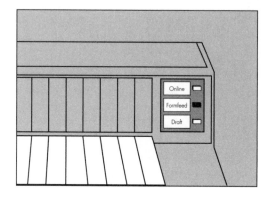

FIGURE 7.12 Buttons found on a typical printer.

Note the button labeled Form Feed. Periodically, depending on the program you are using, the printer may not eject the last page of the printout. To eject the page, press the On-line button to take the printer off-line and press the **Form Feed** button. After the printer ejects the page, place the printer back on-line.

Color Printer

Recently, the decreasing prices of color printers is making such printers a business alternative. Using a color printer you can print spreadsheet graphs or other images using full color, which improves the overall presentation of your entire document. Depending on your needs, there are several ways you can obtain color. If you already own a printer, you can purchase colored ribbons, ink jet cartridges, and even colored laser toner. Using colored inks, you can change the color of your entire document from black to blue or some other desired color.

Unfortunately, you cannot use these techniques to print more than one color at a time. Color printers on the other hand, let you print *multiple* colors at the same time.

There are chiefly two color printer types, *CMYK* printers and *dye sublimation* printers. CMYK printers print the colors *cyan*, *magenta*, *yellow*, and *black* to create different colors. The more expensive dye sublimation printer creates colors using chemical processing similar to that performed for a photograph. In the past, CMYK printers used a special wax-like paper to print on. Recently, many CMYK printers have begun using standard laser printer paper. The price of the CMYK printers is now less than $4,000, whereas dye sublimation printers cost almost twice as much.

When you shop for colored printers, you have the same considerations you have for laser printers, such as printer resolution and the average cost of each printed page. Pages printed on the wax-like paper currently cost about 50 cents a page. Dye sublimation printed pages, on the other hand, cost about $2.00 a page.

Understanding a Grayscale Printout

As you have just learned, many newer printers support color printouts. If your printer does not support colors, you can often print grayscale images that represent different colors using different shades of black and white. For example, Figure 7.13 illustrates a grayscale printout of a color image.

FIGURE 7.13 A grayscale image printout.

Understanding Printer Memory

Before a printer can print text or graphics, the corresponding information must reside in your printer's memory. Most printers come with 512Kb of memory.

When your program sends information to the printer, the program normally does so until it fills the printer's memory. Then, your program must wait until the printer prints information and frees up memory. Unfortunately, while your program waits, you must often wait as well.

By increasing the amount of memory in your printer, you increase the amount of information your program can send to the printer before the program (and you) must wait. If you plan to make extensive use of your printer, you will want to add more memory. Likewise, if you plan to print complex graphics, you will want to increase your printer memory.

Understanding Network Printers

If you work in an office that uses a *local area network*, you may share one or more printers with other users. In the past, the network administrator attached the shared printer to a PC that was connected to the network as shown in Figure 7.14. The PC to which the printer is attached is called a *printer server*.

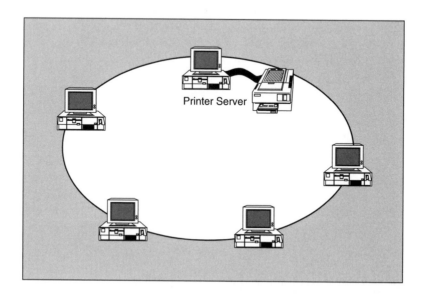

FIGURE 7.14 Connecting a printer to a network PC.

Today, however, as shown in Figure 7.15, many newer printers can be directly connected to the network itself.

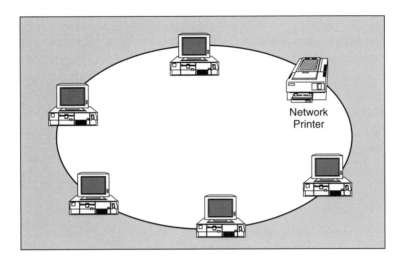

FIGURE 7.15 Connecting a printer directly to a printer.

The advantage of connecting a printer directly to the network, as opposed to connecting the printer to a server PC, is improved performance. Because the information to be printed does not have to travel through the server PC, data gets to the printer sooner. Also, if the server PC is being used by another user to run other programs, the PC is no longer slowed down by the server operations.

If you plan to attach a printer directly to your network, you need to ensure that the printer supports your network type and that your network software supports your printer. Most network printers support an Ethernet connection.

Understanding Printer Drivers

A *device driver* is special software that lets your operating system (Windows or DOS) access a device, such as a printer or mouse. When you purchase a new printer, you will normally receive a floppy disk that contains the printer's device driver software. Follow the instructions that accompany the floppy disk to install and to select the printer device driver.

Printer Buyer's Guide

As the cost of laser and ink jet printers decrease, your choice of printers becomes more difficult. As before, compare the printer prices you are given with those listed in computer magazine advertisements. Use the following list as a guideline when you shop for your printer:

❖ How many pages do you expect the printer to print each day? Is printer speed important?

❖ Where will the printer be located? Is noise a factor?

❖ What will you use the printer for? Do you need letter quality or graphics capabilities?

❖ How much will the printer cost to maintain? Are toner or ink cartridges too costly?

❖ Does the printer provide the fonts you need? If not, are font cartridges or soft fonts available?

❖ Is the printer compatible with your software or does it need special device driver software?

❖ What is the warranty and where can you get the printer serviced?

❖ Do you have an available port to which you can attach the printer? Do you have the necessary cable?

❖ Do you need to print multipart forms? If so, you need an impact printer.

❖ Do you need to print 132 column documents?

❖ Do you need to print labels?

❖ Do you need to print transparencies?

❖ Do you need color printouts?

❖ What is the cost per page?

❖ What printer speed do you require?

❖ Does the printer support PostScript?

❖ How much memory does your printer require? How much data will you send to the printer at one time?

❖ Do you want to share the printer with two or more users?

❖ Do you have a local area network to which you can directly connect the printer?

Putting It All Together

There are two primary printer types: impact and non-impact printers. Impact printers such as the dot matrix and daisy wheel create letters by pressing an ink ribbon against the paper. Because they are mechanical, impact printers are slower and noisier than non-impact. The two most common non-impact printers are the laser and ink jet. In addition to having a higher cost, the laser printer periodically requires a new toner cartridge and the ink jet a new ink cartridge. Table 7.1 summarizes the capabilities of these four commonly used printer types.

TABLE 7.1 SUMMARY OF PRINTER CAPABILITIES.

PRINTER QUALITY	LETTER SUPPORT	GRAPHICS	NOISE	SPEED
Dot matrix	Near	Yes	Loud	150-300 characters per second
Daisy wheel	Yes	No	Loud	10-75 characters per second
Laser	Yes	Yes	Quiet	6 to 20 pages per minute
Ink jet	Near	Yes	Quiet	120-240 characters per second

Glossary

bursting	The process of tearing off the proper tractor-feed from a sheet of paper.
CMYK	An abbreviation for cyan, yellow, magenta, and black—the four colors used to print color images.

CPS	An abbreviation for characters per second, a unit of measure used to describe printer speed.
device driver	Special software that lets the operating system or Windows use a program.
DPI	An abbreviation for dots per inch, a unit of measure used to describe printer resolution.
grayscale image	A black and white representation of a color image whereby different colors are represented using different shades of grey.
hard copy	A paper printout from a computer.
multipart form	A form that consists of two or more pages that contain the same information. Using an impact printer, you can print data to each page.
pica	A standard typewriter character size that compounds to ten characters per inch.
point	A unit of measure used to describe the size of a font. A point is equal to 1/72 of an inch.
PostScript	A printer programming language.
PPM	An abbreviation for pages per minute, a unit of measure used to describe laser printer speed.
printer driver	Software that allows an application program to use your printer.
toner	The powder-like ink used by a laser printer or copy machine.

Lesson 8: Getting to Know Your Disk

To store information from one user session to the next, the computer records information on disk. The PC uses two primary disk types: a fast, non-removable disk called a *hard disk*, and a slower removable floppy disk. This lesson examines how your computer stores information on a disk, as well as the different disk types you can use with a PC.

Storing Information on Disk

The computer stores information on disk by magnetizing the information onto the disk's surface, in much the same way a tape recorder records a song on a cassette tape. Like a song on a cassette tape, you can access the disk's information immediately, after a few days, or even years later, provided you don't erase or overwrite the information. The information you store on disk may contain a letter or report you created with a word processor, a budget worksheet you created with a spreadsheet program, or a computer program.

When you use the computer to create a letter or report, you must store your document on disk. If you don't, you lose your work when you exit the word processing program, or when you turn off your computer. The same holds true for spreadsheets, drawings, or databases. In other words, the computer only "remembers" the information you are working with until you exit the current program. If you need the information later, save it to disk.

Just as you store information in an office in paper folders, the information you store on your disk is placed in a file. Lessons 13 and 14 examine electronic files in detail.

Understanding Disk Storage

The files you store on your disk may contain a wide range of information: word processing documents, worksheets, database files, and even programs. To provide a uniform way of discussing file sizes, the term *byte* is used. Conceptually, a byte is the amount of space required to store a character of information. The word *floppy*, for instance, requires 6 bytes. Today, a floppy disk can store over one million bytes of information. Rather than referring to a file or disk space in millions of bytes, users often use the term *megabyte (Mb)*. Although most users think of a megabyte as one million bytes, a megabyte is actually 1,048,576 bytes. A 1.44Mb floppy disk, therefore, can store over 1,500,000 bytes (1.44 x 1,048,576).

A hard disk can store several million bytes of information. In a similar way, the term megabyte or Mb is used. One megabyte is actually 1,048,576 bytes. A 300 Mb hard disk can store 314,572,800 bytes (300 x 1,048,576).

If you work with older floppy disks (that can store less data), you will find that users express the disk sizes in terms of *kilobytes* (Kb). Although users normally equate a kilobyte with 1,000 bytes, a kilobyte is actually 1,024 bytes. As such, a 360Kb floppy disk, for example, can store 368,640 bytes (360 x 1,024).

Disk Drive Types

As discussed, the PC uses two disk drive types: hard disks and floppy disks. As shown in Figure 8.1, the system unit houses the disk drives.

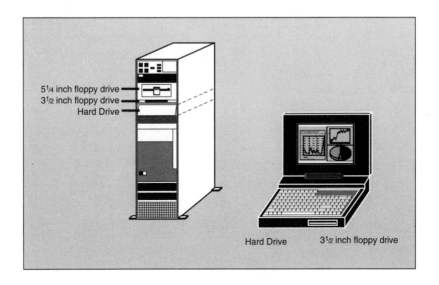

5¼ inch floppy drive
3½ inch floppy drive
Hard Drive

Hard Drive   3½ inch floppy drive

FIGURE 8.1 The system unit can hold multiple disk drive types.

Hard Disk Drives

As discussed, the hard disk is non-removable. If you could look inside the hard disk, you would see several round platters, on which the disk records information. Figure 8.2 illustrates a cut-away of the hard disk.

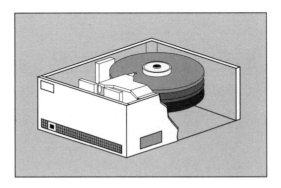

FIGURE 8.2 A hard disk contains several non-removable storage platters.

A hard disk is much faster and can store many more times as much data as a floppy disk. Within the drive, the circular platters spin at a rate of 3,600 *revolutions per minute* (*RPMs*). To record or read information stored on the disk, the disk drive has a read/write head similar to the needle on a record player, that moves in and out to access the entire disk.

Hard disks store several million bytes of information. A 30 Mb hard disk (small by today's standards) can store up to 7,500 single-spaced typed pages of text. When you buy new software, the program normally comes on floppy disk. Before you use the software, you load it onto your hard disk as discussed in Lesson 21.

Today, most new PCs come with 300Mb of disk space or more. If you shop for hard disks, you will encounter the term *gigabyte* (*Gb*). Although most users equate a gigabyte with one billion bytes, a gigabyte is actually 1,073,741,824 bytes. When you first price gigabyte drives, you will find that the drives are still quite expensive. To better appreciate the cost of a gigabyte drive, you need to consider the costs in terms of cost per byte (or Mb). Assume, for example, that a 300Mb hard disk costs $300. In this case, your cost per Mb disk space is $1.00. Next, assume that a 1Gb drive costs $600. In this case, your cost per megabyte becomes $0.60. As such, the cost per Mb for the 300Mb disk is almost twice as much as that of the 1Gb drive.

Floppy Disk Drives

Every PC typically has at least one floppy disk drive. As shown in Figure 8.3, floppy disks come in two sizes: 5.25-inch and 3.5-inch. The original IBM PC used the 5.25-inch floppy. Today, because of their increased storage capacity and durability, more PCs use the 3.5-inch microfloppy disk.

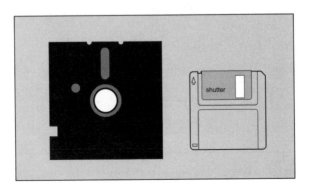

FIGURE 8.3 Floppy disks come in two sizes—5.25-inch and 3.5-inch.

Floppy disks store information by magnetizing the information to the surface of a specially coated flexible plastic disk. Compared to a hard disk, floppy disks are much slower and store much less information. When you insert a floppy disk into the drive, the floppy disk spins at about 300 RPMs. Depending on the floppy disk type, a floppy disk can store from several hundred thousand to slightly over a million characters of information.

To access the information a floppy disk contains, you must insert the disk into a floppy disk drive. If you are using a 5.25-inch floppy disk, you must remove the disk from its protective paper envelope and gently insert the disk into the drive, so that the side of the disk containing the disk label is facing up and the end of the disk inserted last. As shown in Figure 8.4, you must then close the disk drive latch.

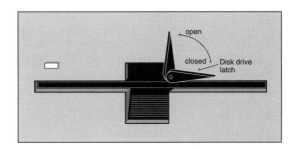

FIGURE 8.4 After you insert the floppy disk, close the disk drive latch.

Never force a floppy disk into the drive. Doing so may damage the disk. To remove the floppy disk from the drive, unlock the drive latch and gently slide the disk out of the drive. Return the disk into its protective paper sleeve.

If you are using a 3.5-inch floppy disk, insert the disk into the drive such that the end of the disk containing the label is inserted last, and the disk's spindle is facing down as shown in Figure 8.5.

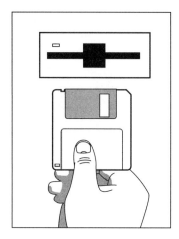

FIGURE 8.5 Insert a 3.5-inch disk with the label end last and the disk spindle facing down.

To remove the 3.5-inch floppy from the drive, press the drive's eject button. As discussed in Lesson 18, laptop computers make extensive use of 3.5-inch disks.

Disk Activation Light

If you look at your hard and floppy disk drives, you see a small light called the *disk activation light*. The disk drive illuminates this light when it reads information from, or writes information to, its disk. Never remove a disk or turn off your computer while a disk activation light is on. Doing so may damage the disk, losing the information the disk contains.

Taking a Closer Look at the Disks

Figure 8.6 illustrates the different parts of a floppy disk. When you remove a floppy disk from its protective paper envelope, you must be very careful not to touch the disk's surface. Touching the surface may scratch the disk, destroying its contents. When you insert a disk into the drive, the drive essentially grabs hold of the center of the disk to spin it. The small metal disk hub at the center of the floppy provides the disk with reinforcement.

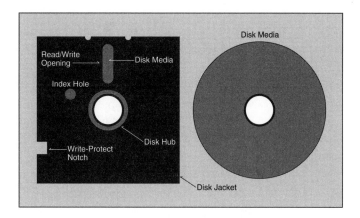

FIGURE 8.6 The different parts of a 5.25-inch disk.

Most 5.25-inch disks have a small write-protect notch in their upper right corner. When this notch is visible, the disk drive can read or write information to the disk, or erase information from the disk if you desire. In some cases you may have a disk whose contents should never change, such as a disk containing an original newly purchased software program. If you cover the disk's write protect notch using a write protect tab (each time you buy a box of disks, the box contains a small sheet of write protect tabs), you *write protect* the disk which prevents the disk drive from being able to write to the disk. The disk drive can still read the disk's contents. However, the drive cannot change the contents in any way. By write protecting your disks whose contents never change, you provide a level of disk protection. Figure 8.7 illustrates how you write protect a 3.5-inch floppy disk.

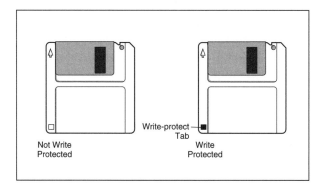

FIGURE 8.7 Using a write-protect tab to protect a 3.5-inch floppy disk.

Figure 8.8 illustrates the front and back sides of a 3.5-inch floppy disk. Unlike the 5.25-inch floppy that has a flexible cover, the 3.5-inch floppy disk is protected by a hard plastic sleeve. As a result, the 3.5-inch disk is less susceptible to damage from bending or having other objects placed on top of it. When you insert a 3.5-inch disk into the disk drive, the drive slides the disk's metal shutter to the left, exposing the disk's storage media. The drive uses the disk spindle on the bottom of the disk to spin the disk. The 3.5-inch floppy does not have a write-protect notch. Instead, it has a write-protect opening you can cover or expose by moving a small plastic slide up and down. When the opening is exposed, and you can see through the opening, the disk is write-protected. When the opening is covered, the disk drive can read or write to the disk.

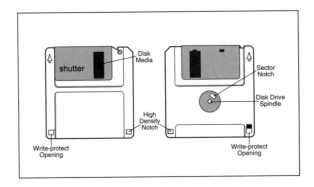

FIGURE 8.8 The different parts of a 3.5-inch floppy disk.

Caring For Your Floppy Disks

As discussed, you should never touch the floppy disk's surface, or force the disk into the drive. When you are through using a floppy disk, always place the disk into its protective paper sleeve. Do not expose your disk to smoke or dust. Such particles can get on the disk's surface and scratch it, destroying the information the disk contains. To help them remember the disk's contents, users place labels on their disk as shown in Figure 8.9. Do not write on a label once you have attached the label to the disk. If you need to change labels, write on a new label and place the new label on top of the existing label. Lastly, if the disk contains important files, make a back-up copy of the disk's contents, just in case the first disk is lost or damaged.

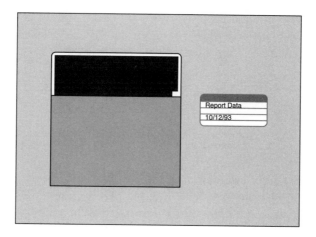

FIGURE 8.9 Always write on your disk labels before you attach the label to the disk.

Storing Your Floppy Disk

Regardless of whether you are using 3.5- or 5.25-inch floppy disks, you should store the floppy disks in a safe location when the disk is not in use. Ideally, you should place the disk into a disk holder similar to the ones shown in Figure 8.10.

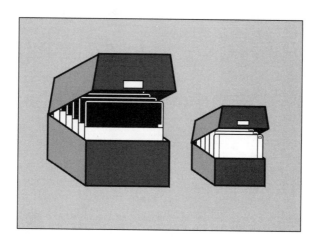

FIGURE 8.10 Storing floppy disks in disk storage containers.

Next, place your disk storage containers in a safe location, away from direct sunlight, your telephone, and other large electronic devices (such as a pencil sharpener) that may emit a magnetic flux that could destroy the disk's contents.

Understanding Floppy Disk Sizes

When the IBM PC first released in 1981, floppy disks were capable of storing 160 Kb (160,000 characters) of information. As disk storage capabilities increased, the amount of information the floppy disk could store grew to 180 Kb, to 320 Kb, to 360 Kb, to eventually 1.2 Mb. Today, the most common 5.25-inch, floppy disk sizes are either 360 Kb or 1.2 Mb. In a similar way, 3.5-inch disks can store either 720 Kb, 1.44 Mb, or 2.88 Mb.

Most 5.25-inch disk drives bought today are 1.2 Mb drives, capable of reading all 5.25-inch disk sizes. Most 3.5-inch disk drives are 1.44 Mb. The reason you must understand floppy disk sizes is to make sure you buy the right disk for your disk drive type. Table 8.1 summarizes the common floppy disk sizes.

TABLE 8.1 COMMON FLOPPY DISK SIZES.

Disk Type	Disk Size	Number of Characters	Number of Single-spaced, Typed Pages
5.25	360 Kb	368,640	92
3.5	720 Kb	737,280	184
5.25	1.2 Mb	1,213,952	303
3.5	1.44 Mb	1,457,664	364
3.5	2.88 Mb	2,915,328	729

If you are using 5.25-inch floppy disks, the only way to tell if a disk is a 360 Kb or 1.2 Mb disk is to examine the label attached to the disk. If the disk is unlabeled, the two disk types appear identical. If you are using 3.5-inch disks, however, you can use the high-density disk notch to determine a 1.44 Mb disk from a 720 Kb floppy. Figure 8.11 illustrates the 3.5-inch floppy high-density notch.

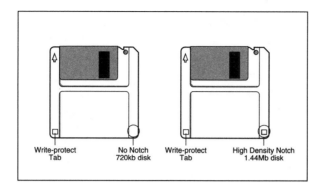

Write-protect Tab — No Notch 720kb disk — Write-protect Tab — High Density Notch 1.44Mb disk

FIGURE 8.11 The 1.44 Mb floppy disk has a high-density notch.

Disk Drive Names

Each of your disk drives has a unique single letter name such as A, B, C, and so on. If your computer has two floppy disk drives, the drives are named A and B. Your computer's hard disk is typically named drive C. Figure 8.12 illustrates several system units, each with different disk drive configurations.

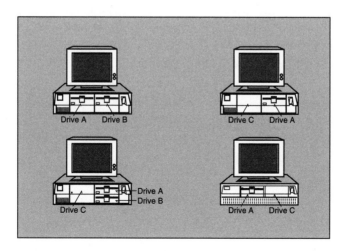

Drive A   Drive B   Drive C   Drive A

Drive A
Drive B
Drive C   Drive A   Drive C

FIGURE 8.12 Each of your computer's disk drives has a unique single letter name.

Common Disk Terms

This section examines several terms you hear used when users discuss disks. As discussed, the disk drive stores information by magnetizing the information to the disk's surface. The disk divides its surface into several storage locations. First, the disk is divided into several circular tracks as shown in Figure 8.13. For floppy disks, the number of tracks is typically 40 or 80. For hard disks, the number of tracks may be several hundred or more depending on the disk's capacity.

FIGURE 8.13 A disk contains several circular tracks.

The best way to visualize the disk tracks is to picture them as being similar to the grooves in a record album. Just as you can move the phonograph's needle to a specific groove in a record, the disk drive can move its read/write head to a specific track.

Each track is further divided into *sectors* that make up the disk's actual storage locations. In most cases, a sector stores 512 bytes of information. Figure 8.14 illustrates disk sectors. Depending on the disk type, the number of sectors per track is typically 8 to 18. Every disk track contains the same number of sectors.

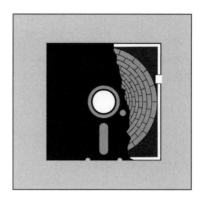

FIGURE 8.14 Each disk track is divided into sectors.

Preparing a Disk for Use

Normally, when you buy a box of floppy disks, or even if you purchase a hard disk, the disk manufacturer has no idea of the type of computer with which you intend to use the disk. As a result, you must prepare a disk for use before you can use the disk to store information. The process of preparing a disk for use is called *disk formatting*. DOS, the PC operating system, provides the FORMAT command for this purpose. If you are using Windows, you can format disks using the File Manager.

When you format a disk, the DOS FORMAT command examines the disk for any defective locations that are unable to store information. FORMAT marks these locations as unusable so DOS doesn't try to use them to store information.

The best way to visualize the formatting process is to assume that a disk, prior to formatting, is completely blank, and after formatting, has its tracks and sectors defined. For more information on the formatting process, refer to the

FORMAT command in a DOS book or in the DOS user manual that accompanied your system.

For a floppy disk, the formatting process may take about two minutes. To save you time, many stores now sell floppy disks specifically formatted for use by an IBM PC or PC compatible. As you shop for floppy disks, look for disks that are preformatted.

Two Drives in One

If your system is short on drive bays, but you need to use both 3.5- and 5.25-inch floppies, you can purchase a dual floppy drive similar to the one shown in Figure 8.15. By combining two floppy drives into the single bay, you make more room for a tape drive or CD-ROM.

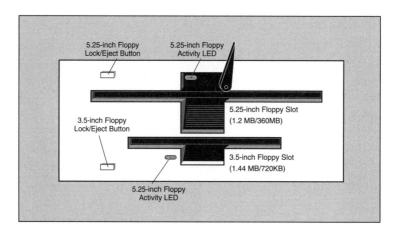

FIGURE 8.15 A 3.5- and 5.25-inch floppy in a single drive bay.

As you can see, the drive supports both floppy disk sizes. Depending on how you cable the drive, you can make the 3.5-inch floppy drive A and the 5.25-inch floppy drive B or vice versa.

Understanding Hard Disk Speeds

As you shop for hard drives, you will encounter the terms *access time* and *transfer rate* which describe the disk drive's speed. The access time specifies how long, on average, it takes the disk to retrieve the requested information. Access times typically fall into the range 7 to 15ms (milliseconds or 1/1000 of a second). The lower the access time, the faster the disk. The disk's transfer rate specifies how much data the disk drive can store or retrieve in a given period of time (normally one second). The higher the transfer rate, the better your disk's performance.

As you shop, you will find that the faster the disk, the higher the disk's cost. Because the disk is a mechanical device (one with moving parts), your disk is much slower than the computer's electronic components (such as the CPU and memory). As you shop for a disk, make sure you purchase one that is fast enough to complement your system. However, if you don't run programs such as a database that makes extensive use of the disk, you may not need a high performance disk.

Understanding SCSI Disks

Within your PC system unit, you will normally find a ribbon cable that connects your hard drive to a disk's controller card as shown in Figure 8.15. Some disk drives, called *IDE* (*integrated drive electronics*) drives, however, contain their own built-in controller that you cable directly to the motherboard.

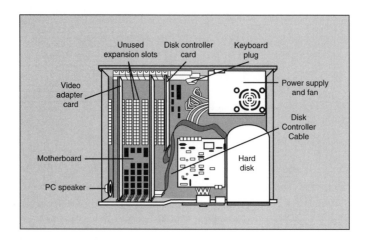

FIGURE 8.16 You connect a disk drive to a drive controller or the motherboard.

Over the past two years, hard drives that connect to *SCSI* (*small computer system interconnect*) connections have become very popular. The SCSI interface is convenient because you can use it to connect multiple devices such as a CD-ROM drive, scanner, and a hard disk to your computer. Lesson 28 discusses SCSI devices in detail.

SCSI hard drives can be internal or external drives. Before your computer can use a SCSI drive, however, your computer must have a SCSI adapter card.

Disk Drive Buyers Guide

If you are purchasing a floppy disk drive, you must first decide if you want a 5.25-inch drive or a 3.5-inch drive. Ideally, your system will have two floppy disk drives, one of each type. As a rule, you want to buy the floppy disk drive with the highest capacity. For example, if you buy a 1.2 Mb 5.25-inch drive, the drive can read 1.2 Mb floppy disk as well as 360 Kb floppies. If you are adding a disk drive to your system, make sure your existing disk controller supports the drive.

If you are purchasing a hard disk, you need to determine how big a disk you need. To begin, make a list of all the programs you plan to load on your hard disk, and each program's disk storage requirements. Next, estimate the amount of data such as letters, reports, worksheets, and possibly temporary files you need to store. Add the amount of space you need for data to the amount of space your programs use. Multiply the result by three (a growth factor). The final result is the smallest hard disk size you should consider.

As you shop for disk drives, use the following list as a guideline:

❖ Can you afford to buy both a 5.25-inch and 3.5-inch floppy drive? Having both is very convenient. Make sure you purchase a 1.2 Mb 5.25-inch drive and a 1.44 Mb 3.5-inch drive.

❖ Do you already have a large collection of 5.25-inch or 3.5-inch disks?

❖ Is the disk drive compatible with your existing disk drive controller?

❖ If you are purchasing a hard disk, what is the disk's average access time? The faster the disk's average access time, the faster the disk's performance.

❖ How much disk space do you need?

❖ Is the disk compatible with your computer's BIOS (see Lesson 42)?

❖ What is the disk manufacturer's warranty and technical support policy?

❖ Does the disk require a special device driver?

❖ If you are adding a disk, what are the installation costs?

❖ Can you purchase a dual floppy drive that contains both a 3.5- and 5.25-inch floppy drive?

❖ Do you have an existing SCSI adapter to which you can connect a new drive? If not, what is the cost of the SCSI adapter?

❖ What is the hard drive's cost per byte (or megabyte)?

Putting It All Together

Disks let you store information from one computer session to another. If you don't save information to disk, the information is lost when you end the current program or turn off your computer.

Disks come in two primary types: fast non-removable hard disks and slower removable floppies. Hard disks provide tremendous storage capacity. A typical hard disk provides storage for up to 30 million characters of information. Floppy disks, on the other hand, typically store from several hundred thousand to slightly over 1 million characters. Floppy disks come in two sizes: 5.25-inch and 3.5-inch. Most newer computers use 3.5-inch floppy drives because of the disk's storage capacity and durability.

107

Glossary

byte	A unit of information that corresponds to a character of the information.
cylinder	For the purpose of this book, a cylinder is a track on a hard disk.
density	A measure of how much information a disk can store in a fixed area. As disk technology has improved, double-density and quad-density disks are able to fit twice as much and four times as much information in a fixed area as the PC's original floppy disk.
disk formatting	The process of preparing a disk for use for a specific operating system, such as DOS.
dual-floppy drive	A floppy disk drive that combines a 3.5-inch and 5.25-inch floppy drive into a single unit that consumes only a single drive bay.
Gb	An abbreviation for gigabyte. OneGb is approximately one billion bytes.
IDE	An abbreviation for integrated drive electronics. An IDE drive contains its own disk controller electronics and does not require a disk controller card. An IDE drive connects directly to the motherboard.
Kb	An abbreviation for kilobyte. One Kb is 1,024 bytes.
Mb	An abbreviation for megabyte. One Mb is approximately one million bytes.
SCSI	An abbreviation for small computer system interconnect. The SCSI standard provides a way for users to connect different hardware devices, such as a disk drive or CD-ROM, to their PC.

transfer rate

The speed, in megabytes per second, at which a disk can transfer information to or from the computer's memory.

write-protected disk

A disk whose contents can be read by a disk drive, but cannot be changed or erased.

Lesson 9:
Of Mice and Men

As we have discussed, your different software programs provide a wide variety of capabilities. One of the common trends in newer software is to make programs easier to use by supporting the *mouse*. The mouse is a small hand-held device that many programs let you use to select menu options, choose a specific document, or even to select a paragraph, word, or phrase with a document for special processing. This lesson introduces the mouse, discusses several of its common uses, and steps you may need to perform to use the mouse.

Building a Better Mouse

As shown in Figure 9.1, mice come in different sizes and shapes. To use a mouse, you must be running a program that supports it.

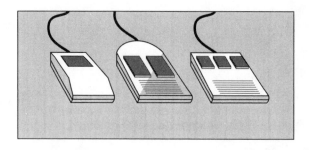

FIGURE 9.1 Several commonly used mouse sizes and shapes.

A program that supports the mouse displays a small, moveable shape on your monitor called the *mouse pointer*. Most text programs display a rectangular mouse pointer, about the size of an uppercase letter. Programs running in graphics mode may display a mouse pointer shaped like an arrow, or even a hand with the index finger extended. Microsoft Windows is the program most responsible for the mouse's current popularity. Within Windows, the mouse pointer appears as an arrow.

To move the mouse pointer on your screen, you simply move the mouse forward, back, right, or left along your desk. The mouse is very responsive, so a little movement of the mouse on your desk results in considerable movement of the mouse pointer on your screen.

Moving and Using the Mouse Pointer

In general, you move the mouse across your desk to aim the mouse pointer at a specific menu item or object that appears on your screen. Next, you press and release (called *clicking*) the mouse select button to choose the option. If the mouse has two or more buttons, most software programs define the left mouse button as the select button. Using a word processor, for example, your screen might display a list of reports or memos. By clicking the mouse on the document name you desire, you can quickly select the document for editing. Using a spreadsheet program, you might use the mouse to quickly select several values you want to total.

Click Versus Double-Click

When you use a mouse within your programs, different operations require that you click the mouse one time on an object. For example, to select a menu you would aim the mouse pointer at the menu and press and release the mouse select button. Other operations, however, require that you *double-click* the mouse. To *double-click* your mouse you press and release the mouse select button two times in quick succession as shown in Figure 9.2.

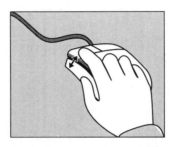

**FIGURE 9.2 To double-click your mouse, press and release
the mouse select button twice in quick succession.**

Within Windows, for example, you can highlight an icon by clicking on the icon with your mouse. However, if you double-click on the icon, Windows runs the program associated with the icon. Figure 9.3 shows the mouse pointer displayed by Windows.

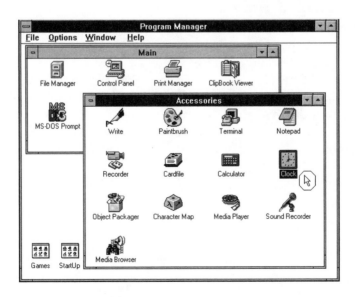

FIGURE 9.3 Microsoft Windows displays the mouse pointer as an arrow.

Using a Mouse Pad

If you turn a mouse over, you'll find it has a small round ball that spins as you move the mouse across your desk. This ball (called the *mouse trackball*) generates the signals that cause the mouse pointer to move across your screen. Depending on your desk's surface, the trackball may not be able to grip the desk well enough to spin. Many users purchase a small rubber pad (less than $10) on which they move the mouse. Figure 9.4 illustrates a mouse on a mouse pad.

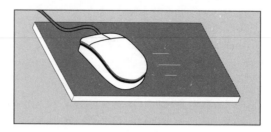

FIGURE 9.4 A mouse pad provides the mouse trackball with better traction.

Connecting a Mouse

Like a monitor and printer, the mouse connects to the system unit. There are two types of mice: a *serial* mouse, and a bus mouse. To the user, both mouse types look the same; their difference is how they attach to the system unit. A serial mouse connects to one of the system unit's serial ports (Lesson 10 discusses ports in detail). A bus mouse usually requires its own adapter board, similar to a video adapter card discussed in Lesson 6. In general, you can simply match the plug at the end of the mouse cable to a port on the back of the system unit as shown in Figure 9.5.

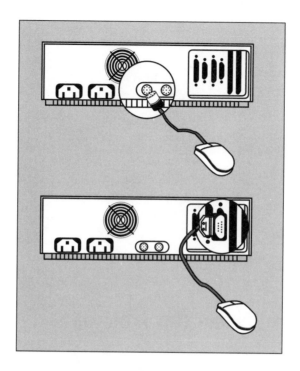

FIGURE 9.5 Connecting the mouse to the back of your system unit.

If you have not yet purchased a mouse, the bus mouse may be slightly faster and leaves a serial port available for another device such as a modem. If your system unit is running out of expansion slots (see Lesson 10) into which you add a hardware card, you may not want to consume a slot with the bus mouse adapter card.

When your mouse is not in use, you may find that a mouse holder (mouse trap) similar to the one shown in Figure 9.6 is very convenient.

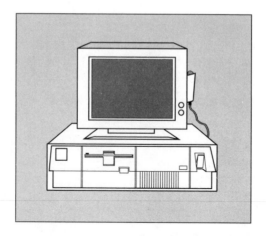

FIGURE 9.6 Storing your mouse when it is not in use.

The Mouse Versus the Trackball

If your work area does not have enough room for you to use a mouse, you may find that a *trackball* meets your needs. Figure 9.7 illustrates a trackball, which looks similar to a mouse turned upside-down. Unlike the mouse, the trackball does not move. Instead, you move the pointer on the screen by spinning the trackball with your fingers.

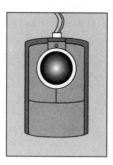

FIGURE 9.7 A trackball lets you move the screen pointer by spinning the small ball with your fingers.

The trackball has become popular for use with laptop and portable computers that are often used in places (such as airplanes) where the user does not have room for a mouse. Newer trackballs even snap onto the sides of a laptop computer. In addition, newer laptop computers provide a small electronic sensor within the keyboard that lets you control the mouse cursor without having to move your hands from the keyboard. Figure 9.8 illustrates common laptop trackballs.

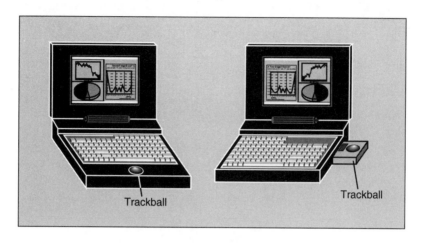

FIGURE 9.8 Trackballs are very common with laptop computers.

Special Software is Required

Before an application program such as your word processor can use your mouse, you need to load special software, called a *device driver* that tells your computer you have a mouse attached. The device driver software must run each time your system starts. Depending on your mouse type, you may need to make an entry in a special DOS file named CONFIG.SYS or AUTOEXEC.BAT. For more information on these files, refer to an introductory book on DOS or the DOS user manual that accompanied your computer. If you use a mouse, make sure the retailer provides you with the mouse device driver software on a floppy disk.

Controlling Your Mouse Within Windows

Lesson 20 discusses Microsoft Windows in detail. Within Windows, you perform most operations using a mouse. Using a special program within Windows called the *Control Panel*, your can customize your mouse settings. For example, if you are left handed, you might configure your mouse to swap select buttons. Likewise, depending on your preferences, you might increase or decrease the speed at which your mouse pointer moves across your screen. Also, if you are using a laptop computer whose screen makes it difficult for you to locate the mouse pointer, you may want to enable *mouse trails* that highlight your mouse pointer's movement as shown in Figure 9.9.

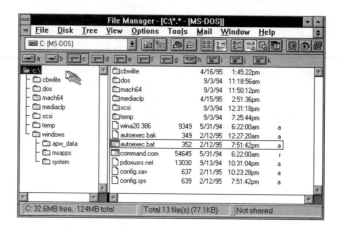

FIGURE 9.9 Mouse trails highlight the mouse pointer's movement across the screen.

Mouse Buyer's Guide

Because of its popularity, many retailers include a mouse when you purchase a new computer. If you are considering purchasing a mouse, use the following checklist as your guide:

❖ Does your software support a mouse? How many mouse buttons does the software support?

❖ What is the cost difference between a bus and serial mouse?

❖ Do you have an unused serial port? (See Lesson 10.)

❖ Do you have an unused expansion slot to hold a bus mouse adapter card?

❖ Do you need a mouse pad? The pad improves the performance and feel of most mice.

❖ Would a trackball better suit your needs?

❖ Did you get the necessary mouse device driver software?

❖ Take time to demo one or more mice with your retailer to get a feel for the mouse's responsiveness.

Putting It All Together

A mouse is a hand-held hardware device many application programs support to make the program easier to use. When you use a mouse, the program displays a small shape on the screen called the mouse pointer. As you slide the mouse along your desk, the mouse pointer moves across your screen in the same direction. By aiming the mouse pointer at a menu option, document name, or other object and pressing the mouse select button, you can quickly choose different program options.

Not all software programs let you use the mouse. However, because of the mouse's current popularity, most newer software does.

Glossary

bus mouse	A mouse that connects to your PC using an expansion slot card that plugs into your PCs bus as opposed to using a serial port.
clicking	The process of aiming the mouse pointer at a screen object, pressing, and releasing the mouse select button.
device driver	Special software that lets the operating system (DOS) or Windows use a hardware device such as a mouse.
double-clicking	The process of aiming the mouse pointer at a screen object and quickly pressing and releasing the mouse select button twice. Many programs require you to double-click the mouse on an object to select it.

hi-res mouse	A mouse capable of responding to precise movements. Hi-res mice are useful for creating detailed computer aided drawings.
mechanical mouse	A traditional mouse that moves the mouse pointer by spinning a rubber trackball.
mouse select button	The mouse button you click (or double-click) to perform an operation within Windows.
mouse trackball	The small ball underneath the mouse that detects (tracks) the mouse movement across the surface of your desk.
mouse trails	The use of multiple graphic mouse pointers that appear to chase the mouse pointer across the screen. Mouse trails highlight the mouse pointer's movement across the screen.
mouse trap	A small plastic holder with which you can place your mouse when it is not in use. Most mouse traps connect to your monitor.
optical mouse	A mouse that uses a special reflective pad that moves the mouse pointer by optically (based on light reflections on the pad) tracking its movement.
point and shoot	Another term for positioning and then clicking the mouse select button.
serial mouse	A mouse that connects to the PC using a serial port such as COM1.

Lesson 10: Understanding Computer Ports

In Lesson 3 you learned that the monitor and printer connect to ports at the back of the system unit. In this lesson you learn how to recognize the different port types and you learn common uses for each port type. In addition, you learn the steps you must perform to install a new hardware board within your computer.

Understanding Port Types

As discussed in Lesson 3, the system unit typically has a *video adapter* port to which you attach your monitor, *a serial port* to which you can attach a serial printer, mouse, or modem, and a *parallel port* to which you can attach a printer. Figure 10.1 illustrates several different port types you may encounter.

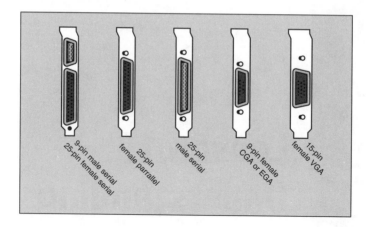

FIGURE 10.1 Common PC port types.

Users classify ports and cables as either male or female based on whether they plug into, or are plugged into. Figure 10.2 illustrates a female parallel port and a male serial port. Note the difference in the receptacle types.

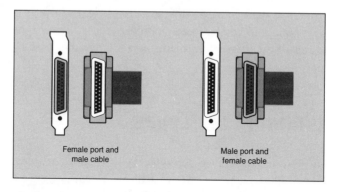

Female port and male cable

Male port and female cable

FIGURE 10.2 Ports and cables are classified as either male or female.

The following section examines different port types you may encounter.

Serial and Parallel Ports

Serial and parallel devices differ in how they exchange information. A *serial device* sends or receives information over one wire. A *parallel device*, on the other hand, sends or receives information over eight wires at a time, and as such, is much faster. Figure 10.3 illustrates how parallel and serial devices transfer data.

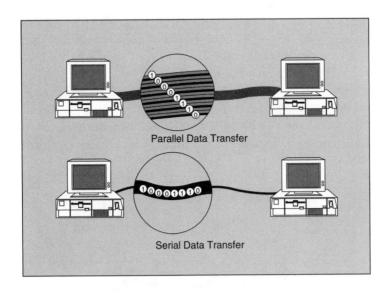

Parallel Data Transfer

Serial Data Transfer

FIGURE 10.3 Parallel devices transfer 8 bits of data at one time while serial devices transfer 1 bit at a time.

Almost every PC comes with at least one serial port to which you can attach a serial printer, mouse, modem (see Lesson 19) or other hardware device. As shown in Figure 10.1, serial ports can be either 9-pin or 25-pin ports.

Serial ports are also called *RS-232* or *COM* (COM is an abbreviation for *communications*) *port*s. The PC can hold up to four serial ports (COM1 through COM4). When you attach a device such as a printer to a serial port, you must insure the port and device are communicating at the same speeds. If you attach a serial printer to a computer and the printer does not print, refer to the printer manual to determine the printer's speed and data communications settings. Use the DOS MODE command to assign these same settings to the serial port.

In addition to a serial port, most computers have one parallel port. Parallel ports normally only connect printers. The PC can hold three parallel ports (LPT1 through LPT3). Because parallel ports often connect line printers, they are often called *LPT* (LPT is an abbreviation for *line printer*) *ports*.

Because the device types communicate differently, you cannot attach a serial device to a parallel port or vice versa.

SCSI Ports

SCSI (pronounced *scuzzy*) stands for *Small Computer System Interface*. If present, you can attach SCSI devices such as an external hard disk, a CD-ROM drive, or a tape back-up system to a SCSI port. In fact, if you connect a hard disk to the SCSI port, you can connect another device such as a tape back-up or the hard drive, connecting up to as many as seven devices in this manner. In other words, you might plug an external SCSI disk drive into the SCSI port, then plug your SCSI CD-ROM into the external disk drive, and then possibly *plug* an external SCSI tape drive into the CD-ROM. Figure 10.4 illustrates how you might connect (*cascade*) multiple devices to one SCSI port. Lesson 28 discusses SCSI devices in detail.

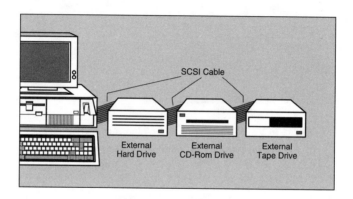

FIGURE 10.4 SCSI ports can support up to eight devices.

The SCSI port is very fast with the ability to send several million characters of information per second. A serial port, in comparison, typically transfers several thousand characters per second. Most PCs do not have a SCSI port. Instead, you must buy a SCSI adapter board which you insert into your system unit as discussed later in this lesson. Figure 10.5 illustrates a SCSI port.

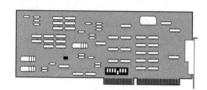

FIGURE 10.5 SCSI ports typically use 50-pins.

Video Ports

As discussed in Lesson 6, you must connect your monitor to a video adapter card. Figure 10.1 illustrates the 9-pin (CGA and EGA) and the 15-pin (VGA) video adapter port types. When you buy a new monitor, you must make sure it is compatible with your video adapter card.

Other Port Types

If, after comparing your computer's ports to those shown in Figure 10.1, you still have ports you cannot identify, the ports very likely connect to a bus mouse, a *joystick* (used for computer games), or a similar device. Refer to the documentation that accompanied your computer for a diagram describing the port use.

Installing New Hardware

If you examine the back of the system unit, you may find several unused slots next to the existing ports. These slots are called *expansion slots* because the hardware you place in them expands your computer's capabilities. When you buy a hardware device such as a bus mouse or an internal modem, you may have to install a hardware board into one of the expansion slots. Figure 10.6 illustrates a hardware card.

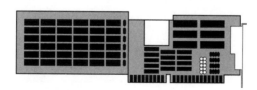

FIGURE 10.6 A hardware board you install in a system unit expansion slot.

If possible, have your computer retailer or an individual who is very familiar with PCs install the board for you. If you must install the board yourself, carefully follow the steps discussed next.

First, to avoid electrical shock or damage to your computer's internal parts, unplug your system unit. Next, as shown in Figure 10.7 remove the screws that

125

connect the system unit cover and gently remove the cover. Be very careful to make sure the cover does not tug or pull on any of the system cables as you remove it.

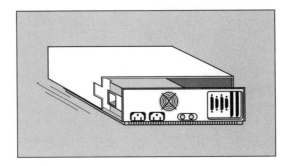

FIGURE 10.7 Gently remove the system unit cover.

Locate the expansion slots. As shown in Figure 10.8, unscrew and remove the cover of an unused connector opening. Place the slot cover in a safe location.

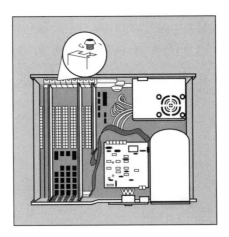

FIGURE 10.8 Select an unused expansion slot and remove its cover.

As shown in Figure 10.9, use both hands to gently slide the board into the slot. Make sure the board slides tightly into place.

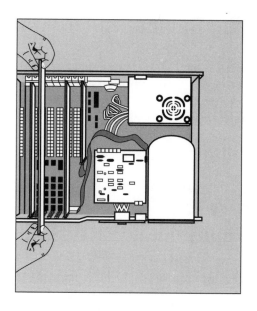

FIGURE 10.9 Gently slide the board into place.

NOTE

To reduce the chance of an electrical shock damaging the sensitive electronic chips contained on the card, always first ground yourself by touching your PC's system chassis before you touch a hardware card or your PC's motherboard.

Gently slide the system unit cover back into place and replace the screws you removed earlier. You can now connect the cable to your new device and plug in your system unit.

NOTE

Some hardware boards may require that you set small switches on the board to prevent conflicts with your existing hardware. Such hardware installations should be performed by your retailer or a very experienced user.

Understanding Cables

As shown in Figure 10.10, the PC uses two primary cable types: a *standard* and *ribbon* cable. Ribbon cables are so named because they are wide and flat. When you purchase serial and parallel cables, you have a choice between standard and ribbon cables. The function of both cables is identical.

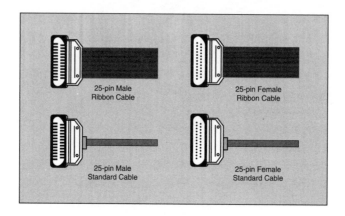

FIGURE 10.10 The PC uses standard and ribbon cables.

When you connect a cable to your system you normally align the cable's plug with the port. If the port does not have a unique shape that controls how you connect the plug, you can normally look very closely at the port and plug and find small numbers. Simply align pin 1 on the port to pin 1 on the cable. If you are using a ribbon cable, the pin 1 cable is normally darker than the rest of the cable as shown in Figure 10.11.

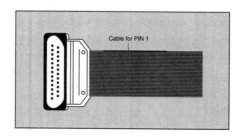

FIGURE 10.11 Pin 1 on a ribbon cable normally appears darker than the rest of the cable.

Understanding DIP Switches and Jumpers

As discussed, some hardware boards may require change switches or jump settings. Figure 10.12 illustrates DIP switches and a jumper on a hardware board. As a rule, you only let very experienced users make jumper or DIP switch settings. Before changes are made, make sure you write down the board's original settings in case your changes do not work.

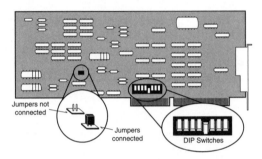

FIGURE 10.12 DIP switches and jumpers on a hardware board.

Working with Laptop Computer Ports

If you are using a laptop computer, you will normally find the computer's ports behind a small plastic cover at the back of computer as shown in Figure 10.13.

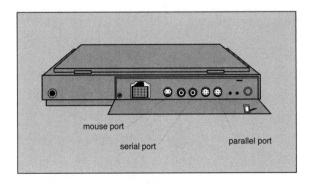

FIGURE 10.13 Locating a laptop computer's ports.

129

Many older and less expensive laptop computers will not let you add additional ports. Newer laptop computers, however, let you extend their hardware capabilities through the use of PCMCIA cards. As you will learn in Lesson 29, a PCMCIA card is slightly larger than a credit card and contains the electronics for a specific device, such as a modem or network card.

Buyer's Guide

If you are planning to purchase a new printer, keep in mind that a parallel printer receives information faster than a serial printer. Also, remember you must have an available port of the same type (serial or parallel) to which you attach the printer.

❖ If you are planning to buy a bus mouse or an internal modem, make sure you have an available expansion slot to hold the hardware board.

❖ When you buy a cable for a new device, pay attention to the port's sex to which you must attach the cable to ensure you purchase the correct cable type.

❖ Lastly, if you are buying a second serial or parallel card, tell your retailer you have an existing port and ask the retailer to change the board's switch settings as required.

Putting It All Together

Ports let you connect external devices such as your printer, monitor, or a mouse to your system unit. A port is actually a cable connection to a hardware board (sometimes called a *card*). Many devices connect to a serial port. Serial devices send and receive information over one wire. Most printers attach to a parallel port. Parallel devices are faster than serial devices because they send and receive information over eight wires at a time.

Glossary

card	Another term for interface card.
cascade	The process of connecting one device to a SCSI adapter and then connecting a second device to that device and a third device to the second. A SCSI card lets you connect up to seven devices.
DIP switches	Small switches found on a hardware device or interface card.
expansion slot	A connection inside the system unit into which you insert an interface card.
interface card	The hardware board containing a device port that you place inside your system unit that lets you attach a device to your computer.
joystick	A small hand held device a user can use to interact with many game programs.
parallel device	A device that communicates with the computer by sending or receiving 8-bits of data (a byte) over 8 wires. A parallel ribbon cable, for example, contains 25 wires.
ribbon cable	A thin (flat) cable that contains several wires. A parallel ribbon cable, for example, contains 25 wires.
serial device	A device that communicates with the computer one bit at a time over a single wire. Most mouse devices, for example, are serial devices.
standard cable	A cable that wraps (bundles) its wires into a single cable.

Lesson 11: Understanding the Different PC Types

Throughout the previous lessons, telling the differences between PCs has been easy: basically, a PC was either IBM compatible or a Macintosh. Because they function in the same way, we have been able to group the IBM PC, the IBM PS/2 line of computers, and IBM compatibles under the term PC. In this lesson you learn there are actually several different types of PCs, distinguished by their *central processing unit* (CPU or *microprocessor*). We describe each of these PC types using a unique number such as 8088, 286, 386, 486 or the Intel Pentium. By the end of this lesson you will understand the differences among these PC types and be able to select the one that best fits your needs and budget.

The Microprocessor Controls the Computer

As discussed, your computer's system unit contains the electronics that make the computer run. In particular, the system unit contains the *microprocessor*, the computer's electronic brain. The microprocessor controls and performs every computer instruction. The microprocessor is an integrated circuit or chip, that, in terms of size, is smaller than a dime. Every microprocessor has a name. When the IBM PC released in 1981, the PC used a microprocessor called the *8088*.

Just as software developers are constantly working to develop newer and better programs, the same is true for microprocessor designers. In 1984 when IBM announced the IBM PC AT, the computer contained a newer, more powerful microprocessor called the *80286* (or 286 for short). Not only was the 286 faster than the 8088, it provided new capabilities, while still maintaining the ability to run programs written for the 8088 (in other words, it remained PC compatible).

Since that time, the *80386* (386 for short), the *Intel 486* (486 for short), and recently, the *Intel Pentium* have been introduced. In each case, the newer microprocessors are faster and more powerful, while still maintaining full compatibility with the original 8088.

If you find all these numbers frustrating, don't worry. For now, just remember the microprocessor controls the computer's processing, and each microprocessor has a unique name. Most PCs sold today use the 386 or 486. Although the microprocessor is your computer's most powerful component, the chip that holds the microprocessor may only be a one inch by one inch square.

How Do Microprocessors Differ?

The two most obvious ways microprocessors differ are speed and cost. A computer using a 486 microprocessor may be up to 50 times faster than the original IBM PC and the Pentium several hundred times faster! However, a computer housing a Pentium may cost five times as much. In addition to running faster, the newer microprocessors support more memory and provide features that let you run several programs at the same time.

Understanding PC Speed

Within the microprocessor is a tiny clock that controls when each operation can occur. As chip designers create ways to improve performance, they can increase the clock's speed. The faster the clock ticks, the faster the computer can perform its operations.

When discussing clock speeds, we refer to the number of clock ticks per seconds (or *hertz*). Because the clocks are so fast, we often use millions of clock ticks per second (*megahertz*). Hertz and megahertz are often abbreviated as Hz and MHz. A 4.77 MHz clock ticks 4,770,000 times per second. Likewise, a 33 MHz clock ticks 33 million times per second. If you are considering buying a 486, for example, you may encounter 486s with the speeds 25MHz, 33MHZ, 66MHz, up to 100MHz, each priced differently. Remember, the faster the clock ticks, the faster the computer.

In addition to the microprocessor's clock rate, a second factor that influences the computer's speed is how fast the computer can transfer information between its internal components. In general, the computer sends information over a set of wires as electronic signals. The set of wires is a *bus*. Depending on the computer's type, the number of wires in the bus is either 8, 16, 32, or 64. Assuming the computer needs to send 32 pieces of information from one component to another, it would take a computer with an 8 wire bus four times as long as it would a computer with a 32-wire bus. You may hear a retailer discuss a computer's bus size. Now you know why. Table 11.1 lists the bus sizes of commonly used microprocessors.

TABLE 11.1 COMMON MICROPROCESSOR BUS SIZES.

MICROPROCESSOR	BUS SIZE
8088	8
8086	16
80286	16
80386SX	16
80386DX	32
486	32
Pentium	64

Understanding the Microprocessor's Memory Capabilities

Lesson 16 discusses your computer's electronic memory in detail. In general, each time you run a program, the program must reside in your computer's memory.

As program capabilities increase, so does the program's size. If you are running a spreadsheet program that uses a large worksheet containing thousands of values, the more memory your computer contains, the faster the spreadsheet runs.

Understanding Protected Mode

When the IBM PC first released, IBM intended for users to run one program at a time. As software capabilities increased, many users found they needed to exchange information between programs.

For example, a user creating a budget report with a word processor might need to look up sales information using a spreadsheet. For years, the user would have to end the word processing program, start the spreadsheet program to look up the figures, end the spreadsheet program, and restart the word processor. As you can guess, this was not only a time-consuming process, but also very frustrating.

As a solution, users can now load several programs into their computer's memory, quickly switching between programs as their needs require (see Microsoft Windows in Lesson 12). Although its ability to load and run several programs at once is very convenient, it can cause a few problems. If one of the programs you load has an error and fails, it may cause the other programs to fail as well.

To prevent one program from harming another in this way, the 286, 386, 486, and Pentium provide a mode of operation called *protected mode*. In protected mode, one program cannot harm another.

PC and Macintosh Processors Differ

If you are using an IBM PC or a PC compatible, the computer's processor is a 486, Pentium, or one of the other Intel-based processors previously discussed. The Macintosh, on the other hand, uses a Motorola processor, such as the 68030. When you talk to Macintosh users, they use the term $680x0$ to describe their processor, such as 68000, 68020, and so on, just as PC users use the term $80xxx$. In both cases, the letter x is replaced with the processor's number.

The Intel $80xxx$ and the Motorola $600x0$ are chips from two different and unrelated families of processors. As such, you can't run a program written for a Mac (a $680x0$ processor) on a Pentium (an $80xxx$ based processor). The two processors use different instructions.

Using a Math Coprocessor

As discussed, *software* (computer programs) is nothing more than a list of instructions the computer performs to accomplish a specific task. The computer's microprocessor actually performs each instruction. Because many programs perform complex mathematics, special processors that perform only mathematical instructions have been created. These processors are called *math coprocessors*. When your program needs the result of a square root or possibly the trigonometric sine or cosine of an angle, the program uses the math coprocessor. Because the math coprocessor specializes in mathematical instructions, it performs the operations very quickly. Without the math coprocessor, your computer's microprocessor might have to perform hundreds of instructions to determine a value's square root, a much slower process. Unfortunately, most computers do not come with a math coprocessor. Instead, you must buy the processor and install it on your computer's motherboard. Math coprocessors normally use a number very similar to your computer's microprocessor but ending with the number 7. For example, the math coprocessor for the 80286 is the 80287. Likewise, the math coprocessor for the 80386 is the 80387. If you are using a 486DX or a Pentium chip, the math coprocessor is built into the chip. If you're using a 486SX, however, the math coprocessor is not provided. The Pentium chip contains a built-in math coprocessor.

A math coprocessor does not improve the performance of every program you run. Instead, it only improves the speed of programs that perform complex mathematical operations, such as CAD or other engineering software. If you only use your computer for word processing, a math coprocessor will not improve your system's performance.

Understanding Multiprocessors

The microprocessor is your computer's CPU or electronic brain. The IBM PC and PC compatibles use one microprocessor. Larger and more expensive computers that use more than one CPU are called *multiprocessors*. In the future, as the price of computer chips continues to drop, PCs will become multiprocessors, which increases their speed and capabilities. For example, one processor runs your word processor, a second listens for and processes your voice commands, while a third displays the news or another TV program in a window on your screen. For now, however, simply understand that a multiprocessor is a computer that uses more than one CPU.

Upgrading Your Computer's Processor

Depending on your computer's processor type, there may be times when you can upgrade the processor chip within your computer to a newer, faster processor. For example, if you are using a 386-based processor, you may be able to replace the processor with a 486. Likewise, if your computer is using a 486 processor, you may be able to replace the 486 processor with a faster, and more powerful Pentium. To upgrade your processor, you remove the processor chip from your system's motherboard and plug in the new processor as shown in Figure 11.1.

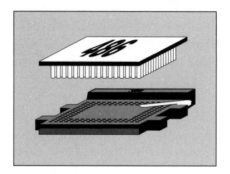

FIGURE 11.1 Replacing a processor on a motherboard.

Depending on your computer type, you may not be able to replace your processor in this way. Contact your PC's manufacturer for more information on your ability to upgrade the processor. If your system contains an upgradeable processor, have a very experienced user assist you, or a computer hardware service perform the upgrade for you.

Microprocessor Buyer's Guide

Every IBM PC and PC clone uses a microprocessor such as the 8088, 286, 386, 486, or Pentium. Before you buy any computer, make sure you know the microprocessor type and speed.

Due to their slow performance, very few PCs with the original 8088 are sold today. In most cases, the least expensive computer retailers offer is an IBM PC AT compatible using the 386. Cost-wise, the 386-based system is very attractive. However, be aware that the 386 will be very, very slow compared to newer processors. As a result, you should strongly consider a 486- or Pentium-based computer instead of the 386.

If you are considering a 486-based computer, you can reduce your costs by purchasing a computer with a slower clock speed, or a 486SX does not include a math coprocessor. Although the system may run slower, it fully supports existing software and should support future software. If you are considering a Pentium-based computer, systems with several different clock speeds are available.

Use the following list as a guide as you shop for a computer:

❖ What is the system cost?

❖ What is the clock speed? Remember, the higher the clock speed, the faster the computer.

❖ Do you require a math coprocessor?

❖ What is the bus size? The larger the bus size, the better the performance.

❖ Does the system run your existing software?

❖ What software won't the system run?

❖ Is your current processor upgradeable?

❖ Is upgrading your processor cost effective?

Also, see the Memory Buyer's Guide in Lesson 16.

Putting It All Together

PCs are classified based on their microprocessor type. The microprocessor controls every operation the computer performs. Over the past 10 years, the speed, capabilities, and name of the microprocessor has changed.

Although newer microprocessors run older software programs, many of the newer, multimedia-based software that will release over the next few years may require a 486 or a Pentium to give you adequate performance. Before you buy a computer, make sure you know its processor type.

Glossary

bus	A collection of wires over which the computer sends information.
CPU	An abbreviation for central processing unit. The computer's microprocessor.
Hz	An abbreviation for hertz that is the number of cycles per second. Microprocessor clock speeds are measured in hertz. The more hertz, the faster the clock.
math coprocessor	A specialized microprocessor that can improve your system performance for programs that perform complex math operations.
MHz	An abbreviation for megahertz or millions of cycles per second.
micro-processor	The computer's electronic brain that oversees every operation the computer performs.
multiprocessor	A computer that uses more than one CPU.
protected mode	A special mode of operation for which the processor protects (prevents) one program from interfering with another. Windows 95 supports protected mode processing while DOS does not.

Lesson 12: Understanding the Operating System

As discussed in Lesson 4, each time your computer starts, it loads a special program from disk into memory called the *operating system*. The operating system oversees your work with the computer, letting you use your printer, store information on disk, and run other programs. This lesson takes a look at the primary functions the operating system provides. DOS is the most commonly used PC operating system. Recently, however, other operating systems such as Microsoft Windows NT, IBM OS/2 and UNIX are being used on PCs. In the near future, Windows 95 will become the newest mainstay operating system. Unlike Windows 3.1, Windows 95 does not require you to run DOS. This lesson takes a brief look at these operating systems. Lesson 15 provides an introduction to DOS.

Operating System Functions

When computers were first introduced in the 1940s and 50s, every program written had to provide instructions that told the computer how to use devices such as the printer, how to store information on disk, as well as how to perform several other tasks not necessarily related to the program. The additional program instructions for working with hardware devices were very complex, and time-consuming. Programmers soon realized it would be smarter to develop one program that could control the computer's hardware, which other programs could use as they needed. With that, the first operating system was born.

Today, operating systems control and manage the use of hardware devices such as the printer or mouse. They also provide disk management by letting you store information in files. The operating system also lets you run programs such as your word processor. Lastly, the operating system provides several of its own commands that help you use the computer.

Operating Systems Other than DOS

DOS is the most commonly used PC operating system, with over 100 million users. Just as you have a choice of word processors, the same is true for operating systems. However, your choice of operating systems is very important. Normally, different operating systems cannot run one another's programs or even read the same disks. If you plan on changing operating systems, plan on buying a lot of new software. Table 12.1 lists several operating systems that run on the PC. Note, several of the operating systems listed may require a 386 or higher.

TABLE 12.1 PC OPERATING SYSTEMS.

OPERATING SYSTEM	DOS COMPATIBLE
DR DOS	Yes
Windows NT	Yes
OS/2	Yes
UNIX	No
XENIX	No
CP/M	No
Windows 95	Yes

Understanding Multitasking

DOS is a *single tasking operating system*, which means DOS lets you run one program at a time. Several of the operating systems listed in Table 12.1, however, provide *multitasking* capabilities, meaning you can run two or more programs at the same time. Assume, for example, that you are running a spreadsheet program that needs to perform a time-consuming calculation. While the spreadsheet is calculating, a multitasking operating system lets you run another program, such as your word processor, possibly allowing you to create a memo in the time you would have otherwise been waiting for the spreadsheet to complete its task. Likewise, using multitasking, you could have one program using a modem and phone lines to get information on your favorite stocks. A second program could be graphing changes in stock prices in a window on your screen. Meanwhile, you could be running a third program, perhaps a word processor, creating a report or even a chapter of a book. The ability to run several programs at once makes you more productive and makes multitasking operating systems very desirable.

Although DOS itself does not provide multitasking capabilities, you can achieve some multitasking capabilities by running Microsoft Windows, which is discussed later in this lesson.

Your User Interface

The operating system provides a way for you to run other programs. The way you communicate with the operating system is called your *interface*. As you will learn, the interface can be character based, so that you can type keyboard commands. Secondly, the interface can be picture based, allowing you to run programs by clicking your mouse on icons. If you are using DOS, for example, your screen may contain the DOS prompt for a command, similar to the one shown here:

```
C:\>
```

DOS displays this prompt when it is waiting for you to type in a command. Assuming that you start your word processor by typing the letters **WP**, you would type these letters at the DOS prompt and press **Enter** as shown.

```
C:\> WP <Enter>
```

DOS, in turn, runs your word processor. When you later end the word processing program, DOS redisplays its prompt, and waits for the next command. Although this discussion has centered on DOS, most of the operating systems listed in Table 12.1 display a prompt for and process your commands in this same way. Several of the operating systems, however, also provide a graphic (or picture) based interface that makes it much easier for you to run programs. Rather than having to remember many different commands, you simply click your mouse on different icons.

A Shell Interface Makes the Operating System Easier to Use

Although you won't need to use all of them, DOS provides over 80 commands. Each command has a unique name, and expects you to include specific values in the correct order. That's a lot to remember. To make their computers easier to use, many users run menu-driven programs (called *shells*) as soon as the operating system starts. From within the shell, the user can use menus to run the programs they desire, or simply click on the programs using their mouse. Figure 12.1 illustrates the shell interface provided with DOS version 6.0.

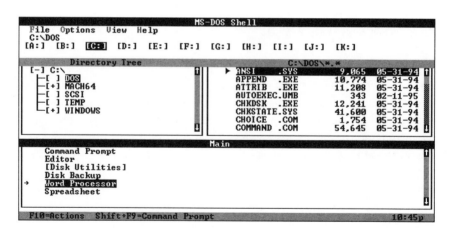

FIGURE 12.1 The DOS Shell interface.

A shell exists to make the computer easier to use. Figure 12.2 illustrates the user interface provided by the very popular Microsoft Windows. As you can see, Windows uses meaningful pictures, called *icons*, to represent your commonly used programs. To run a program within Windows, you simply double-click on the corresponding icon using your mouse.

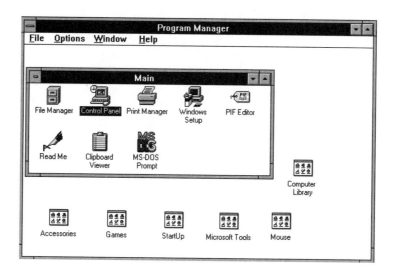

FIGURE 12.2 The Microsoft Windows user interface.

In addition to using a graphical interface, Windows provides multitasking capabilities, letting you run several programs at the same time.

PC-DOS, MS-DOS, and DOS Version Numbers

DOS is an abbreviation for *disk operating system*. DOS was developed by a company named Microsoft. MS-DOS, therefore is an abbreviation for Microsoft DOS. When IBM first released the IBM PC in 1981, IBM licensed DOS from Microsoft for use on the PC and called it PC-DOS. If you are using an IBM computer such as an original IBM PC or a PS/2, you are probably using PC-DOS. If you are using a PC compatible computer, you are probably using MS-DOS.

From the user's perspective, PC-DOS and MS-DOS are the same, each providing the same capabilities and commands.

The version of DOS released in 1981 was 1.0. Over the past decade, DOS has undergone several changes. Each time the DOS developers release a new version of DOS, they increment the version number. Table 12.2 lists the version changes MS-DOS has experienced since its release in 1981.

145

TABLE 12.2 DOS VERSION NUMBER CHANGES SINCE 1981.

DATE	VERSION
1981	1.0
1982	1.25, 2.0, 2.01, 2.11, 2.25
1984	3.0, 3.1
1986	3.2
1987	3.3
1988	4.01
1991	5.0
1993	6.0
1994	6.1, 6.2
1995	6.22

As you can see from Table 12.2, the DOS developers are constantly working on ways to improve DOS. Because DOS effects the behavior of every program you run, you probably want to upgrade to the latest version of DOS.

Looking at Windows NT

Windows NT (new technology) is an operating system developed by Microsoft. NT is an enhanced version of the popular Microsoft Windows programs. NT requires a 386 or greater and 8 Mb to 12 Mb of RAM. For the best NT performance, you want to use a 486 with about 16 Mb. Unlike Windows that is constrained by the fact that it runs on top of DOS, Windows NT is an operating system itself. As such, NT does not require DOS to exist on your system. However, NT is DOS compatible, which means it can run DOS programs and read disks created by DOS. To the user, NT appears very much like Windows. In fact, NT runs Windows-based programs. The advantage of using NT over Windows is that NT makes better use of the PC's memory management capabilities. In addition, Microsoft has written NT so that is runs on non-Intel based computers, such as the DEC Alpha. In this way, NT may eventually run on a wide variety of computers, not just PCs.

Figure 12.3 illustrates the Windows NT user interface. As you can see, Windows NT looks very much like Windows 3.1.

FIGURE 12.3 The Windows NT user interface.

Looking at OS/2

OS/2 is a PC operating system created by IBM. Like NT, OS/2 is DOS compatible and provides a graphical user interface that lets you run programs with the click of a mouse. Also like NT, OS/2 performs best when you are using a powerful system such as a 486 or Pentium that has abundant memory. Many IBM-based PCs ship with OS/2 preinstalled. As you can see, OS/2 provides a graphical user interface similar to Windows.

Looking at UNIX

All of the operating systems discussed thus far, DOS, Windows NT, and OS/2 are *single user systems*, meaning only one person can use the system at any given time. UNIX is a multiuser operating system that allows multiple users to access the system. There are currently about eighteen million UNIX users, which places UNIX second only to DOS. Traditionally, UNIX was run on larger minicomputers to which users accessed the system using terminals (not PCs) as shown in Figure 12.4. The terminals connected to the minicomputer were normally not computers themselves. As such, all the programs were run on the minicomputer. UNIX allowed each user to simultaneously run the program they desired. Unlike NT and OS/2, UNIX is not DOS compatible. Most users would not purchase UNIX for their own use. However, users who work in an office environment may encounter UNIX. The point to remember is that, UNIX, like all other operating systems, exists to let you run programs, use devices such as printers, and to store information in files that reside on disks.

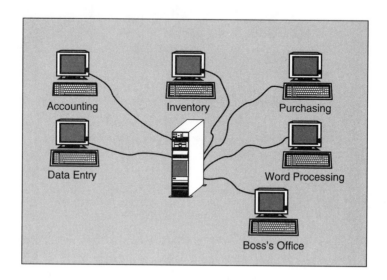

FIGURE 12.4 Terminals connected to a minicomputer.

With the tremendous power and speeds of 486- and Pentium-based computers, UNIX can now be run on a PC. Depending on the user needs, one user can run UNIX at a time or multiple users can connect to the PC (given the proper hardware), treating the PC much like a minicomputer. Lesson 30 introduces the Internet, today's information highway. To date, UNIX is the most widely used operating system found on the Internet.

Looking at Windows 95

Since the release of version 3.1, Windows has become the most widely used graphical user interface in the world. Using Windows, you can run programs by simply clicking your mouse on a program icon. For years, Windows has been constrained by the fact that it runs on top of the DOS operating system. As such, Windows 3.1 is not an operating system, but rather, a user interface.

Windows 95 is an operating system and a graphical user interface that replaces DOS and Windows 3.1. As such, Windows 95 takes over the responsibility of such tasks as storing files, running programs, and controlling devices. Windows 95 is a 32-bit operating system which requires a 386-based system or higher.

Although Windows 95 still uses a graphical user interface, the interface has evolved from Windows 3.1 to appear more like the Mac interface. Figure 12.5 illustrates the Windows 95 user interface.

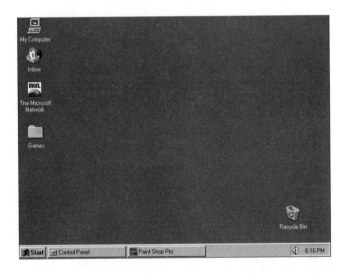

FIGURE 12.5 The Windows 95 user interface.

Using Windows 95, you can run the same programs that you used under Windows 3.1 and DOS.

Installing the Operating System

The operating system is software, and like all other programs, must be installed on your disk before your computer can run it. When you purchase a new PC, your retailer may install DOS on your hard disk for you. If you must install the operating system yourself, follow the installation instructions provided with your system documentation, or refer to a book. If you are using any of the operating systems listed in Table 12.1 you will be able to find a large collection of books specific to each. Unlike software programs such as a word processor that you can add to the programs that already reside on your disk, an operating system installation normally overwrites any information on your disk. Luckily, however, your computer retailer normally installs the operating system on to your hard disk for you.

Operating System Buyer's Guide

Most users won't change from using DOS to a different operating system such as OS/2 or UNIX without a significant amount of research on the benefits and disadvantages of making such a change. As such, the following list provides guidelines you should keep in mind when you consider upgrading to a new version of DOS.

- ❖ Is the new version fully compatible with your existing hardware and software?

- ❖ Does the new version have additional hardware requirements (such as more memory)?

- ❖ What capabilities does the new version provide? How many of those capabilities will you use?

Although some new versions may not appear to provide considerable new features, they may fix errors that exist in your current version, or they may improve the operating system's performance.

Putting It All Together

Each time your computer starts, it loads and runs a special program called the *operating system*. The operating system controls your computer's resources, letting you use the printer, store information on disk, and most importantly, run other programs. DOS is the most commonly used PC operating system.

Glossary

DOS   An abbreviation for disk operating system. DOS
                                   is the most commonly used PC operating system.

DOS prompt

The message DOS displays when it is ready for you to type your next command. The DOS prompt typically contains the current disk drive letter and possibly the current directory, such as:

`C:\>`

multitasking

The ability to run two or more programs at the same time.

operating system

A special software program the computer runs that lets you use your printer, disks, and run other programs.

shells

A special program from within which the user runs other programs. Shell programs are often menu driven and easy to use.

Lesson 13: Understanding Files

In Lesson 8 you learned that if you don't store the information with which you are working to disk, you lose the information when you exit the program, or turn off your computer. To organize the information you store on disk, the operating system places the information files, much like you would group information in a paper file folder in an office. Files on your disk might contain a letter, report, worksheet, or even a computer program. As you will learn, every file on your disk must have a name. Likewise, many of the operations you perform on paper files in an office, such as copying, viewing, renaming, and later discarding, also apply to files stored on your disk. This lesson introduces you to working with files.

Understanding File Names

Every file on your disk has a name. If you are using DOS, a file's name consists of two parts: an eight-character base name and a three-character extension. The file name should describe the file's contents. The file's three character extension should describe the file's type. If a file contains a letter, you might use the extension LTR. Likewise, for a memo you can use MEM., and for a word processing document DOC. Table 13.1 lists several commonly used file extensions.

TABLE 13.1 COMMONLY USED FILE NAME EXTENSIONS.

FILE EXTENSION	FILE'S PROBABLE CONTENTS
LTR	A letter
DOC	A word processing document
RPT	A report
MEM	A memo
COM	A command
EXE	An executable program
SYS	A DOS system file

The file's eight-character base name should provide you with specifics about the file, such as who the letter or memo the file contains is written to. DOS lets you use one to eight characters in the base name. Keep in mind, however, that a single-letter base name is probably not too meaningful. When you use a file name, you must separate the base name from the extension using a period. For example, you might name a file that contains a report about your company's 1996 budget as BUDGET96.RPT. Table 13.2 lists several meaningful file names that describe a file's contents.

TABLE 13.2 MEANINGFUL FILE NAMES THAT DESCRIBE A FILE'S CONTENTS.

FILE NAME	FILE CONTENTS
MAY96IRS.LTR	A letter to the IRS written in May 1996.
VACATION.MEM	A memo containing a company's vacation policy.
WORDPROC.EXE	The file containing an executable word processing program.
LESSON13.DOC	A word processing document containing this lesson's text.

Filenames Under Windows 95

As you may know, Windows 95 is a new operating system that replaces DOS and Windows 3.1. Windows 95 eliminates the short filename restriction DOS users have had to work with for years. Under Windows 95, your filenames can contain up to 255 characters! The following list, for example, illustrates several filenames that take advantage of Windows 95 long filename support:

COMPANY_BUDGET_FOR_1996.XLS

CUSTOMERS_WHO_HAVE_PURCHASED_IN_1995.MDB

LESSON_13_OF_THE_BOOK_WELCOME_TO_PERSONAL_COMPUTERS.DOC

Understanding File Operations

As discussed, you perform many of the same operations on your disk files you might perform on paper files. This section examines several common file operations, including a brief discussion of the DOS commands you would use to perform each operation.

Copying a File's Contents to a New File

Just as you might make a copy of a paper file for another person to read, the same holds true for the files on your disk. For example, to create this book, I created files on my hard disk containing the text for each lesson. When I was done with a lesson, I copied the file containing the text from my hard disk to a floppy disk I then sent to the publisher. When the publisher received the floppy disk, they in turn made copies of the file for their editors, art department, and proofreaders. To copy a file using DOS, you issue the COPY command. The following COPY command copies the file named LESSON13.DOC from drive C to the floppy disk in drive A.

```
C:\PCBOOK> COPY LESSON13.DOC A:LESSON13.DOC   <Enter>
```

As you can see, the command includes the name of the file you want to copy (LESSON13.DOC) and the name or location of the new file (A:LESSON13.DOC). The letters A: tell COPY to place the new copy on drive A.

Renaming a File

As discussed, a file's name should describe the file's contents. Should you change a file's contents, you may need to change the file name. If you are using DOS, the RENAME command lets you change a file's name. The following RENAME command, for example, renames the file POLICY.MEM to PARKING.MEM.

```
C:\> RENAME POLICY.MEM PARKING.MEM  <Enter>
```

The format of the RENAME command is simply RENAME OldName NewName.

NOTE

Do not rename files whose contents or purpose you don't fully understand. If you rename a file needed by one of your programs, the program may not be able to run.

Examining a File's Contents

If you create a file using your word processor or a spreadsheet program, you probably have to view the file's contents using the same program. Such programs place special characters in their files that may select a special attribute such as bolding or underlining. Although these characters are meaningful to the program that created the file, other programs won't understand them, and as a result, probably can't display the file's contents.

If you have a file that only contains letters and numbers (often called an *ASCII* file) and no special formatting codes, you can use the DOS TYPE command to display the file's contents. The following TYPE command displays the contents of a file named CONFIG.SYS.

```
C:\> TYPE CONFIG.SYS  <Enter>
```

As before, if you create a file using a specific program, you can use the same program to print a copy of the file's contents. If the file contains only letters and numbers, you can use the DOS PRINT command as shown here:

```
C:\> PRINT CONFIG.SYS  <Enter>
```

Files with the .COM or .EXE extension contain command or program instructions in a format you cannot display or print.

Discarding a File When it is No Longer Needed

Just as you would discard a paper file in your office when the file is no longer needed, the same is true for files on disk. When you remove a file from disk, you make the disk space the file consumed available for use by other files. Using DOS, the DEL (short for *delete*) command removes a file from your disk. The following DEL command removes a file named REPORT.OLD.

```
C:\> DEL REPORT.OLD   <Enter>
```

If you accidentally delete one or more wrong files, you may be able to "undelete" the files using a disk utility program. See Lesson 40 for a list of disk utility program names.

NOTE

Listing the Files on a Disk

To help you organize your files, DOS lets you group related files into lists called *directories*. The best way to visualize directories is as drawers in a filing cabinet. Using directories, you can group your word processing documents in one location, and your spreadsheet files in another. The DOS DIR (short for *directory*) command displays the names of files that reside in a directory.

```
C:\> DIR   <Enter>
```

For more information on directories within DOS, refer to Lesson 14 that discusses the CHDIR, MKDIR, and RMDIR commands.

Files Within Your Applications

With almost any application program you run, you create one or more files. For example, when you use a word processor, you create files that contain your documents, possibly letters, memos, or reports. Likewise, if you use a spreadsheet program, you store your data in a file. As you create files within your applications, you are normally given the opportunity to assign the file's name. As discussed, use meaningful names that describe the file's contents. In that way, you can quickly find the files you require at a later time.

Files Within Windows

When you run programs within Windows, you create files as just discussed. Most Windows applications let you work with files in a consistent way, providing a menu of file options similar to those shown in Figure 13.1.

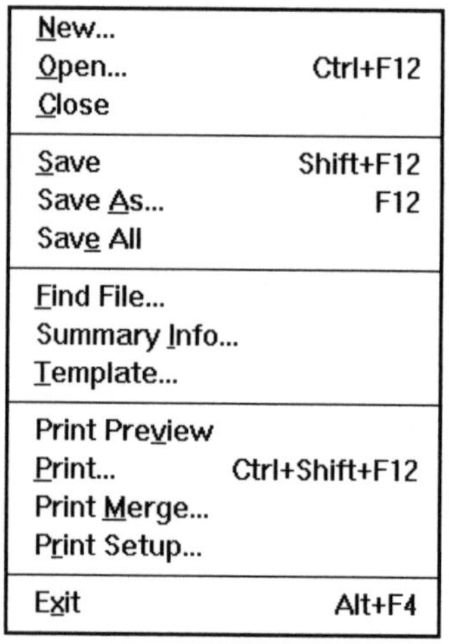

```
New...
Open...                    Ctrl+F12
Close

Save                       Shift+F12
Save As...                      F12
Save All

Find File...
Summary Info...
Template...

Print Preview
Print...               Ctrl+Shift+F12
Print Merge...
Print Setup...

Exit                        Alt+F4
```

FIGURE 13.1 The File menu within a Windows application.

As you can see, the File menu lets you open an existing file, create a new file, print the file, or save your work to a file. If you select the **Save As** option, Windows displays the dialog box shown in Figure 13.2 asking you for the desired filename.

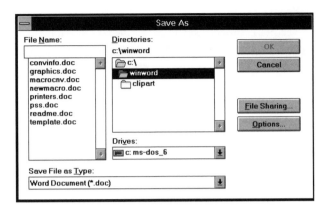

FIGURE 13.2 The Save As dialog box within Windows.

From within the Save As dialog box you can type in the filename you desire, specifying a meaningful filename. If you simply type in a filename, Windows stores the file on the current disk. If you want to store the file on a different disk, simply precede the filename with the drive letter and colon, such as A:FILE-NAME.EXT. Likewise, if you later need to access the file, you can open and display the file's contents using the **Open** option. When you select the **Open** option, Windows displays the Open dialog box as shown in Figure 13.3.

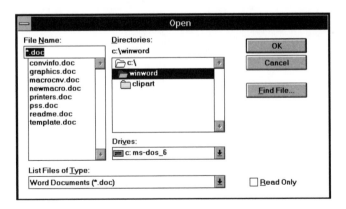

FIGURE 13.3 The Open dialog box.

Within the Open dialog box you can type in the filename and press **Enter** to open and display the file's contents. If the file resides on a different disk, precede the filename with a drive letter and colon. If the file resides in a different directory (see Lesson 14), you can click on the desired directory using your mouse and then type in the desired filename. It is important that you understand the Save As and Open dialog boxes because you encounter these in each Windows application you run.

Copying, Renaming, and Deleting Files within Windows

As you learned earlier in this lesson, you can use the DOS COPY, RENAME, and DEL commands to manage files on your disk. Most users, however, work from within Windows. As the number of files you create within Windows increases, you eventually need to move, copy, or delete one or more files. To help users perform these file operations, Windows provides a special program called the File Manager, as shown in Figure 13.4

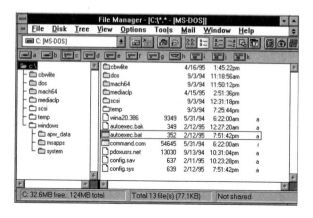

FIGURE 13.4 The Windows File Manager.

Using the File Manager you can click your mouse on the desired file and then perform the desired operation.

Putting It All Together

If you don't save your work to a file on disk, you lose your work when you exit the program or turn off your computer. Every file on your disk has a name. The file name should describe the file's contents. Using DOS, filenames consist of two parts: an *eight-character base name* that provides specifics about the file, and a *three-character* extension that describes the file's type. In general, the operations you perform on disk files are almost the same as those you would perform on paper files in an office. To help you perform these operations, DOS provides the COPY, RENAME, DEL, TYPE, and PRINT commands.

A directory is a list of related files. Using directories, you can organize your files on disk. The DOS DIR command displays a list of names of files in a specific directory. Table 13.3 summarizes the DOS file manipulation commands.

TABLE 13.3 DOS FILE MANIPULATION COMMANDS.

FUNCTION	COMMAND	EXAMPLE
Display a file's contents	TYPE	TYPE BUDGET.DAT
Print a file's contents	PRINT	PRINT BUDGET.DAT
Copy one file to another	COPY	COPY BUDGET.DAT, BUDGET.SAV
Rename a file	REN	REN OLDNAME.DAT, NEWNAME.DAT
Delete a file from your disk	DEL	DEL OLDFILE.DAT

To perform similar operations within Windows, you must use a special program called the Windows File Manager.

Glossary

ASCII file	A file that contains only characters and digits. A word processing document, for example, contains hidden formatting characters and as such, is not an ASCII file.
directory	A list of related files. Directories help organize your disk by grouping related files, just as you might place related files in the same filing cabinet drawer.

file	A named collection of information stored on a disk.
file extension	The three character portion of a filename that describes the file's type, such as MEM for a memo, DOC for a document, or RPT for a report.
File Manager	A special program provided with Windows that helps you manage files on your disk by copying, renaming, moving, printing, or even deleting the files.

Lesson 14: Organizing Your Files Using Directories

In Lesson 13 you learned that between user sessions you can store information in files. For example, if you start a word processing document late Monday afternoon, you can store the document in a file so that on Tuesday you can continue your work. Over time, you create a huge number of files. To help you keep your files organized, operating systems let you create directories. The best way to visualize a directory is as a drawer within a filing cabinet into which you place related paper files. As you will learn, the directories on your disk use unique names, such as BUSINESS, SCHOOL, NOTES, FAXES and so on. When you need to store or retrieve a specific file, you simply specify the directory within which you want the file stored. This lesson examines the directories under DOS and Windows. If you are working with a different operating system, the concepts presented and many of the commands are still the same.

Understanding Directories

A directory is a storage location on your disk into which you can place related files. When you first use a disk, the disk contains only one directory, called the *root*. The root directory is so named, because, like the root of a tree, all your directories grow from it (as shown in Figure 14.1).

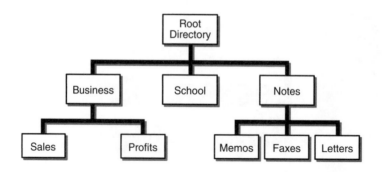

FIGURE 14.1 The directories on your disk grow from a special directory called the *root*.

If you are using DOS, Windows NT, OS/2, or even Windows 95, the root directory is represented using a backslash character (\). To create the directory named BUSINESS, for example, you use the MKDIR command as shown here:

```
C:\> MKDIR  \BUSINESS  <Enter>
```

Pictorially, your directory hierarchy would appear similar to that shown in Figure 14.2.

FIGURE 14.2 Creating the directory business.

To create the additional directories SCHOOL, NOTES, and FAXES, you would use the additional MKDIR commands shown here:

```
C:\> MKDIR  \SCHOOL  <Enter>
C:\> MKDIR  \NOTES  <Enter>
C:\> MKDIR  \FAXES  <Enter>
```

As you can see, to create the three directories, you had to issue three MKDIR commands. Note the backslashes that precede the directory names. When you specify a directory name, you essentially specify a road map the operating system follows to locate the directory. In this case, by preceding the directory name with a backslash, you tell the operating system to start at the root directory. Pictorially, your directory structure would now appear similar to that shown in Figure 14.3.

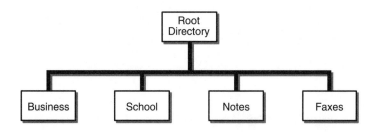

FIGURE 14.3 Adding three additional directories to the directory structure.

Assume, for example, that you want to further organize your school files by subject, including the directories MATH, SPANISH, and HISTORY as shown in Figure 14.4.

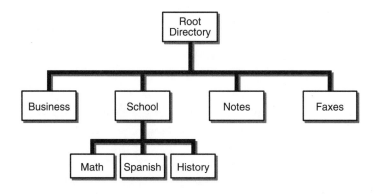

FIGURE 14.4 Creating subdirectories within the school directory.

To create the subdirectories, you would use the following MKDIR commands:

```
C:\> MKDIR  \SCHOOL\MATH  <Enter>
C:\> MKDIR  \SCHOOL\SPANISH  <Enter>
C:\> MKDIR  \SCHOOL\HISTORY  <Enter>
```

If you follow the directory road map, you start at the root directory (\), move to the SCHOOL directory, and then create the desired directory.

NOTE In addition to helping you organize your files, directories also help you protect your files. For example, if you issue a DEL command to delete files, the command only affects files in the directory specified. Files in other directories are not deleted. Likewise, if you issue a COPY command, the command only affects files in one directory.

Selecting the Current Directory

When you store files in a filing cabinet, you normally open a specific drawer and store or retrieve files. In a similar way, when you work with files, you can select the current directory. To select the current directory, you use the CHDIR command. In short, the CHDIR command is similar to opening the filing cabinet drawer labeled BUSINESS, SCHOOL, or FAXES. The operations you perform within the drawer only affect those files. For example, the following command selects the BUSINESS directory as the current directory:

```
C:\> CHDIR  \BUSINESS  <Enter>
C:\BUSINESS>
```

Note how the directory name that appears in the DOS prompt changed when you selected the BUSINESS directory. In most cases, the prompt changes to reflect the current directory name. After you select the BUSINESS directory, you can issue file manipulation commands such as DIR, TYPE, DEL, or RENAME that only affect files in the BUSINESS directory. In a similar way, the following command would select the FAXES directory:

```
C:\> CHDIR \FAXES  <Enter>
```

Lastly, the following command selects the subdirectory SPANISH within the SCHOOL directory:

```
C:\> CHDIR \SCHOOL\SPANISH  <Enter>
```

Note how each CHDIR command specifies a complete road map to the desired directory, beginning with the root (\).

Removing a Directory

Just as there are times when you need to delete files you no longer require, the same is true for directories. To remove a directory, you use the RMDIR command. For example, to remove the directory FAXES, you use the following command:

```
C:\> RMDIR \FAXES  <Enter>
```

In a similar way, the following command would remove the subdirectory SPANISH from the SCHOOL directory:

```
C:\> RMDIR \SCHOOL\SPANISH  <Enter>
```

Most operating systems do not let you remove a directory until you have deleted the files it contains.

NOTE

Understanding Relative and Complete Directory Names

When you specify a directory name, you can do so in one of two ways. First, you can specify a complete directory name, beginning with the root directory as shown in each of the commands presented so far. However, when you select a directory as the current directory, you can then refer to the subdirectories it contains by name. For example, assume you select the directory SCHOOL as the current directory using the following CHDIR command:

```
C:\> CHDIR \SCHOOL  <Enter>
```

You could then use the following CHDIR command to select the directory SPANISH:

167

```
C:\SCHOOL> CHDIR SPANISH  <Enter>
C:\SCHOOL\SPANISH>
```

When you want to select a directory that resides beneath the current directory, you can simply specify the directory name, as opposed to a complete path name. If you want to select the directory BUSINESS, you must specify a complete path-name to the directory because BUSINESS does not reside beneath the directory SCHOOL\SPANISH:

```
C:\SCHOOL\SPANISH> CHDIR \BUSINESS  <Enter>
C:\BUSINESS>
```

Directories Within Windows

As you will learn in Lesson 20, Windows replaces commands such as CHDIR and RMDIR with menu options and visual directory trees. For example, Figure 14.5 illustrates how Windows displays the directories you have created in this lesson.

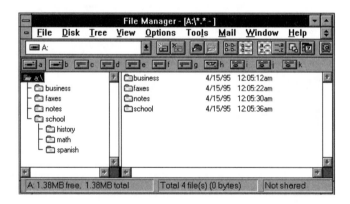

FIGURE 14.5 Viewing directories using the Windows File Manager.

To select a directory within Windows, you simply click your mouse on the directory name within the directory tree. The Windows File Manager lets you create and remove directories as you require. As you select different directories, many Windows programs display the files the directory contains. Assume for example, that you are using a Windows-based word processor. When you want to save your document, Windows displays the Save As dialog box shown in Figure 14.6.

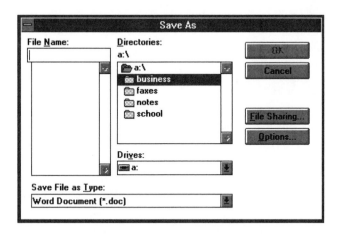

FIGURE 14.6 The Windows Save As dialog box.

To place the file in a specific directory, click on a directory from the list of available directories and then type in the file name. Likewise, when you later need to open the file, Windows displays the Open dialog box shown in Figure 14.7.

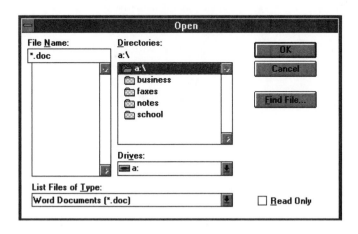

FIGURE 14.7 The Open dialog box.

To open a file that resides in a specific directory, click your mouse on the desired directory and then click on the desired file. As you can see, storing a file within a directory on your disk is similar to opening a folder within the drawer of a filing cabinet and inserting a piece of paper into the folder. When you later need to use the paper (file), you again open the directory and open the file.

Putting It All Together

Directories help you organize the files that reside on your disk. To create a directory you use the MKDIR command. To select a directory, you use the CHDIR command. Selecting a directory with CHDIR is similar to opening the drawer of a filing cabinet. To remove a directory that is no longer needed, you use the RMDIR command. If you work within Windows, you can use the File Manager to create, select, and remove directories. As you store or retrieve files within most Windows-based programs, you can use the Save As and Open dialog boxes to select the desired directories.

Glossary

directory
: A location on your disk within which you store related files.

root directory
: A special directory with which all disks start and from which each directory you create grows. The root directory is so named because your other directories grow from root much like branches of a tree.

subdirectory
: A directory that appears within another directory.

Lesson 15: Getting Started with DOS

In Lesson 14, you learned that *DOS*, an abbreviation for *disk operating system*, is a special software program your PC runs each time it starts. DOS lets you use hardware devices such as your printer or mouse, store files on disk, and run other programs. In addition, DOS provides over eighty of its own commands. This lesson introduces you to DOS, teaching you how to execute several different DOS commands.

Starting DOS

Each time your computer successfully completes its power-on self-test discussed in Lesson 4, the computer first searches the floppy disk drive A for a disk containing DOS. The computer looks for DOS on drive A first for two reasons. First, not all computers have a hard disk. Second, if your computer has a hard disk, and the disk becomes damaged, you need a way of starting DOS. Because the computer looks on drive A first, you can start DOS by placing a DOS floppy disk in drive A.

To start DOS, the disk must contain several special files. If the floppy disk in drive A does not contain these files, your screen displays the following message:

```
Non-System disk or disk error
Replace and strike any key when ready
```

If this message appears, remove the floppy disk and let your computer start DOS from the hard disk, or insert a floppy disk that contains DOS.

As you will learn in Lesson 16, your computer loads DOS from the disk into its electronic memory. As you will learn, DOS lets you define several commands it should automatically run each time it starts. Depending on the individual who installed DOS on your system, DOS may ask you to type in the current system date as shown here:

```
Current date is Sat 09-30-95
Enter new date (mm-dd-yy):
```

If the date DOS displays is correct, press **Enter** to continue; otherwise, type in the correct date. DOS may then ask you to type in the current time as follows:

```
Current time is 8:5:13.33a
Enter new time:
```

If the time displayed is correct, press **Enter** to continue; otherwise type in the correct time. DOS only requires you to specify hours and minutes such as 8:30.

DOS may simply display a set of letters similar to the following that are called the DOS *prompt*:

```
C:\>
```

DOS displays its prompt to tell you it's ready for you to type in a command.

To make DOS easier to use, DOS versions 4 and later menu-driven programs, called *shells*, from within which you can run other programs and work with your files. For information on using the shell, refer to a DOS book.

If you are using a DOS version 6, DOS may display its shell interface as shown in Figure 15.1. If this shell appears, press your keyboard's **F3** function key to exit the shell. DOS displays its prompt.

As discussed in Lesson 5, press the **Alt-F3** keyboard combination by holding down the **Alt** key and pressing **F3**. DOS ends the shell program, and displays its prompt.

Depending again on your system, DOS may run a different shell program from those shown here. In any case, exit the program to the DOS prompt.

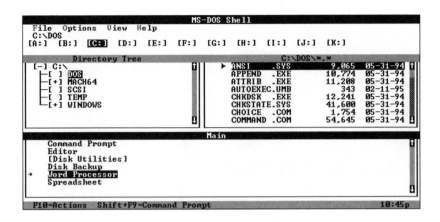

FIGURE 15.1 The DOS Shell interface.

Issuing DOS Commands

As discussed, DOS displays its prompt when it is waiting for you to issue a command. When you type in a command and press **Enter**, DOS performs the command. When the command ends, DOS again displays its prompt and waits for your next command.

The DOS VER (short for *version*) command directs DOS to display its version number on your screen. To run the VER command, type the letters **VER** and press **Enter**. In the case of DOS version 6.22, DOS displays the following:

```
C:\> VER <Enter>
MS-DOS Version 6.22
```

If you mistype a letter, use the **Backspace** key as discussed in Lesson 5 to erase the letter. Although most books show DOS commands entered in all uppercase letters, DOS does not care if you use uppercase, lowercase, or a combination of both. The following command, for example, invokes VER using lowercase letters.

```
C:\> ver <Enter>
MS-DOS Version 6.22
```

DOS command names can only contain up to eight characters. As a result, many DOS commands use abbreviated names. The DOS CLS command, for example, is an abbreviation for *clear screen*. When you invoke CLS, DOS erases your current screen contents and displays its prompt in your screen's upper-left corner.

```
C:\ > CLS <Enter>
```

Internal and External Commands

DOS provides two types of commands: *small internal commands* DOS keeps in your computer's memory, and *larger external commands* that DOS stores on disk. As you will learn in Lesson 16, your computer has a fixed amount of memory it can use for running programs. Because DOS has over eighty commands, it cannot possibly fit all its commands into memory. As a result, DOS places many of its larger commands on disk. When you issue one of these commands, DOS loads the command from disk into memory. The command remains in memory as long as it runs. When the command ends, DOS can run a different command using the same memory locations. Because these commands don't reside in memory at all times, they are called *external* commands. DOS keeps smaller commands such as VER, CLS, and DIR in memory at all times, making them *internal* commands.

Your DOS external commands reside in a directory on your disk named *DOS*. Use the following DIR command to display their names:

```
C:\> DIR \DOS <Enter>
```

If the file names scroll past you on the screen faster than you can read them, include the characters /P in the DIR command as shown here:

```
C:\> DIR \DOS /P <Enter>
```

DOS pauses, waiting for you to press any key each time your screen fills with directory names. Under DOS 6.22, the command displays a screen similar to the following:

```
C:\>DIR \DOS /P <Enter>
Volume in drive C is DOS DISK
```

```
Volume Serial Number is 1A73-5E09
Directory of C:\DOS
                          <DIR>        09-03-94    11:18a
                          <DIR>        09-03-94    11:18a
ATTRIB          BIN      11,208        05-31-94     6:22a
CHKDSK          EXE      12,241        05-31-94     6:22a
COUNTRY    SYS  26,936   05-31-94      6:22a
COUNTRY    TXT  15,920   05-31-94      6:22a
DEBUG           EXE      15,718        05-31-94     6:22a
DOSSETUP   INI  3,114    05-31-94      6:22a
EDIT            COM      413           05-31-94     6:22a
EXPAND          EXE      16,129        05-31-94     6:22a
FDISK           EXE      29,336        05-31-94     6:22a
FORMAT          COM      22,974        05-31-94     6:22a
KEYB            COM      15,750        05-31-94     6:22a
KEYBOARD   SYS  34,598   05-31-94      6:22a
MEM             EXE      32,502        05-31-94     6:22a
NLSFUNC    EXE  7,036    05-31-94      6:22a
README          TXT      60,646        05-31-94     6:22a
NETWORKS   TXT  17,465   05-31-94      6:22a
Press any key to continue...
[end cc]
```

The files in the directory listing with the EXE (short for *executable program*) and COM (short for *command*) contain the DOS commands.

Changing Disk Drives

As discussed in Lesson 8, each of your computer's disk drives has a unique name. Your hard disk is normally drive C, and your floppy disks, drives A and B. DOS lets you use each of the disks by using the drive's name. DOS lets you select one disk drive as the current drive. Normally, the DOS prompt contains the drive letter of the current drive. Given the following prompt, the current drive is the hard disk, drive C.

Unless you tell DOS to look elsewhere, DOS looks for files and commands on the current drive. Assume you have a floppy disk in drive A, and you want to know what's on the disk. As you know, the DIR command lists the names of files on a disk. However, unless you tell DOS to do otherwise, it uses the current drive, which is drive C.

To view the files on the floppy disk in drive A, you have two choices. First, you can include the drive letter followed by a colon (A:) in the DIR command as shown here:

```
C:\> DIR A: <Enter>
```

Because you've told DIR to look specifically on drive A, DIR lists the floppy disk's files as you desire.

Your second option is to select drive A as the current drive. To select a specific drive, type the drive letter followed by a colon at the DOS prompt and press **Enter**. The following command selects drive A as the current drive:

```
C:\ A: <Enter>
A:\>
```

Note how DOS changes its prompt to include the letter A, which corresponds to the new current drive. Unless you tell DOS to do otherwise, DOS only looks on drive A for files and commands. To change the current drive back to drive C, perform the following command:

```
A:\> C: <Enter>
```

Turning Off Your Computer

As you have seen, each time a command ends, DOS redisplays its prompt and waits for your next command. As a rule, only turn your computer off while DOS is displaying its prompt. Some programs wait until you end them to save your work to disk. If you turn off your computer while one of these programs is running, your work may be lost. If you only turn off your computer when DOS displays its prompt, you eliminate the chance of losing information this way.

DOS Error Messages

Lesson 36 examines the causes for and solutions to the most common DOS error messages. When you encounter error messages while working with DOS, turn to Lesson 36 first. If the lesson does not discuss the error message, refer to the DOS User Manual that accompanied your computer.

DOS and Windows 95

As discussed in Lesson 12, Windows 95 is a new operating system that replaces DOS and Windows 3.1. As such, when you use Windows 95, you may never have the need to work with DOS commands. Instead, you will run programs, copy files, and perform other operations by clicking your mouse on graphic icons. However, to let you still run your DOS-based programs, Windows 95 will still support your older DOS programs as well many DOS commands.

Putting it All Together

DOS is the most commonly used operating system. DOS lets you use hardware devices such as your printer or mouse, store information in files on disk, and run programs. Each time your computer starts, it loads DOS from disk into memory. Depending on who installed DOS, your system may ask you to type in the current date and time, it may display a menu driven shell program, or it may simply display the DOS prompt.

The DOS prompt is a message, normally similar to the C:\> that DOS displays on your screen when it is waiting for you to type in a command. To run a command, type in the command's name and press **Enter**. DOS lets you type in your command's name in upper or lower case letters. When the command ends, DOS displays its prompt and waits for you to type in the next command. As a rule, only turn off your computer while DOS is displaying its prompt.

Glossary

command line	The information typed at the DOS prompt to execute a command. The command contains a command name and possibly other information such as a file name.
executable program	Any computer program—such as your word processor, spreadsheet, or even Microsoft Windows.
external command	A larger DOS command whose instructions DOS stores in a file on disk. Before DOS can execute an external command, DOS must load the command from disk into memory.
internal command	A small command whose instructions DOS keeps in memory at all times.

Lesson 16: Understanding Memory

The PC has two ways to remember information. First, for the PC to remember something long term, after a program ends or you turn off your computer, you must first store the information on disk, as discussed in Lesson 8. When you run a program, the computer places the program (the list of instructions) and the program's data in short term, electronic memory. This *short term memory*, or *RAM* as it is often called, is where your computer holds your word processing documents or spreadsheets until you store them on disk. If your computer loses power, the contents of its electronic memory are lost. Likewise, when you end one program and start another, the previous contents of the computer's electronic memory are overwritten. This lesson examines the computer's electronic memory, its uses, and characteristics. In addition, this lesson discusses the different memory types your PC can use, providing a list of guidelines you can follow when you add memory to your computer. PC memory is a very important concept and entire books have been dedicated to covering it in detail. As such, only the essentials are covered here.

What Does Memory Look Like?

Lesson 8 presented illustrations of different floppy disk types. Because you remove floppy disks from the computer when you don't need to use them, most users have seen what a floppy disk looks like. On the other hand, because the computer's electronic memory resides *inside* the system unit, most users have never seen it. As shown in Figure 16.1, the computer's electronic memory is made up of chips.

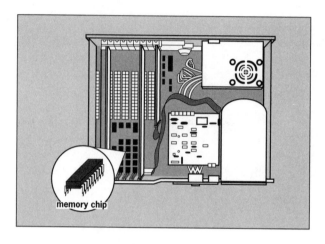

FIGURE 16.1 The computer's electronic memory consists of chips.

Understanding Memory Size

As was the case for disk sizes discussed in Lesson 8, the size of your computer's memory is described in terms of *bytes*. You can think of a byte of information as a character of information. As before, the letters *Kb* are an abbreviation for kilobyte or 1,024 bytes. Likewise, the letters *Mb* are an abbreviation for megabyte or 1,048,576 bytes. Most PCs sold today have at least 4Mb of memory. As you will learn, depending on your computer's microprocessor type, the amount and type of memory the computer can hold and use differ.

Using the DOS MEM command, you can determine how much (and which type of) memory your PC contains:

```
C:\> MEM  <Enter>
    655360 bytes total conventional memory
```

```
 655360 bytes available to MS-DOS
 593744 largest executable program size
1048576 bytes total EMS memory
1048576 bytes free EMS memory
7602176 bytes total contiguous extended memory
      0 bytes available contiguous extended memory
1048576 bytes available XMS memory
        MS-DOS resident in High Memory Area
```

Also, as discussed in Lesson 4, during the power on self test, the PC normally displays a count of the amount of memory it contains.

How Much Memory Do You Need?

In most cases, the programs you plan to run dictate how much memory your computer needs. As a rule, the more memory your computer has, the better your programs perform. Because your computer's memory is electronic as opposed to your mechanical disks, memory is very fast. If, for example, you are working with a large worksheet all of which fits in your computer's memory, the spreadsheet program performs much faster than if it has to continually bring parts of the spreadsheet in and out of memory from disk.

Likewise, if you plan to use Microsoft Windows, the more memory Windows has available to let programs use, the better your performance. If you place two 486 or Pentium systems side by side, one having 4Mb of memory and one 8Mb, you will be amazed by the performance of the computer with 8Mb.

How Programs Use Memory

When you first turn on the computer, its electronic memory is empty. As discussed in Lesson 4, after it successfully completes its self-test, the computer loads DOS from disk into memory. DOS remains in your computer's memory the entire time your computer is on. As shown in Figure 16.2, DOS only consumes a small portion of the memory, leaving the rest available for program use.

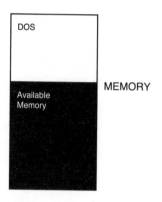

**FIGURE 16.2 Once loaded, DOS remains in memory,
leaving memory space available for program use.**

Before a program can run, the program must be in memory. Assuming you run a word processing program, the word processor consumes part of the memory to hold its program instructions, and another part to hold the document with which you are working. As shown in Figure 16.3, the word processor may use only a portion of memory depending on document size.

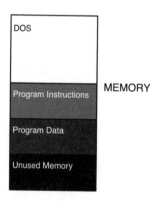

FIGURE 16.3 Programs require memory space for their instructions and for your data.

When you end a program and start another, the new program's instructions overwrite the previous program's memory locations. The best way to visualize RAM is as a chalkboard. As an instructor discusses a topic, the instructor writes information on the chalkboard. When the instructor moves to a new topic, the instructor writes new information on the chalkboard replacing the previous information. In this same way, when you run a program, the program resides in your computer's RAM. When the program ends and you run a new program, the new program replaces the old one in RAM.

Understanding Memory Types

Depending on the PC type, a PC can use three different memory types. When the IBM PC was first released in 1981, 64Kb of memory was considered quite a bit of memory. The original IBM PC, however, had the ability to use (or address) 1Mb of memory. Of this 1Mb, the PC developers reserved 384Kb of the PC's address space for video hardware and future uses, leaving 640Kb of memory space for DOS and your programs. This 384Kb region is often called *reserved* or *upper memory*. Initially, 640Kb was more than enough memory for PC programs. Over time, however, as program capabilities increased, so too did their size, and 640Kb soon became a barrier.

When IBM released the 286-based PC AT, it had the ability to address up to 16Mb of memory. To distinguish the PC's memory capabilities from those of the AT, the terms *conventional* and *extended* memory were born. *Conventional memory* is the memory from 0 to 640Kb. All computers have some (not all older systems have 640Kb) conventional memory. Memory above 1Mb is *extended memory*. A 286-based AT computer could have 16Mb of extended memory. Figure 16.4 illustrates conventional and extended memory.

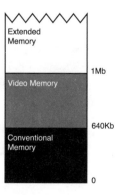

FIGURE 16.4 Conventional memory is from 0 to 640 Kb. Extended memory begins above 1 Mb.

To date, all DOS program instructions run in conventional memory. If the program uses large amounts of data, the program can use the extended memory to store the data.

Keep in mind that the original 8088-based IBM PC could not address memory above 1Mb. As a result, it could not use extended memory. To allow PC users with 8088 machines to add more memory, hardware developers created a memory board called expanded memory. By combining the hardware with special software, *expanded memory* tricked the PC into believing it was addressing memory within the 1Mb range when it really wasn't. Using expanded memory, the PC can now access up to 32Mb of memory! Today, most newer computers use the 486 or the Pentium processors.

The 386, 486, and Pentium have the ability to access 4Gb (over 4 billion bytes) of extended memory. In essence, you would empty your pocket book long before you filled these systems with memory.

Table 16.1 briefly summarizes the three primary PC memory types.

TABLE 16.1 PC MEMORY TYPES.

MEMORY TYPE	DESCRIPTION
Conventional memory	The memory from 0 to 640Kb found in all PCs.
Upper memory	The 384Kb region that resides between the 640Kb and 1Mb used for video memory and other hardware devices.
Extended memory	The memory above 1Mb, available on the 286, 86, and 486.
Expanded memory	A combination of hardware and software that lets the 8088 access more that 1Mb of memory. All PCs can use expanded memory.

Other Memory Considerations

When you want to add memory to your PC, you first need to know which type of memory you need (conventional, extended, or expanded). Next, you need to know the memory speed. Memory chips have an assigned speed, normally measured in *nanoseconds* (millionths of a second). If you are planning to use existing memory chips, your new chips should match (or be lower than) your existing chip's speed. For example, if your computer is using 80 nanosecond chips, you can install and use 60 nanosecond chips as well.

Depending on your PC type, the system unit board that contains the micro-processor (called the *motherboard*) may have available slots to which you can add memory. If not, you may need to buy a memory expansion card that plugs into a system unit expansion slot. For specifics, refer to the system unit documentation that accompanied your computer.

Today, hardware developers reduce the amount of space memory chips consumed by packing several memory chips in a compact *single in-line memory module* (called a *SIMM*). Although the discussion of SIMMs is beyond the scope of this book, if your retailer uses the term, know a SIMM is a way of *packaging* memory. Some boards support SIMMs and some do not. Figure 16.5 illustrates SIMM chips.

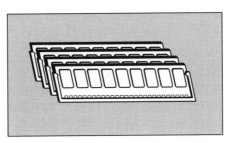

FIGURE 16.5 Simm chips within the computer.

SIMM chips have become very popular because they are easy to work with. Normally, you can simply insert a SIMM chip into its holder. However, should you accidentally break the SIMM holder, you may not be able to get the holder replaced. As such, you may want your computer retailer to install the SIMM chips for you. The money you spend having the chips installed is much, much less than the amount of money you would spend for a damaged SIMM holder.

What is Memory Management?

As you have learned, the PC can use expanded or extended memory. To take advantage of these memory regions, your computer must use special software (called *memory management device drivers*). Beginning with version 5, DOS has provided considerable memory management capabilities that let you make better use of your computer's memory. In addition to the DOS software, you can purchase third-party memory management software. Such memory management lets your PC use extended and expanded memory and maximizes the amount of the 640Kb of conventional memory available to DOS. The memory management software often uses the 384Kb upper-memory region to free up the 640Kb conventional memory for use by DOS programs. To learn more about DOS memory management, refer to the documentation that accompanied your computer or a DOS book.

RAM and ROM

RAM is your computer's electronic memory which holds your program instructions and data as the program executes. RAM is also called *read/write memory* because its contents can be read or written to (changed).

Your computer has a second kind of memory called *ROM* or *read-only memory*. As discussed in Lesson 1, computer programs tell the computer's hardware what to do. When your computer starts, it needs to know enough to perform its self test and load the operating system from disk. ROM is preprogrammed memory that provides these needed instructions. Unlike RAM, whose contents can be overwritten, the contents of ROM cannot change.

Memory Use and Windows 95

As you have learned, if you are using DOS, the first program your computer loads into memory is DOS. The DOS operating system, in turn, loads the other programs you run into memory. The DOS operating system restricts programs to running within the conventional memory area. As you have learned in this lesson, using special memory management software, your programs can store data within extended memory.

Windows 95 is a new operating system that replaces DOS. Windows 95 eliminates the distinction between your PC's conventional and extended memory.

In this way, Windows 95 can place data and programs in any memory location. However, because Windows 95 and the programs it runs are large and complex, you will want to add more memory to your system. In the near future, most PCs will use 16Mb of memory or more!

Memory Buyer's Guide

Upgrading your computer's memory capabilities may not be as easy as you might guess. Most users should let their retailer perform the upgrade for them. Use the following list as a guideline as you begin shopping for memory:

- ❖ Will your programs use the additional memory? If you can't use it, don't add it.
- ❖ Does your computer need extended or expanded memory? The 286, 386, 486, and Pentium can use both. Extended memory, however, provides better performance.
- ❖ How much memory does your software require? Does the software require a specific memory type: extended or expanded?
- ❖ Do you plan to use existing memory? If so, what is its speed?
- ❖ Do you have space for memory on the motherboard or do you need a memory board?
- ❖ Do you need SIMMs or SIPPs?
- ❖ How much will the memory installation cost?
- ❖ What is the warranty? Where can you get service?

Putting It All Together

Before a program can run, the program must reside in your computer's electronic memory. Most PCs have 640Kb of conventional memory. As programs become more complex, their size is growing to fill this 640Kb. Depending on their PC type, users can add either extended or expanded memory to their system.

Glossary

conventional memory	PC memory from 0 to 640Kb.
expanded memory	A memory expansion technique that combines hardware and software to let 8088-based PCs access more than 1Mb of memory. Although it was initially developed for the 8088, all PCs can use expanded memory.
extended memory	Memory above 1Mb in 286, 386, or 486 machines.
motherboard	Your computer's primary electronic card that houses the CPU and random access memory (RAM).
RAM	An abbreviation for random access memory, the computer's electronic memory.
ROM	An abbreviation for read-only memory, the computer's pre-programmed memory.
SIMMs	An abbreviation for single inline memory module —a small hardware module that contains multiple RAM chips.
upper memory	The 384Kb memory region between 640Kb and 1Mb.

Lesson 17: Looking Inside the System Unit

L esson 10 examined computer ports and the steps you must perform to install a hardware board in your system unit. As discussed in Lesson 10, new users normally don't have a need to open their system unit. Because the system unit's electronic components can be easily damaged, you should only open the system unit when you have a need to do so. This lesson discusses the various parts the system unit contains. Use the illustrations this chapter presents to satisfy your curiosity about what's inside the computer.

Common System Unit Components

Figure 17.1 illustrates the most common hardware components the system unit may contain. The following sections briefly describe the function each component performs.

Should you open your system unit, never touch any of your system components without first grounding yourself by touching your system chassis. By grounding yourself in this way, you greatly reduce the chance of an electrical shock damaging your PC's delicate electronics.

NOTE

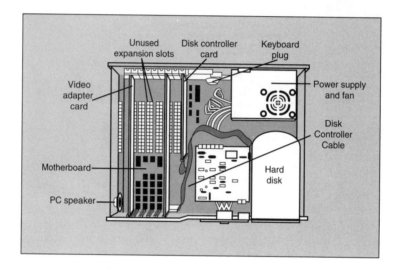

FIGURE 17.1 Common system components.

Power Supply

The largest system unit component is the *power supply* into which you plug the system unit's electrical cord. The power supply is responsible for distributing power to each of the computer's internal components. To meet the demands of today's more powerful devices, most PCs use a 150 to 200 watt power supply. The power supply for the original IBM PC provided 65 watts. The power supply houses a fan that tries to keep cool air moving throughout the system unit. As they run, the system unit's electrical devices generate heat. The fan attempts to remove this hot air. Figure 17.2 illustrates a PC power supply.

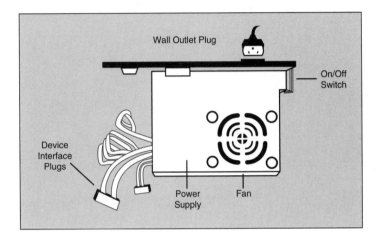

FIGURE 17.2 A PC power supply.

Disk Drives and Disk Controllers

Next to the power supply, the hard and floppy disk drives are the largest system unit components. The disk drives have power cables that attach to the power supply. In addition, the drives normally have cables that connect them to a board in an expansion slot called a *disk controller*. The disk controller contains the electronic circuitry that oversees all disk operations. Some new hard disk drives, called *IDE drives* (*Integrated Drive Electronics*), have a disk controller built in and do not require a controller card. As discussed in Lesson 10, your PC may use a *SCSI port* to which you can connect an internal or external hard drive. Figure 17.3 illustrates how you might connect a drive to a drive controller.

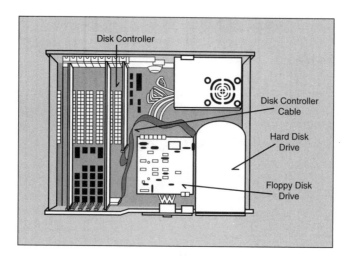

FIGURE 17.3 Connecting a disk drive to a drive controller.

Motherboard

If you look at the bottom of the system unit, you see a large circuit board that holds the expansion slots and contains many different chips. This board, called the *motherboard*, houses the microprocessor (CPU), computer's memory, and other essential chips such as a math coprocessor. The motherboard is the computer's primary circuit board. Figure 17.4 illustrates a PC motherboard.

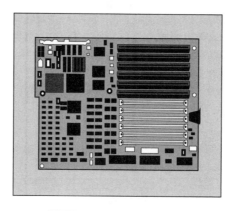

FIGURE 17.4 A PC motherboard.

Expansion Slots

As discussed in Lesson 10, *expansion slots* let you add hardware boards to your computer. Each expansion slot connects directly to the motherboard, which lets the computer's microprocessor communicate with each device. In most cases, several of the expansion slots will be in use, holding a video adapter, a disk controller, as well as serial and parallel ports. As shown in Figure 17.5, you can install hardware boards into your PC expansion slots.

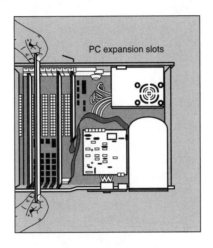

FIGURE 17.5 A PC expansion slot.

Memory

Lesson 16 examined your computer's memory in detail. Depending on your computer type, the motherboard provides some space for memory chips. When the motherboard's memory space is full, you can add memory by purchasing a *memory board* that slides into one of the expansion slots. As shown in Figure 17.6, most newer PCs use memory chips called *SIMMs* that contain large amounts of memory.

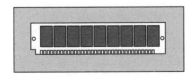

FIGURE 17.6 Newer PCs use SIMM chips.

CMOS Battery

Many systems have a battery-powered memory that stores the current date and time, as well as system configuration information such as the hard disk size and type when you turn off the computer. This memory is the computer's *CMOS* memory. In most cases, the battery that powers the CMOS memory lasts several years. If, during your computer's power-on self-test, your monitor displays a message about invalid set up information, you may need to replace the CMOS battery. Have your computer retailer or an experienced user replace the battery for you. When the new battery is in place, you will probably need to update the computer's set up information to its original settings. CMOS batteries come in one of two types: a *small nickel-CAD battery* and *small battery pack*. Figure 17.7 illustrates the two CMOS battery types.

FIGURE 17.7 CMOS battery types.

Putting It All Together

The system unit houses the computer's most essential components. As a rule, you should not open the system unit unless you have a specific need to do so. Many of the system unit components are easily damaged. If you must open the system unit for any reason, make sure you first unplug it.

Glossary

CMOS	An abbreviation for complementary metal oxide semiconductor. Many computers use a battery-powered CMOS memory to remember the system configuration and date and time.
disk controller	A circuit board that oversees and controls disk operations.
memory board	A hardware expansion slot card that contains RAM chips. Many older (286- and 386-based) systems use memory cards. Newer systems use SIMMs.
motherboard	The large system unit circuit board that contains the microprocessor, memory, and other essential chips.
ribbon cable	A wide, multi-wire cable. A ribbon cable connects the disk drive to the disk controller card.
SIMMs	An abbreviation for single inline memory module —a small hardware module that contains multiple RAM chips.

Lesson 18: Understanding Laptops and Portables

After the IBM PC released in 1981, it didn't take business people long to realize just how much they relied on their PC, and how much more productive they could be if they could only take their PC on the road with them. Compaq Corporation was one of the first companies to provide a *portable PC*. Weighing in at over 25 pounds, the first portable computers were about the size of a medium-size suitcase. Although users could use these early portable computers once they arrived at their destination, users could not use them during their commute. Eventually, smaller (10- to 12-pound) battery-powered, floppy disk-based portables became available. With a battery life of several hours, users could operate these smaller portables on cross-country flights, or cross-city subway commutes. Although these computers were an improvement, their lack of a hard disk limited their capabilities.

Today, technology has not only reduced the laptop's weight (4 to 8 pounds), and allowed for a hard disk, it has provided laptops with the ability to use the latest and most powerful microprocessors. In general, a *laptop computer* is one you can fit in your briefcase, and has the computing power of the full size PC that sits on a desk! As the size of these computers continues to decrease, many users have started calling them *notebook computers*. This lesson takes a look at the differences between laptop and desktop PCs.

Hardware Differences

Functionally, a laptop computer contains the same hardware as a desktop computer: a screen, keyboard, and ports for other devices such as a printer, modem, or mouse. In addition, most newer laptop computers have a hard disk and one or two floppy disk drives. Figure 18.1 illustrates a typical laptop computer.

FIGURE 18.1 A typical laptop computer.

Keyboard Differences

As discussed in Lesson 5, the keyboard consists of four major parts: the standard typewriter keys, function keys, cursor movement keys, and the numeric keypad. Because of the laptop's small size, its keys are much closer together and the cursor movement and numeric key pad keys may be the same, requiring you to press the **NumLock key** (as discussed in Lesson 5) to select one or the other. Figure 18.2 illustrates a typical laptop computer keyboard layout.

FIGURE 18.2 A typical laptop computer keyboard.

Many newer laptops provide a port for a standard-size keyboard, allowing users to attach a larger keyboard to the laptop when they use the computer at their office.

Disk Sizes

Today, most laptop computers support hard disks. In fact, most laptops ship with a hard disk from 80Mb-100Mb hard disk. Most laptop computers use the 3.5-inch floppy disks discussed in Lesson 8. Depending on the laptop type, the location of the floppy disk drive will differ. As shown in Figure 18.3, most laptop computers have their disk drives along the right or left side.

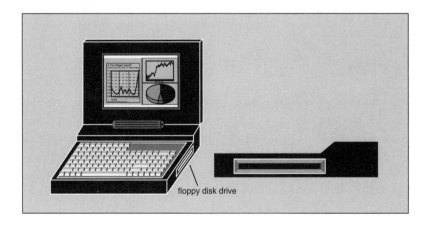

FIGURE 18.3 Location of the laptop's floppy disk drive.

Video Display Types

To reduce the battery consumption, laptops use *LCD* (*liquid crystal display*) screens. Early LCD screens were often poorly lit and difficult to read.

Most new laptops have improved screen quality. In fact, most provide VGA resolution. Most newer laptop computers support color displays. If you are shopping for a laptop with a color monitor, look for a system with an *active matrix display*. Although the active-matrix display costs more than its *passive-matrix display* counterpart, you will be very happy with the sharpness of the color it displays.

Many laptops, however, provide a video adapter, to which you can attach a color monitor. In this way, you can use a color screen at home or work, and the laptop's screen when you travel.

NOTE If you travel with your laptop computer and you work with your computer on an airplane, you might consider purchasing a passive-matrix video display. If you compare active- and passive-matrix displays, you will find that the passive displays have poor display quality if you are not looking directly at the screen. However, if you are working with your computer on an airplane, the passive-matrix display's poor side display prevents passengers who are sitting to your right or left from reading your notebook's screen.

Battery Use

Because users may want to use their laptop computer at any time or place, the length of the laptop's battery life becomes a key consideration. Several factors affect how long a laptop can run on battery power: the *display type*, *battery type*, and the *usage and related power consumption of internal devices* such as a hard disk drive. Although many manufacturers will advertise longer battery lives, common battery lives for 486- and Pentium-based laptops with hard disks and VGA quality output range from 2.5 to 5 hours.

Depending on the laptop type, its battery pack may be removable. If so, you can buy extra battery packs and have them available for longer trips. If the battery pack is not removable, you must recharge the battery by plugging the computer in. Recharging a laptop computer's battery is not quite as simple as you would think. As a rule, you normally want the battery to completely drain its power before you recharge it. Rechargeable batteries such as those in a laptop or portable cellular phones have a unique quality called *memory effect.* If you recharge the battery before it drains completely, the battery changes its ability to recharge, thus decreasing the battery's life time. If you recharge the battery too early once or twice, you probably won't harm the battery. However, if you do so on a regular basis, you eventually reduce the battery's lifetime to such an extent that you have to replace it.

Modem Support

Lesson 19 discusses modems in detail. Most laptops provide built-in modems. If a laptop that you are using does not, you'll probably want to buy a small external modem you can attach to the laptop's serial port. A modem is very important to your success with a laptop computer. Using a modem, you can access files stored at your office, home, or other locations as you travel. In addition, you can send and receive faxes. When you shop for a laptop, therefore, make sure that you purchase one having a fax modem.

Mouse Support

As discussed in Lesson 9, you can attach a mouse to a serial port. In many cases, however, the locations at which you want to use your laptop may not provide a desktop or surface on which you can work a mouse. As shown in Figure 18.4, a clip-on track ball can provide you with the mouse capabilities you need.

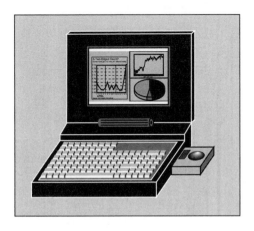

FIGURE 18.4 A clip-on trackball provides laptop users with mouse capabilities.

Laptop Computer Ports

As discussed in Lesson 10, most laptop computers provide *serial* and *parallel ports* you can access at the back of your computer. Figure 18.5, for example, illustrates a laptop's serial and parallel ports. Using these ports you can quickly connect a printer, mouse, or modem to your system.

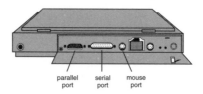

parallel   serial   mouse
port   port   port

FIGURE 18.5 Ports on a laptop computer.

Laptop Docking Stations

Today, many business people take work home with them on their laptop computer. When they return to their office, however, they probably want to use a larger desktop computer, which provides a standard screen, keyboard, and possibly a CD-ROM drive and sound card. To relinquish the user from having to buy a personal computer, many laptop PCs support *docking stations* into which users can plug in the laptop computer as shown in Figure 18.6.

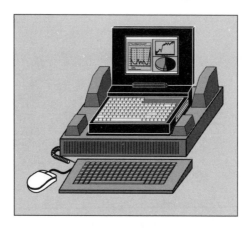

FIGURE 18.6 Plugging a laptop computer into a docking station.

As you can see, the docking station has a full-size monitor and keyboard. The docking station uses the laptop computer's motherboard and CPU to control all operations. By using their laptop and the docking station in this way, the user does not have to purchase a laptop *and* desktop computer. As you shop for a laptop, you might purchase a docking station which provides a floppy disk, hard disk, or possibly a SCSI controller.

Software Differences

Provided they have enough memory, laptop computers run all the same programs you can run on your desktop computer. Depending on your screen type, you may have to view color screens as various shades of gray.

Lesson 15 discussed ROM, your computer's read-only memory. As notebook computers become even smaller, many computers that don't have hard disks are providing DOS and other key programs such as a word processor or spreadsheet built into the computer's ROM. In so doing, the programs are available as soon as you turn the computer on, eliminating your need to use multiple floppy disks. Unfortunately, the only way to upgrade these programs is to upgrade the computer's hardware.

Traveling with Your Laptop

If you cannot fit your laptop safely in your briefcase, buy a carrying case that protects it as you travel. In most cases, the carrying case provides storage for the laptop's power cable, mouse, and a few floppy disks.

One of the most common questions users ask is whether or not the security x-ray machine at the airport can damage their laptop or its disks. In theory, the answer is no. In practice, I always ask for a hand search of my laptop's case, rather than risking my disk. Some newer laptops have warnings not to subject them to x-rays.

Improving Your Laptop's Performance

As you examine available laptop computers, you may find that the laptop computer's processor speed is slower than that available for desktop computers. For example, if you are shopping for a 486 laptop, you may find many 25MHz systems are slower than their 66MHz desktop counterparts. Laptop computers are normally slightly slower than their desktop counterparts to reduce their power consumption when they are using a battery. As such, if you are consumed about improving your laptop computer's performance, the easiest way to do so is to add memory. If you are using Windows, for example, you immediately experience improved system performance by adding memory to your system.

Simplifying Laptop File Transfers

If you travel with a laptop or notebook computer and then return to your home or office and use a desktop computer, you can transfer files between the two systems using floppy disks. If the number of files you need to transfer is very large, you can connect the two computers using a *NULL-modem cable* between the computer's serial ports as shown in Figure 18.7. Next, by running a special software program on both systems, you can quickly copy files between the two systems using disk drive letters and directory names. If you are using DOS 6, you can use the INTERLNK and INTERSVR commands to copy files between your laptop and desktop computer. Performing such file operations is very easy and much faster than if you copy to and from floppy disks.

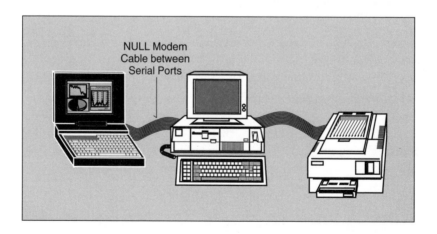

FIGURE 18.7 Connecting a laptop and desktop computer.

Adding Hardware Capabilities to Your Notebook

To add hardware to a desktop or tower PC, you insert a card into one of the PC's expansion slots. Notebook computers, on the other hand, don't have expansion slots. Instead, many notebooks support docking stations or let you take advantage of one or more *PCMCIA cards*. Lesson 29 discusses PCMCIA cards in detail. In short, a PCMCIA card is a credit card sized card that contains the electronics for a specific device. For example, you might buy one PCMCIA card that contains a modem, a second that contains a SCSI interface, and a third that contains a network adapter. As shown in Figure 18.8, you insert the PCMCIA card into a slot on your notebook, much like you would insert a game cartridge into a TV video game.

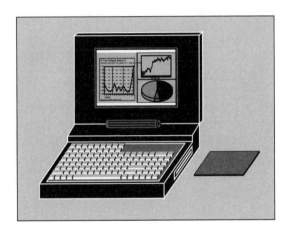

FIGURE 18.8 You insert a PCMCIA cards into a notebook slot to improve notebook capabilities.

Depending on the notebook type, the number of PCMCIA cards you can use at one time will differ.

Laptop Buyer's Guide

Over the next few years, laptop computers may become the fastest selling class of personal computers. Use this list as a guide when you shop for a laptop.

❖ When do you plan to use the laptop? Is a long battery life necessary?

❖ What programs do you plan to run on the laptop? How much disk space will you need?

❖ What is the CPU type and speed? (See Lesson 11.)

❖ How much RAM does the laptop have? Can it hold more?

❖ Does the laptop have a built-in modem?

❖ Can you attach a standard keyboard and monitor to the laptop?

❖ Does the laptop have a serial and parallel port?

❖ Is the battery pack replaceable? If so, how much do replacements cost?

❖ What is the warranty? Where can you get the laptop serviced?

❖ What is the technical support policy?

❖ What software comes with the laptop?

❖ What is the screen display type and resolution? Does it display color?

Putting It All Together

Because they provide users with the ability to use the computer at any place and time, laptop computers are becoming very popular. In general, the laptop computer behaves no differently from a PC that sits on a desktop, with the ability to run the same software. The primary differences between different brands of laptops is weight, disk size, video capabilities, and cost.

Glossary

active-matrix display
A monitor that uses small microprocessors to manager (control) pixels in a small region (a matrix of pixels) on the screen—improving the monitor's picture quality.

docking station
A hardware chassis into which you can plug in your notebook computer. A docking station may provide a screen, keyboard, CD-ROM, and sound card which in turn, the notebook's processor can access.

laptop computer	A computer with battery power, that you can unfold and work with on your lap. A laptop computer may weigh from 10- to 20-pounds.
LCD	An abbreviation for liquid crystal display. Many laptop computers use an LCD monitor due to compact electronics.
memory effect	A physical characteristic of rechargeable batteries that causes them to lose storage capacity if they are recharged while they still have a charge.
notebook computer	A small laptop computer that, when closed, is about the size of a notebook. Notebook computers may weigh from 6- to 10-pounds.
passive-matrix display	A monitor that uses a single microprocessor to manage all the pixels on the entire screen. Passive matrix displays have lower picture quality than their more expensive active matrix counterparts.
PCMCIA card	A credit card sized electronic card that contains the electronics for a specific device such as a modem or network card. PCMCIA cards provide a way to expand a notebook PC's hardware.
portable computer	A computer whose system unit, screen display, and keyboard you can easily move from one location to another. A portable computer may weigh from 20- to 25-pounds, and is not battery-powered.

Lesson 19: Understanding Modems and Telecommunications

A *modem* is a hardware device that lets two computers exchange information over phone lines. This process of using telephone lines for computer communications is *telecommunications*. Using a modem, you can exchange information with other users by calling computer bulletin boards, or you can connect to worldwide information services such as CompuServe, as discussed in Lesson 34. In addition, many business people who travel with their laptop computers use modems to access their corporate computers to send and receive electronic mail, or to access other information. Each day, more people who work at home access their company computers from their home PC by using a modem. This lesson examines how modems work, and the factors you should consider when you shop for a modem.

How Modems Work

As discussed, modems let two computers exchange information over phone lines. As shown in Figure 19.1, to communicate, both computers must have a modem.

The word modem is an abbreviation for the terms *modulator-demodulator*, which describe how a modem works. To begin, the modem *transmitting* (sending) information converts the computer's digital signals into wave-like *analog signals* that can be sent over the phone lines. The receiving modem translates its incoming signals back into digital form. This process of changing signal formats is *modulating* and *demodulating*.

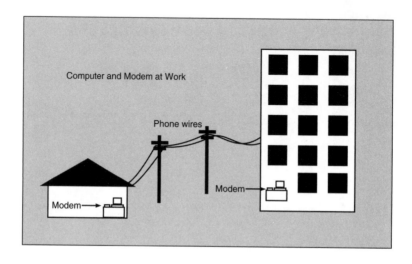

FIGURE 19.1 Modems allow two computers to communicate over normal telephone lines.

Internal versus External Modems

Modems come in two types: *internal* and *external* modems. Internal modems are hardware boards you plug into an expansion slot in the system unit. External modems, on the other hand, sit outside your system unit and connect to a serial port, as shown in Figure 19.2.

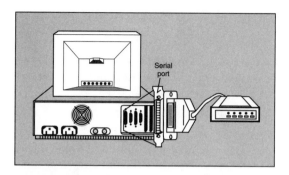

FIGURE 19.2 External modems connect to a serial port.

External modems are slightly more expensive than internal modems, but they offer the advantage that you can quickly move the modem from one computer to another.

Regardless of whether you are using an internal or external modem, the modem has two jacks for phone cables. As shown in Figure 19.3, the first jack connects the modem to the phone's wall jack, providing the modem with access to the phone lines while the second jack connects the modem to the phone. The modem-to-phone connection lets, the phone access the wall jack as well, allowing you to still use your phone.

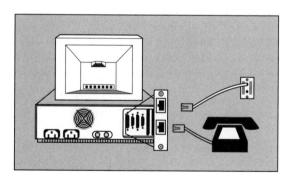

FIGURE 19.3 Phone cable connects the modem to the phone jack on the wall and to the phone.

Using the Modem

To use your modem, you need to run data communication software that lets you assign the modem's speed and other communications settings, and when you later access another computer, the software lets you exchange files and other information. Figure 19.4 illustrates how a data communications program might appear on your screen.

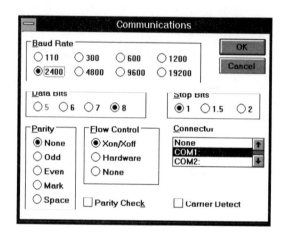

FIGURE 19.4 To use a modem, you must run a data communications program as shown here.

Before two computers can communicate using modems, the computers must agree on the speed at which they send and receive information (called the *baud rate*), as well as the data format. The speed and data format settings are often called *data communication parameters*. To access another computer, you must know the values the computer uses for its communication parameters as well as the computer's phone number.

Using a data communication program, you can direct your modem to call the other computer. In fact, most data communication programs let you create a list of modem phone numbers and settings. When you need to access another computer, you simply select the computer from the list.

Depending on the computer to which you are connecting, your system may display a menu of options or a prompt for you to type in your user name. After you are done accessing the computer, you can use the data communication software to end the phone call (essentially hanging up).

Using a modem is no different than placing a phone call. If you call a local number, there is no extra charge. If you place a long distance call, however, the phone company bills you for the call at its normal rate.

Sites You Can Visit

Lesson 30 introduces you to the Internet, today's information highway. In addition, Lesson 34 introduces the on-line services such as Prodigy, America Online, or CompuServe. Using your PC's modem and telecommunication software, you can access these services. For example, Figure 19.5 illustrates a site on the Internet's World Wide Web.

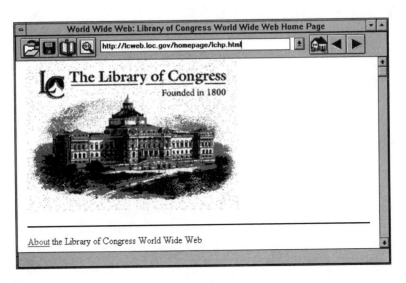

FIGURE 19.5 A site on the Internet's World Wide Web.

Likewise, Figure 19.6 illustrates a screen from the CompuServe on-line service. As you will learn in Lesson 34, you can use the on-line services to send electronic mail to other users, chat with users electronically, research different topics, or even shop!

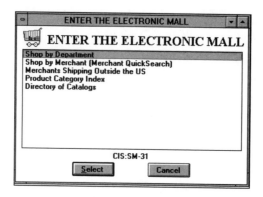

FIGURE 19.6 The CompuServe on-line service.

How Does a Modem Differ From a Fax Machine?

The fax (*facsimile*) machine has quickly become one of the most popular office machines. A fax is almost a cross between a copy machine and a modem. Using the fax, the user dials the phone number of a fax at the location to which the user wants to send a document. After the two fax machines connect, the sending fax machine makes a copy of the document, converting the copy to a set of signals it sends over the phone lines. The receiving fax converts the incoming signals back into an image that it prints.

If you have not yet bought a modem, you should buy a modem that provides fax capabilities. Using software that accompanies the modem/fax, your computer can receive and print incoming faxes and send documents stored on disk to other fax machines. You could not, however, send a copy of a paper document. For that capability, you would need an actual fax machine. If you travel with your computer, the ability to send and receive faxes using your computer is essential. When you purchase a fax modem, you receive software that lets you send and receive faxes. Figure 19.7, for example, illustrates a fax software program.

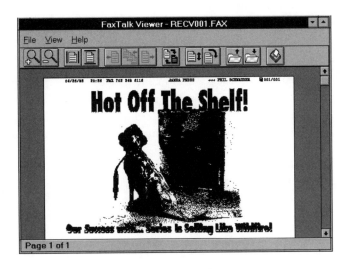

FIGURE 19.7 Sending a fax using fax software.

Understanding Modem Speeds

As discussed, when two computers use modems to communicate, they must agree on the communication speed or baud rate. Common baud rates include 300, 1200, 2400, 4800, 9600 baud, 14.4Kb (kilobaud), and 28.8Kb. In general, baud rate means *bits* (*binary digits*) per second. To represent a character of the alphabet, the computer uses eight bits. The faster the baud rate, the more characters of information sent each second. Today, the most common baud rates are 9600 baud and 14.4Kb.

When you shop for a modem, you will find that each modem has a maximum speed at which it sends. As the modem's maximum speed increases, so too will its cost. Luckily, however, modem prices have recently dropped. As such, more users have modems capable of speeds of at least 9600 baud. If you purchase a modem, do not purchase a modem slower than 14.4Kb. In most cases, the money you spend to purchase a 28.8Kb modem is money well spent.

A Word on Modems Shipped with New PCs

As you shop for a new PC, you will find that many PCs come with a modem. Unfortunately, in many cases, the modem included with new PCs are old and slow. As such, as you compare PC prices, make sure you compare the speeds the modem each system provides. In most cases, you will find that you must replace the older modem, in turn, spending any money you may have saved on the PC's cost.

Understanding a Modem Operation

When you use a modem to connect to a remote computer, you normally follow these steps:

1. Select the data communication speeds and settings required to communicate with the remote computer.
2. Dial the remote computer.
3. Transfer files to and from the remote computer.
4. Hang-up, ending the remote operation.

Figure 19.4 illustrated how you might specify the data communication settings for a remote computer. Next, you must specify the phone number corresponding to the computer you want to dial. Figure 19.8 illustrates a dialog box that lets you specify the desired phone number.

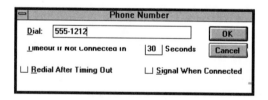

FIGURE 19.8 Specifying a remote computer's phone number.

After you connect to the remote computer, you can transfer files to or from the remote computer. To send a file for example, you must first prepare the remote computer to receive a file. To do so, you normally select an upload menu option. When the remote computer is ready to receive the file, you can begin the file transfer. Figure 19.9, for example, illustrates a dialog box that shows the progress of a file transfer operation.

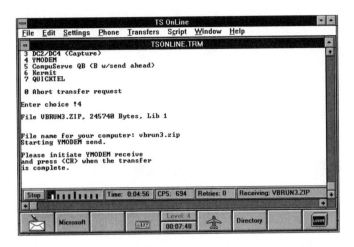

FIGURE 19.9 Watching the status of the file transfer operation.

Lastly, to end the data communication operation, you simply hang-up. Most data communication software programs provide a hang-up option as a keyboard combination or a menu option.

Advanced Modem Operations

When you dial a remote computer, the number you are dialing may be in use by another user. In such cases, you may hear a busy signal and your modem software may display a message telling you the line is busy. Many data communication software programs let you automatically redial the remote computer until you finally get through. If your phone line has call waiting, the beep that normally occurs when you have an incoming call can cause havoc to your data communication software. When you want to perform modem operations, you can disable call waiting by dialing *70 on your phone. To simplify this operation, you may want to include *70 at the start of the phone number you want your modem to dial. Because the operation may require a slight pause, place a comma after the 0 as shown here: *70,555-1212.

To increase the speed at which data is transferred, many modems support *data compression*. Using data compression, the modem transfers the information in a compressed format that requires fewer ones and zeros to be transmitted over the phone line. The receiving modem, in turn, decompresses the data. When you shop for modems, you may encounter terms such as *MNP 5* or *V.42bis*. These terms correspond to modem capabilities. A modem that supports MNP 5 (Microcom Networking Protocol 5) or V.42bis supports data compression. As you shop for modems, use these terms as a guide to a modem's capabilities. If a modem does not support MNP 5 or V.42bis, you should continue your search for another modem.

Be Aware Of Computer Viruses

When you connect to bulletin board systems and download computer programs, do not run any program until you examine it using a virus detection program. In this way, you can reduce the possibility of a virus damaging your computer's disk. If you are connecting to an established bulletin board system such as CompuServe, your risk of obtaining a computer virus is very small.

Modem Buyer's Guide

If you are considering buying a modem, use the following list as your guidelines:

❖ What services or bulletin boards do you plan on accessing with your modem? Do these services have membership dues or long distance costs?

❖ What is the highest baud rate your modem can support?

❖ Does your modem support data compression?

❖ Can your modem send and receive faxes?

❖ Do you have an available serial port to which you can connect an external modem?

❖ Do you have an available expansion slot into which you can insert an internal modem?

❖ Do you have more than one computer to which you might want to attach the modem? Remember, external modems easily connect to a serial port.

❖ Does the modem price include a data communications program? Do you need fax capabilities?

Putting It All Together

A modem is a hardware device that lets two computers communicate over telephone lines. Modems come in two types: an internal modem, which is a hardware board you insert into a system unit expansion slot, and an external modem that connects to a serial port.

To use your modem, you must run a data communications program. To communicate, the two computers must agree on the communication speed or baud rate as well as several other values that define how the computers will exchange information. The data communication software lets you define these settings as well as the phone number needed to call the second computer.

Glossary

analog signals	Wavelike electronic signals. Modems convert data from digital to analog to transmit the signals across phone lines.
baud rate	The number of bits (binary digits) the computer sends per second. The higher the baud rate, the greater the amount of information exchanged per second.
data communication parameters	A set of values, such as the amount of information sent per message, that two computers must agree upon before they can successfully communicate.
data compression	Software and hardware techniques that reduce the amount of data needed to represent information. To reduce the amount of data sent across phone lines, the sending modem might compress data and the receiving modem would decompress it.

demodulating	The process of converting an analog signal to a digital signal the PC understands.
external modem	A modem that resides outside of the PC that typically connects to a serial port.
facsimile machine	A copy-machine-like device that copies a page and transmits the contents across phone lines to a receiving fax machine which in turn, prints the page.
internal modem	A modem whose electronics reside on a hardware card you insert into your PC.
Kb	With respect to modems and data communications, Kb is an abbreviation for kilobaud. A 14.4Kb modem, for example, transfers 14,746 (14.4 x 1024) bits per second.
modulating	The process of converting a digital signal into an analog signal for transmission over phone lines.
telecommunications	The process of exchanging information between computers over telephone lines.

Lesson 20: Why Work with Windows?

As you have learned, *Windows* is a software program that lets you run other programs and perform your computer operations using graphic images called *icons*. This lesson provides a brief overview of the Windows environment. You will learn about icons, dialog boxes, and pull-down menus. One of the major advantages of using Windows is there are very few commands to remember and most of your Windows-based programs run the same way. For example, if you learn to run a Windows-based word processor, learning a Windows-based spreadsheet is very easy.

Getting Started With Windows

Before you can run Windows, your computer must first load DOS. Next, from the DOS prompt, you simply type **WIN** and press **Enter**:

```
C:\> WIN  <Enter>
```

Windows, in turn, displays a screen similar to that shown in Figure 20.1.

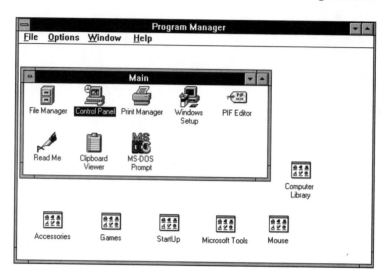

FIGURE 20.1 The Windows interface.

A window is simply a framed region on your screen within which a program can run. In the case of Figure 20.1, the screen contains two windows, one labeled *Program Manager* and one *Main*. Within the windows are small graphic pictures called icons that correspond to programs. To run a program, you simply aim your mouse pointer at the corresponding program and double-click. To help you organize your programs, Windows lets you define program groups, which hold related programs. For example, you might have a program group named *Business* that contains your word processor and spreadsheet, and a second group called *School* that contains programs you use for your school classes. To run the program that resides in a program group, you must first open the program group window by double-clicking on the group icon with your mouse. For example, if you double-click on the Accessories program group, Windows displays the program icons shown in Figure 20.2.

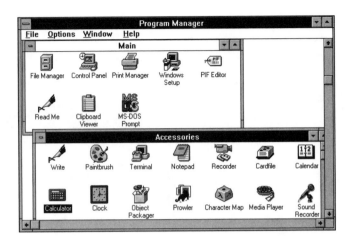

FIGURE 20.2 Program icons within the Accessories group.

To run a program, you simply double-click on the program using your mouse. If you double-click on the Accessories group **Clock** icon, for example, Windows displays a clock (within its own window) as shown in Figure 20.3.

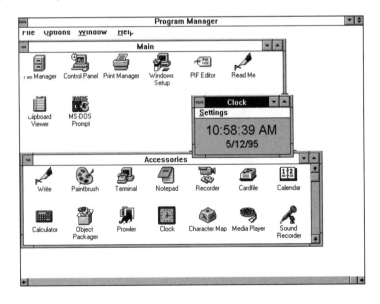

FIGURE 20.3 Running the Windows Clock program.

Windows lets you run two or more programs at the same time. If you double-click on the Accessories group *Calculator* icon, Windows runs the Calculator program as shown in Figure 20.4.

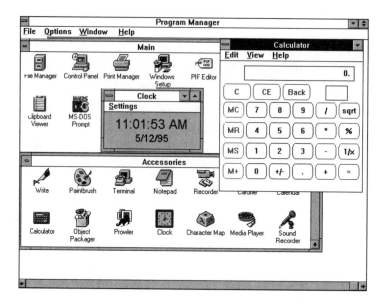

FIGURE 20.4 Running multiple programs within Windows.

When you run multiple programs within their own windows, you can select the program with which you want to work by simply clicking within the program's window. In this way, you can quickly switch from one program to another.

Minimizing and Maximizing Windows

As you run different programs, there may be times when you want the program to fill the entire screen. For example, if you are using a Windows-based word processor, you probably want to work in a full-screen window so you can see more of your document. When you run a program using the full screen, the other active program windows are hidden. Windows refers to the process of enlarging a program window to full screen as *maximizing* the window. In a similar way, there may be times when you won't need to use a program for a while and you simply want to put the program's window aside, out of the way. To do so, you can simply *minimize* the program back to an icon. The program continues to run. Figure 20.5, for example, illustrates the Clock and Calculator icons minimized as icons. When you are ready to use the program again, you simply double click on the icon. Windows opens the window to its previous size. If you look in the upper right corner of each window, you find arrows that face up and down. If you click on the downward facing arrow, Windows minimizes the corresponding window to an icon. If you click your mouse on the upward facing arrow, Windows maximizes the window.

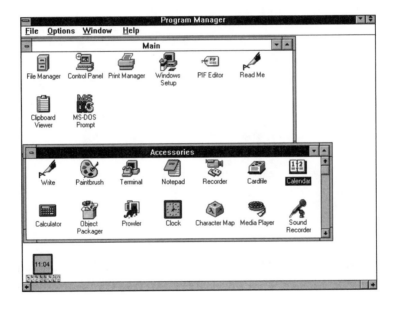

FIGURE 20.5 Minimizing program windows to icons.

As you might guess when you run multiple programs at the same time, your screen could become quite crowded. However, Windows makes it very easy for you to size and move program windows to suit your needs.

Menus and Dialog Boxes

To make your programs easier to use, Windows programs make extensive use of *menus*. For example, most Windows programs provide a File menu similar to that shown in Figure 20.6.

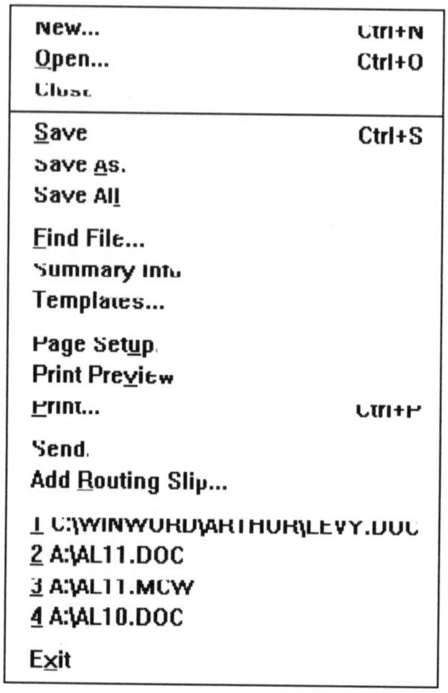

New...	Ctrl+N
Open...	Ctrl+O
Close	
Save	Ctrl+S
Save As.	
Save All	
Find File...	
Summary Info	
Templates...	
Page Setup.	
Print Preview	
Print...	Ctrl+P
Send.	
Add Routing Slip...	
1 C:\WINWORD\ARTHUR\LEVY.DOC	
2 A:\AL11.DOC	
3 A:\AL11.MCW	
4 A:\AL10.DOC	
Exit	

FIGURE 20.6

If you want to open a specific file, you simply click on the **Open** option. Likewise to save your work, you would click on the **Save** option. To print your work, you would click on the **Print** option. Most Windows-based programs make all of their options available through menus.

As you run programs, there will be times when the program needs you to specify more information, such as the name of the file containing your word processing document, or the number of copies you want to print. In such cases, the program displays a *dialog box* similar to that shown in Figure 20.7.

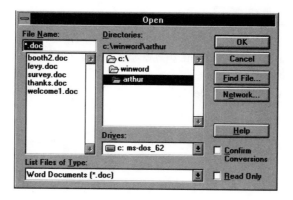

FIGURE 20.7 A dialog box.

Dialog boxes are so named because they provide a way for you and the program to have a dialog (exchange of information). In some cases, a dialog box may display a message telling you to perform a specific action, such as turning on your printer. In other cases, the dialog box may ask you for several pieces of information. Dialog boxes typically have a button labeled OK. After you have read the dialog box message or typed in the required information, click on the **OK** button. In addition, some dialog boxes have a Cancel button. If you click on the **Cancel** button, you can normally end the current operation.

Lastly, to simplify common operations, many Windows-based programs provide a toolbar of icons that appears near the top of the program's window as shown in Figure 20.8. Each icon that appears in the toolbar corresponds to a specific operation. For example, if you want to print your document, you can click on the **Printer** icon. Likewise, to spell check your document's spelling you would click on the button labeled **ABC**.

FIGURE 20.8 The Word for Windows toolbar.

By combining menus, dialog boxes, and toolbars, Windows programs become very easy to use.

Putting It All Together

Windows is a software program that makes your computer easier to use by replacing difficult commands with meaningful pictures you can click on with your mouse. Windows programs take advantage of menus, dialog boxes, and toolbars. An advantage of Windows programs is that they behave in a consistent manner. As such, if you learn how to use a Windows-based word processor, learning how to use a Windows-based spreadsheet is very easy.

Glossary

dialog box	Framed region on your screen that allows an exchange of information between the user and the program, providing messages regarding specific actions, or requesting further information from the user.
icons	Small graphic pictures which represent and correspond to programs.
maximizing	The process of enlarging a program window to full screen.
menu	A list from which the user can select a specific option using their keyboard or mouse.
minimizing	The process of hiding the program's window, or setting it aside by returning it back to an icon.
toolbar	A row of icons that appears near the top of the program's window. Each icon corresponds to a specific operation.
window	A framed region on your screen within which a program can run.

Lesson 21: Understanding External Hard Disks

If you work in an office, there may be times when you have information stored on your disk that you don't want other users to access. For example, you may have important company or salary information other employees should not see. As a general rule, if a user can touch your computer, they can normally get to the files the computer's disks contain. To prevent unauthorized access to your files, you may want to use an *external hard drive* or *disk cartridge*. When you need to leave your office, you can disconnect the drive and either place it in a secure location or even take the drive with you. This lesson examines external hard drives and disk cartridges.

Using an External Hard Disk Drive

As shown in Figure 21.1, an *external hard disk* drive is simply a hard disk that you connect to your computer.

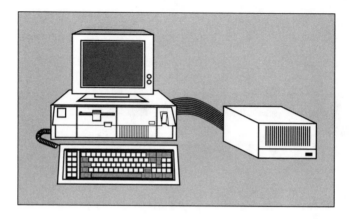

FIGURE 21.1 An external hard disk.

Most external hard disk drives connect to a SCSI port similar to that in Figure 21.2.

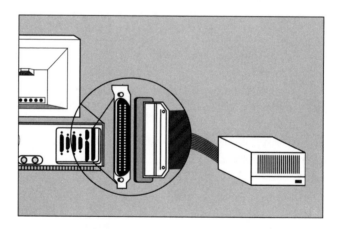

FIGURE 21.2 Connecting an external hard disk drive to a SCSI port.

As discussed in Lesson 10, most PCs do not have a SCSI port. Instead, you must purchase a SCSI *adapter card* and then install the card into your PC as shown in Figure 21.3.

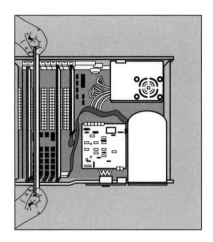

FIGURE 21.3 Installing a SCSI adapter card.

Like internal hard drives, you can purchase external hard drives with different storage capacities and speeds. After you connect the drive to your computer, you must normally install special device driver software for the drive. You can then reference the drive using a standard drive letter such as drive D or E.

Using a Disk Cartridge

When you work with floppy disks, you insert a different disk into the floppy drive as your needs require. In this way, you can store information on a floppy disk and then take the disk with you for use with a different computer or for storage in a safe location. The problem with floppy disks, however, is their limited storage capacity.

Depending on your data storage needs, you may find that disk cartridges are very convenient. A *disk cartridge* is a cross between a hard disk and a floppy disk. Like a hard disk, the disk cartridge can store tremendous amounts of information. In fact, disk cartridges capable of storing 44Mb are very common. Like a floppy disk, you can insert and remove a disk cartridge as you need. Also, like floppy disks, if you are using an 88Mb disk drive, you can read and write data to 88Mb or 44Mb disk cartridges. However, if you are using a 44Mb drive, you can only access 44Mb cartridges. Figure 21.4 illustrates a disk cartridge and drive.

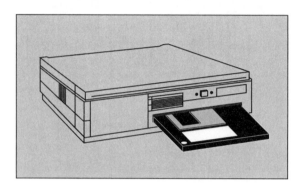

FIGURE 21.4 A disk cartridge and drive.

If you have files that you need to keep private or secure, you can store the files on the disk cartridge and later take the cartridge with you when you leave the office. Like an external disk drive, a disk cartridge uses a device driver that lets you refer to the cartridge using a standard drive letter. Many users store large amounts of information on a single disk cartridge for shipping, eliminating the need to ship dozens of floppy disks. Likewise, if you work at home and the office, a disk cartridge provides a very convenient way to move your files and programs.

The drive for a disk cartridge may connect to a SCSI connector (discussed in Lesson 28), or it may connect to its own custom card that you must install within your computer.

External Storage Device Buyer's Guide

As you shop for an external storage device, use the following as a guideline:

❖ How much information do you need to store?

❖ Is speed or storage capacity a priority?

❖ Does the drive require a SCSI adapter?

❖ Is your SCSI adapter compatible with the drive?

❖ Do you need to use the external storage media to ship files?

Putting It All Together

External hard disk drives and disk cartridges provide large storage capacity and the convenience of disconnecting the storage device from your PC. Users use external storage devices for security and to simplify the shipping or movement of large amounts of information. If a disk contains confidential information, you can disconnect the disk, placing it into a safe and secure location when you are away from your computer.

Glossary

disk cartridge — A floppy disk-like cartridge (but larger) with the storage capacity of a hard disk

external hard drive — A hard drive you can connect and disconnect from your computer.

Lesson 22: Protecting Your Data Using a Tape Backup

When you store information on a disk, the most important operation you must perform on a regular basis is a *disk backup*. Unfortunately, most users do not back up their systems as often as they should. Most users state that backups simply take too much time or that managing the backup floppy disks is a hassle. Tape backup systems eliminate the need to manage a large number of backup floppy disks and allow you to perform backups quickly. If you work in an office that creates many files each day, a tape backup unit is a must.

Using a Tape Backup

As shown in Figure 22.1, tape backup units can be internal or external to your computer.

The advantage of an external tape backup unit is that you can move the unit from one computer to another to back up multiple systems. Unfortunately, external tape backup units still cost considerably more than their internal counterparts. As shown in Figure 22.2, tape backup units copy your disk files onto a small cassette tape, similar in size to the tape used in a video camera.

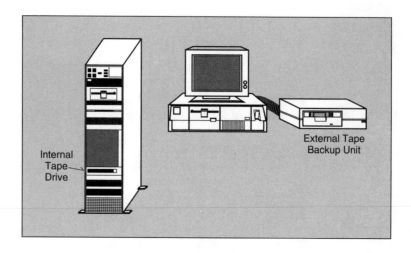

FIGURE 22.1 Internal and external tape backup units.

You can purchase tape backup units that support different tape sizes, such as 125Mb or 250Mb tapes. If your disk drive is larger than the tape, your backups simply require two or more tapes.

FIGURE 22.2 A backup tape.

 One of the most time consuming aspects of performing tape backups is preparing, or *formatting*, the tape for use. When you shop for magnetic tapes, purchase tapes that are preformatted. Although the tapes may cost slightly more than their unformatted counterparts, using the preformatted tapes will save you considerable time.

NOTE

Performing a Tape Backup

When you back up your disk to tape, you can back up your entire disk, or you can back up specific files. As shown in Figure 22.3, tape backup units come with software that let you control the backup.

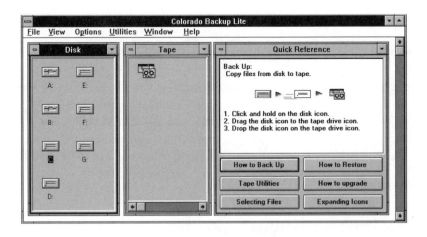

FIGURE 22.3 Tape backup software lets you select the files you want to back up.

Some tape backup software compress files as they are stored on the tape. In this way, a 125Mb tape may be able to store 200Mb of files (or more). An advantage of using a tape backup is that once the backup operation begins, you don't have to monitor its progress, continually inserting new floppy disks. Instead, the backup operation runs on its own, recording information to the large tape. In this way, many users start their backup operation right before they leave for the day, allowing the backup to continue on its own. Tape backup operations are very fast. In fact, you can back up an entire 100Mb disk in less than 30 minutes.

Installing a Tape Backup Unit

Some tape backup units come with their own hardware adapter card that you insert into an expansion slot inside your PC. Some connect to a SCSI port while others connect to an unused disk controller cable. Lastly, some external units connect to a parallel port. As you shop for a tape backup unit, your first consideration should be storage capacity. If you can store your entire disk on one tape, you simplify the backup operations. Next, you must decide on an internal or external unit. As briefly discussed, external units can be shared by multiple computers but cost a little more. Internal units eliminate the need to move the tape drive from one system to another, which simplifies the backup process.

Automating the Backup Process

As a rule, you should back up the files you create or change each day. To simplify your backup chores, many tape backup programs let you automate the entire process. For example, you can direct the software to automatically run at a specific time, such as midnight, and to backup specific files. In this way, before you leave the office, you simply need to place a backup tape into the tape drive. The backup software, in turn, will take care of the backup operation for you.

Tape Backup Buyers Guide

As you shop for a tape backup unit, use the following as a guideline:

- ❖ How much data do you need to back up?
- ❖ Do you need to back up multiple computers?
- ❖ Do you prefer an internal or external tape backup unit?
- ❖ What software comes with the unit? Does the software perform data compression?
- ❖ Does the software let you select specific files for backing up?
- ❖ How does the tape backup unit connect to the system?

Putting It All Together

Tape backup units simplify and speed up backup operations. Because the tape can store a large amount of information, you eliminate the need for multiple floppy disks. As such, some users store large amounts of information on a tape for shipping. Tape backup units can be internal or external. The advantage of external units is that the unit can be moved from one PC to another. Tape backup units come with software that oversees the backup operation. Once you start the backup, it normally runs on its own to completion or until you need to insert a second tape.

Glossary

automated backup
A backup operation that automatically backs up specific files at a predefined time without user intervention.

backup
A set of disks containing duplicate copies of your files.

external tape backup unit
A device which you can move from one computer to another to back up multiple systems.

file compression
The use of special software to reduce the amount of storage space a file requires. Using file compression, backup software may be able to store 200Mb of data on to a 120Mb tape.

formatting
The process of preparing a magnetic tape for use.

preformatted tape
A magnetic tape that is already formatted for immediate use by your tape drive.

Lesson 23: Experiencing Multimedia

Multimedia is the combination of text, sound, and video to display information in the most meaningful way. In general a *multimedia PC* contains a sound board (see Lesson 25), speakers, and a CD-ROM. Ideally, you would want a fast 486 and a video accelerator card. Figure 23.1 illustrates a multimedia PC. If your PC does not have all of these components, you can add them one component at a time as you begin to experience multimedia. This chapter presents several multimedia programs that should give you a better understanding of multimedia and its potential as a learning tool.

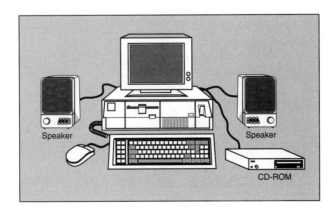

FIGURE 23.1 Components of the multimedia PC.

Looking at Multimedia Programs

As discussed, multimedia programs combine text, sound, and video. Figure 23.2, for example, illustrates a screen from the Compton's Multimedia Encyclopedia CD-ROM. The screen shows an animation of a volcano. As you view the animation, a narrator reads the encyclopedia text describing a volcano. As the narration continues, the volcano animation progresses until an eruption occurs. At that time, you hear actual recordings of a volcanic explosion.

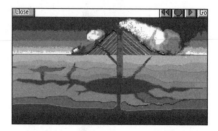

FIGURE 23.2 A multimedia animation of a volcano.

In a similar way, Figure 23.3 illustrates a screen from a National Geographic CD-ROM on animals. The CD-ROM presents pictures, video, text descriptions, and recordings of different animals. In the case of Figure 23.3, the screen shows specifics about giraffes. By combining sounds, video, pictures, and text, the CD-ROM quickly captures your imagination.

FIGURE 23.3 A multimedia animation presentation.

Multimedia is a very powerful learning tool. In the future, students learning about Vietnam will hear sights and sounds of the war, including video. In similar ways, students learning about medicine will use CD-ROM presentations that present and discuss different surgeries or medical procedures. Multimedia is not restricted to encyclopedias and other learning tools. Figure 23.4, for example, illustrates a multimedia game that combines video and sound to present Sherlock Holmes mysteries that you can solve. The ability to integrate sound and video produces a new level of video games.

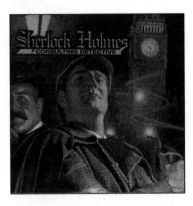

FIGURE 23.4 A multimedia video game.

Figure 23.5 illustrates a multimedia sound *screen saver* that runs when your system has not been used for a certain period of time. As the screen saver changes its screen image, the program plays background sounds.

FIGURE 23.5 A multimedia screen saver.

Buying Multimedia Equipment and Software

Several of the lessons presented in this book discuss different multimedia components. At that time, specific buyer's information is presented. As a general rule, you should look for hardware and software that includes the MPC logo. Hardware and software bearing the MPC 1 logo should be compatible with a PC meeting the system requirements listed in Figure 23.6.

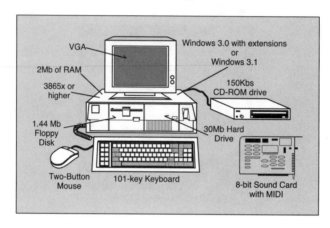

FIGURE 23.6 Requirements of the multimedia PC.

Hardware and software that use the MPC 2 logo should be compatible with a PC meeting the requirements shown in Figure 23.7.

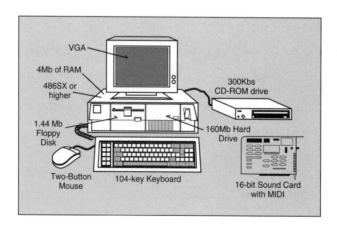

FIGURE 23.7 PC requirements for MPC 2.

Multimedia and Windows

Beginning with version 3.1, Windows provides several simple multimedia capabilities. To begin, Windows lets you assign sounds to different events. For example, when Windows begins, you can sound trumpets. Likewise, when Windows displays a dialog box, you can play the sound of a honking car horn. Windows also provides a MIDI mapper that lets you control MIDI devices (see Lesson 25). Lastly, many multimedia programs are written to run under Windows. Figure 23.8, for example, illustrates a video running under Video for Windows, a new software program from Microsoft.

FIGURE 23.8 Running a video within Video for Windows.

Putting It All Together

Multimedia is the combination of text, sound, and video to present information in the most meaningful way. By combining text, sound, and video, programs present information in ways that capture the user's imagination. When you purchase multimedia hardware and software, look for the MPC logo. Such products should be compatible with one another. For more specifics on multimedia, refer to Welcome to Multimedia, by Linda Tway (MIS:Press, 1992).

Glossary

MPC

An abbreviation for Multimedia Product Council, whose logo helps you determine compatible multimedia hardware and software.

multimedia

The combination of text, sound, and video to present information in the most meaningful way.

Lesson 24:
Scanning Images
and Text

When you create newsletters or multimedia presentations, a hardware device you will not want to be without is a *scanner*. Using a scanner you can quickly make electronic copies of photographs and text. Most scanners can copy color or black and white images. This lesson takes a look at scanner basics and common operations.

In addition, many computer stores now sell photo CD-ROM disks that contain hundreds of photographs that you can integrate into the documents you create. Best of all, you can use the images for free. This lesson takes a brief look at photo CDs you can buy and how you can create your own.

Flatbed and Handheld Scanners

There are two primary scanner types, a *flatbed scanner* shown in Figure 24.1 and a *handheld scanner* as shown in Figure 24.2.

As you can see, a flatbed scanner appears and behaves much like a copy machine. As shown in Figure 24.3, to scan an image, you simply place the image on the scanner and press the **scan** button. Rather than generating a hard copy of the image, the scanner stores the image in a file on your disk. You can later use the image file within a word processing document or newsletter.

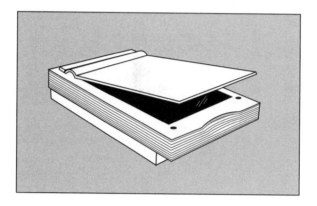

FIGURE 24.1 A flatbed scanner.

FIGURE 24.2 A handheld scanner.

If you are scanning a color image, most scanners make three passes over the image, one using a red light, one with a green light, and one in blue. As shown in Figure 24.4, to scan an image using a handheld scanner, you move the scanner slowly over the desired image or page. A handheld scanner is much less expensive than its flatbed counterpart. However, the scanned image it creates may require more editing touch-ups.

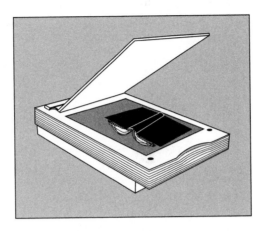

FIGURE 24.3 Scanning an image using a flatbed scanner.

FIGURE 24.4 Scanning an image using a handheld scanner.

Working with Photo Images

When you are scanning photographs, you may need to later touch up the images, possibly correcting colors or by actually editing the images. You can perform such photo editing using a software program such as Photoshop. For example, Figure 24.5 illustrates two scanned photo images.

FIGURE 24.5 Two scanned images.

Using Photoshop, you can edit these images, possibly combining the two images to create a third image as shown in Figure 24.6.

FIGURE 24.6 Using photo editing to create a new image.

Working with Scanned Images

When you scan an image there may be times when you need to "touch up" parts of the image. As such, most scanners come with software that lets you zoom in on and manipulate scanned images.

In addition to letting you edit the scanned image, many software packages let you change image colors and even rotate the image.

Working with Scanned Text

In addition to providing software that lets you work with scanned images, many scanners provide *optical character recognition* (OCR) software that lets you scan a page of text and then extract the text to a word processing file. For example, Figure 24.7 displays a page from this book that contains text and graphics.

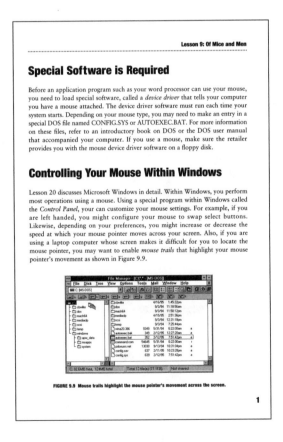

FIGURE 24.7 A page containing text and graphics.

Using OCR software, Figure 24.8 illustrates the text that was extracted from the scanned page.

SPECIAL SOFTWARE IS REQUIRED

Before an application program such as your word processor can use your mouse, you need to load special software, called a device driver that tells your computer you have a mouse attached. The device driver software must run each time your system starts. Depending on your mouse type, you may need to make an entry in a special DOS file named CONFIG.SYS or AUTOEXEC.BAT. For more information on these files, refer to an introductory book on DOS or the DOS user manual that accompanied your computer. If you use a mouse, make sure the retailer provides you with the mouse device driver software on a floppy disk.

CONTROLLING YOUR MOUSE WITHIN WINDOWS

Lesson 20 discusses Microsoft Windows in detail. Within Windows, you perform most operations using a mouse. Using a special program within Windows called the Control Panel, your can customize your mouse settings. For example, if you are left handed, you might configure your mouse to swap select buttons. Likewise, depending on your preferences, you might increase or decrease the speed at which your mouse pointer moves across your screen. Also, if you are using a laptop computer whose screen makes it difficult for you to locate the mouse pointer, you may want to enable mouse trails that highlight your mouse pointer's movement as shown in Figure 9.9.

FIGURE 24.8 Extracting text using OCR software.

OCR software is very powerful. To begin, the software examines the scanned image trying to match the shapes of letters and numbers. To improve the accuracy of the extracted text, the software then typically spell checks the resultant words and sometimes even performs a context or grammatical evaluation. If you are scanning a page that contains sharp text, OCR software should have 95% accuracy or better. In fact, some optical character recognition software can even recognize handwritten text!

Using Photo CD Images

In general, a *photo CD* is simply a CD-ROM disk that contains one or more photographs. To give users an easy way to integrate photographs into newsletters, reports, or advertisements, many companies now sell photo CDs that contain images users can include in their documents royalty free. The advantage of using photo CDs is that you eliminate the need for a photographer or scanner. You can find photo CDs that contain photographs taken on a wide variety of topics. Figure 24.9, for example, illustrates six different photo CD images.

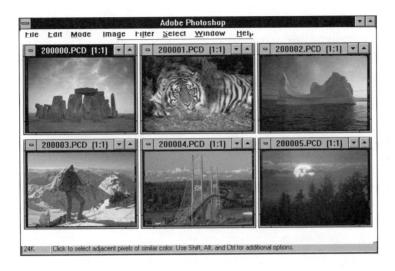

FIGURE 24.9 Photo CD images cover a wide variety of topics.

Creating Your Own Photo CD

If you have one or more photographs you want to include within a document, but you don't have a scanner, you may find that creating a photo CD is a cost-effective alternative. Many companies will scan your photo images for you to produce a photo CD that contains the electronic images. If you price color separations by a professional film processing company, it may cost you $100 or more, *per picture*! On the other hand, having a company produce a photo CD for you may reduce your per picture cost to less than $1.00 per image!

Scanner Buyer's Guide

❖ Will an inexpensive hand held scanner produce the quality image you require?

❖ How many images will you scan per week?

❖ Will you scan black and white, color images, or both?

253

❖ What is the scanner's resolution? The higher the resolution, the sharper the resulting image.

❖ What software accompanies the scanner? Will you get an image editor and OCR software?

Putting It All Together

If you are creating newsletters or other documents that require pictures, a scanner is a must-have hardware device. A flatbed scanner works very much like a copy machine in that you place the image you want to scan on to the scanner and press a scan button. Rather than generating a hard copy, the scanner creates an electronic image. Using software that accompanies your scanner, you can touch up the image or even extract text from the image into a word processing document.

Glossary

optical character recognition (OCR)
Software that lets you scan a page of text and then extract the text to a word processing file.

photo CD
A CD-ROM disk that contains photographic images in an electronic format that a user can integrate into a document.

photo editing
The use of computer software to edit an image stored in an electronic format on disk. Photo editing might include color correction, image elimination, or image combination.

scanner
A hardware device which allows you to quickly make electronic copies of photographs and text.

Lesson 25: Understanding the Sound Board

Multimedia is the combination of text, sound, and video to present information in the most meaningful way. To help your computer present high quality sound, you must install a *sound board*. This lesson presents PC sound boards. As you will learn, sound boards are easy to install and use. As the price of computer hardware has continued to decrease, so too has the price of sound boards. In fact, you can now purchase quality sound for less than two hundred dollars. As shown in Figure 25.1, a sound board is simply a board you install in your computer's expansion slots.

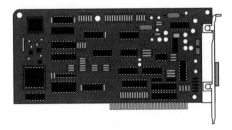

FIGURE 25.1 A PC sound board.

Installing a Sound Board

To install a sound board in your computer, you open your system unit and insert the sound board into an expansion slot, as shown in Figure 25.2.

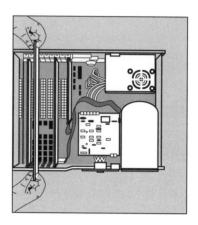

FIGURE 25.2 Installing a sound board.

When you install a sound board, you may need to adjust the board's *interrupt request number* and *memory address* to avoid conflicts with other hardware boards such as a modem or mouse. To help you determine the correct settings, use the MSD program discussed in Lesson 36.

NOTE

Many users have difficulty installing a sound board and resolving conflicts with other hardware boards. As such, you may want your retailer to install the sound board into your system for you, directing him or her to include the correct software with which you need to use the sound board from within Windows.

Looking at the Sound Board

If you examine the back of the sound board, you find several ports similar to those shown in Figure 25.3.

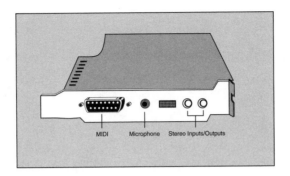

FIGURE 25.3 Common sound board ports.

Figure 25.4 illustrates how you might attach different devices to sound board ports. The use of the MIDI port is discussed in detail later in this lesson.

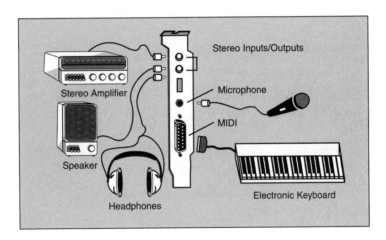

FIGURE 25.4 Connecting devices to sound board ports.

As you can see, you can connect a microphone to your sound board. Using the microphone you can record your own sounds, storing the sounds in a file on disk.

How a Sound Board Works

As you have learned, your computer works with ones and zeros that represent digital signals, similar to those shown in Figure 25.5.

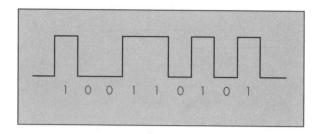

FIGURE 25.5 Using ones and zeros to represent a digital signal.

Sound, however, is represented by a wave, as shown in Figure 25.6.

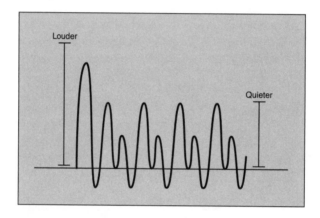

FIGURE 25.6 Sound is represented by an analog wave.

When you run a multimedia program that uses sound, the sound board converts the computer's digital representation of a sound to an *analog wave* that can be played through speakers or a headphone.

Making Music with MIDI

With the success and popularity of multimedia programs, computer users can now create multimedia presentations that include video, sound, and music. *MIDI* is an acronym for *musical instrument digital interface*. In other words, MIDI specifies how you can connect electronic instruments to your digital computer. Most sound boards provide a MIDI port to which your computer can send signals that play an electronic instrument or from which your computer can record instrument sounds. As you will learn in this lesson, there are many different electronic instruments you can connect to a MIDI port, such as a keyboard or saxophone.

Looking at MIDI Devices

As shown in Figure 25.7, most PC sound boards provide a MIDI port.

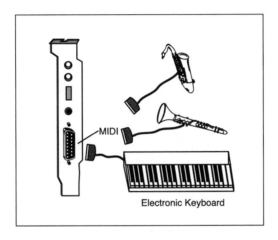

FIGURE 25.7 Most PC sound boards provide a MIDI port.

As discussed, you can use the MIDI port to record sounds from an electronic device. An entire MIDI song is often called a *MIDI score*. Files containing MIDI scores contain instructions that correspond to an electronic instrument. For example, if you are using an electronic keyboard, MIDI instructions might include commands such as "hold down keys C, E, and F" or "release middle C." A MIDI score can contain instructions for several different instruments. Depending on the number of instruments, a one minute MIDI score might consume 10Kb of disk space.

To play a MIDI score, sound boards use a *synthesizer* that converts the MIDI instructions for a specific device to the analog wave signals used by speakers. A synthesizer is a chip that receives electronic signals and converts the signal to an analog wave. If a MIDI score uses three different instruments, the sound board would use three different synthesizer channels. When you shop for sound boards, you may encounter the term *polyphony*, which describes the number of channels into a synthesizer. The larger the polyphony, the more instruments the synthesizer can represent. Windows 3.1 provides a program called the MIDI Mapper that lets you control which devices the synthesizer associates with specific channels. By mapping channels to different devices, you can play songs written for an electronic keyboard using an electronic saxophone.

Sound Boards and CD-ROM Drives

Lesson 27 discusses CD-ROM drives in detail. As you will learn, many multimedia upgrade kits include CD-ROM drives that connect to a sound card. The advantage of connecting the CD-ROM drive to a sound card is *cost*. The kit manufacturer only needs to provide one card (the sound card) as opposed to a separate sound card and CD-ROM drive controller. The disadvantage of connecting the CD-ROM drive to sound card is that should your sound card break, you will not be able to access your CD-ROM drive. Likewise, should you decide to upgrade your sound card in the future, your CD-ROM drive may not be compatible with the new card. As a result, you may have to upgrade your CD-ROM drive as well.

Putting It All Together

To help your computer produce high quality sound, you must install a sound board within one of your computer's expansion ports. After you install the hardware card, you normally need to install a specific software that lets programs use the sound board. Most sound boards provide a common set of ports. These ports let you connect the sound board to speakers, a synthesizer, a microphone, or even MIDI devices. When you purchase a sound board, shop for one that supports MIDI.

Glossary

analog signal   A wave like signal. Normally, sound is represented
                           as an analog wave. The computer, however, must
                           store a digital representation of the sound.

digital signal   A signal represented using ones and zeros.

interrupt request	A signal from a device such as a sound card to the CPU that notifies the CPU that the device needs to be serviced. Each device must have a unique interrupt request line.
memory address	A value that identifies a location in your PC's memory. Devices use unique memory locations to communicate with the CPU.
MIDI	An acronym for musical instrument device interface that lets you connect electronic instruments to your personal computer.
sound board	A hardware board that lets your computer play high quality sounds.
synthesizer	An electronic device that produces (synthesizes) sounds. Sound cards for example can produce sounds that mimic a piano, guitar, and so on.

Lesson 26:
Understanding PC
Networks

A computer *network* consists of two or more computers connected to share data files, printers, or to exchange information. If you are using a PC at home, you probably don't need to worry about understanding networks. However, if you are using a PC at work, the PC may connect to other computers, forming a network. This lesson briefly describes how a network functions, why businesses use networks, and how a network affects the way you work. For information on specific networking software, refer to the MIS:Press book, *Networking Fundamentals*, by Joe Levy and Glenn Hartwig.

Lesson 30 introduces the Internet, today's information highway. As you will learn, the Internet is a worldwide collection of networks (over 30,000 networks).

What is a Network?

A *network* is a collection of computers that connect either by cable (in the case of a *local area network*), or possibly by satellite (in the case of a *wide area network*). Users connect computers within a network to share files and other resources such as a disk drive or laser printer. A network requires hardware such as cables and adapter cards that reside within each computer's system unit, as well as software. Figure 26.1 illustrates a possible network configuration.

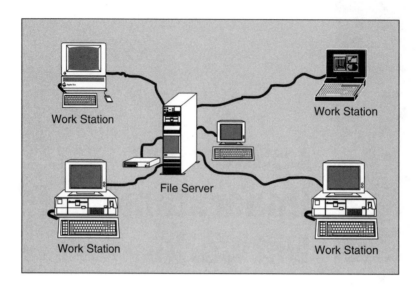

FIGURE 26.1 Workstation computers connect to a server computer to share files and resources.

As you can see, the computers connected to the network don't have to be the same type. Most networks have one or more special computers called *servers*, to which the other computers connect. Server computers typically have a very large hard disk and possibly several printers that users connected to network can share.

User computers that attach to the server are called *workstations*. Although the user may type at the workstation, the information with which the user is working may reside on the server. In this way, many users connected to the server can share the same information, such as a large customer database. In addition, users connected to the server can use the server's printers, eliminating the need for each workstation to have its own printer. If two or more users try to use the printer at the same time, the network software assigns the printer on a first come, first serve basis.

Why Businesses Use Networks

The main reason businesses use networks is to let users share information and resources. If you have 25 users who only periodically print documents, letting the users share network printers may prove more cost effective than buying each user his/her own printer. Likewise, many companies (such as a bank, insurance company, or airline) have large databases of information that many employees must access and possibly update throughout the day. A network provides users with the ability to share information in this way.

One of the most convenient features networks provide is the ability to send and receive electronic mail (often called *e-mail*). Using electronic mail, you can quickly send a memo to one or more users on the network. Electronic mail helps reduce the problem of missed phone calls. Each worker has a unique electronic mail name. To send a message to a specific user, you simply refer to the corresponding e-mail name. If you need to get a message to another worker, you can simply mail it to him. If the user is currently connected to the network, the electronic mail software immediately tells them of the message. If the user is not connected to the network, the electronic mail software waits, telling the user of their new mail as soon as they connect to the network. Figure 26.2, for example, illustrates how you might send an electronic mail message to another user using Microsoft Mail.

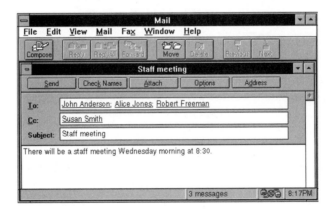

FIGURE 26.2 Using Microsoft Mail.

In addition to electronic mail, many businesses use scheduling programs that let multiple users coordinate their busy calendars electronically to simplify scheduling. Figure 26.3, for example, illustrates Microsoft Schedule+. Using Schedule+, you can specify the users that must attend a meeting. Schedule+, in turn, examines each user's schedule to determine when each is available. In this way, you spend more time performing useful work and less time playing phone tag.

FIGURE 26.3 Scheduling appointments using Schedule+.

Accessing the Network

Depending on your network software, the steps you must perform to access the network differ. To begin, your network administrator assigns you with a user name and a password. When you want to access the network, you run a special program that first prompts you to type in your user name. As you type your user name, the letters you type appear on the screen. Next, the program asks you to type in your password. Your password is private. When you type your password, the letters do not appear on the screen. You can and should tell other users your username. Other users must know your username to send you electronic mail messages. (Lesson 35 discusses electronic mail in detail.) If you correctly type the user name and password, you gain access to the network. *Never* tell another user your password. Should another user obtain your password, that user can access the network just as you would. In other words, the user could access (change or delete) your files, read your electronic mail, or even send money on your behalf.

In Lesson 8 you learned your hard disk is normally drive C, and your floppy disks, drives A and B. When you use a network, the server disk normally uses drive F, G or H. For the most part, you can use the server disk just as you would use any disk drive. Depending again on your network software, the steps you must perform to use printers attached to the server differ. See your network administrator for details. Assume, for example, your business owns only one PostScript or color printer. Using network software, all of the users on the network can use the printers just as if the printer were connected to their own system.

When you no longer need to use the server, you normally run a program that logs you off, or disconnects you from the server.

Understanding Workgroups

When you work within a computer network with other users, it is common for several workers to work on different parts of the same project. Recently, the term *workgroup* has been used to describe the users in a network that work together on the same project. In a similar way, software that helps such users coordinate their work on a specific project is called *workgroup software*. Over the past few years, Windows for Workgroups and Lotus Notes have brought workgroup processing into the spotlight. In the near future, software will let users work on different parts of a same report or project, furthering the workgroup concept.

Understanding Network Security

Computer networks help users share files and printers. Within a network, many workers may have access to one or more files. As a result, a user may change or delete a file other users did not want to change. To prevent such problems, most network software lets you specify which users can access specific files. If all of the users in your network can access the files of everyone else, your network security is poor. In such cases, talk to your network administrator. In general, network users should only have access to those files they need to perform their work. If your network security is high, no other users on the network (other than the network administrator) can access your files. The network administrator is a privileged user who normally has access to all files that reside throughout the network, including yours.

Accessing a Network Remotely

Lesson 19 discussed telecommunications. Using a modem, you learned that you can dial into your computer in the home or your office. Depending on your network software, you may be able to access the network using your modem. The advantage of remote network access is that you can get to network files or even print files on network printers regardless of where you are calling from. The disadvantage of allowing remote network access however, is that unauthorized users (*hackers*) may access your network and the files it contains. As a result, you need to ensure that your network is very secure and the number of files users can access is restricted.

Putting It All Together

A network is two or more computers connected to exchange information, or to share files and resources such as a printer. In general, users working at computers (or workstations) log onto a computer called the network file server. Once attached to the server, users can share files, use server devices such as a printer, or correspond with other users via electronic mail.

Glossary

e-mail	An abbreviation for electronic mail. Using e-mail, network users can quickly exchange memos and other documents with one another.
hackers	Computer users who intentionally and often maliciously try to break into a computer system.
LAN	An abbreviation for a local area network, typically a network whose computers are all contained within the same, or adjacent buildings.
network administrator	The individual responsible for setting up and maintaining a computer network. The network administrator is a privileged user who has complete access to files across the network.

server
: A network computer to which users can connect to receive special services such as file sharing or resource sharing.

WAN
: An abbreviation for wide area network—a computer network whose computers may be dispersed across a city, state, country, or even the world.

workgroup
: Two or more users that collaborate on the same project.

workstation
: A PC from which the user can log into the network. A workstation may have its own disk drives and printer, or it may not have either.

Lesson 27: Understanding CD-ROMs

Over the past two years, the sale and use of CD-ROMs have exploded. As you may know, multimedia programs that contain text, photos, sounds, and video consume tremendous amounts of disk space. A CD-ROM disk can store over 600Mb (megabytes) of data. In other words, a single CD-ROM disk can store 150,000 pages of single-spaced typed text, thousands of full-color photo images, or even over 60 minutes of video.

Using a CD-ROM Drive

Depending on the type of your CD-ROM drive, the steps you perform to use a CD-ROM disk will differ. As shown in Figure 27.1, for example, your CD-ROM drive may have a disk drive that slides in and out, or it may use a disk holder. When you insert a CD-ROM disk either into the drive or a disk holder, you do so with the disk label facing up.

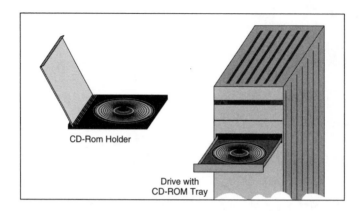

FIGURE 27.1 CD-ROM drives may or may not require the use of a disk holder.

How a CD-ROM Disk Stores Information

CD-ROM is an acronym for *compact disk read only-memory*. The term read-only memory tell you that your computer can read the disk's contents, but your computer cannot change the information the disk contains.

As you learned in Lesson 8, disks store information by magnetizing the data on to the disk's surface. A CD-ROM disk, on the other hand, records information using small pits on the disk's surface. As shown in Figure 27.2, the CD-ROM drive reads the data the disk contains by reflecting a laser light off of the disk's surface. As it turns out, light reflects off the disk's surface differently than it does a pitted area. Because the drive cannot change the pits on the disk's surface, the disk is read-only memory.

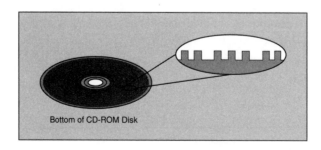

FIGURE 27.2 A CD-ROM disk uses small pits on the disk's surface to record information.

Uses for CD-ROM Disks

Over the next few years, the use of CD-ROM disks will continue to explode. In the past, many software companies shipped their programs using many floppy disks. For example, Windows 3.1 required seven floppies. In the future, software companies will ship their software on a single CD-ROM disk to reduce their costs (the cost to replicate one CD-ROM is very close to the cost of duplicating a single floppy disk) and to simplify the software installation. Also, as discussed, a CD-ROM disk can store over 600Mb of data. As such, a CD-ROM is ideal for storing electronic books, which may contain several thousand pages of reference material. Lastly, as briefly discussed, a CD-ROM disk can hold up to an hour of video. By integrating video into programs such as electronic encyclopedias or computer games, software developers can make their programs much more interesting to the end user.

Understanding Different CD-ROM Drive Speeds

Since CD-ROM drives first became available a few years ago, they have increased significantly in terms of speed. The initial CD-ROM drives, called *single-speed drives*, were capable of transferring 150 Kb of data to the PC per second. Next, manufacturers released *double-speed drives*, capable of transferring 300 Kb per second.

By allowing the CD-ROM drive to transfer more information in less time, the double speed drives let multimedia programs display large video windows whose contents play at more realistic speeds (less jerky motion in the video). Although double-speed drives are the most widely used CD-ROM drive type, quad-speed drives (600Kb per second) are quickly gaining popularity. Again, as CD-ROM drive speeds continue to increase, the video and animations found in multimedia programs will continue to improve. In the near future, all PCs will ship with quad speed drives or faster!

Understanding CD-R Disks

As you have learned, CD-ROM disks are so named because you cannot change the disk's contents. At first glance, a recordable CD-R disk seems to violate this rule. *CD-R* is an abbreviation for *compact disk recordable*. Using a special hardware drive called a *CD burner* (or *recorder*) you can record information onto a special CD-R disk. After you record the data on the disk, however, the disk's contents cannot be changed. Initially, CD-ROM burners were large external drives. Today, however, a burner may fit in a standard *disk drive bay*. However, most burners still cost $1,000 or more. The CD-R disk costs $15 to $20.

CD-ROM burners provide companies with a very convenient way to back up large amounts of data. Because the CD-ROM burner burns pits into the CD-R disk as opposed to magnetizing data on to a disk or tape, the CD-ROM disk is less susceptible to damage. In addition, the small CD-ROM disks consume much less storage space than floppy disks or disk cartridges.

CD-ROM Drives and Notebook Computers

Most users who work with a notebook computer want to have the same capabilities with their notebook as they would have with a desktop computer. As such, notebook computers that contain CD-ROM drives are starting to emerge. Notebook users want their computer to be small and compact. The difficulty with placing a CD-ROM drive within a notebook computer is the drive's size. As such, many notebook computer users connect external CD-ROM drives to their notebook as shown in Figure 27.3.

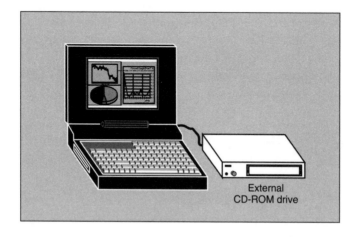

External
CD-ROM drive

FIGURE 27.3 Connecting an external CD-ROM drive to a notebook computer.

Most external CD-ROM drives connect to a SCSI connector. If your notebook computer supports PCMCIA cards, you can purchase a PCMCIA-based SCSI connector. Likewise, you can buy a hardware device that converts the computer's parallel port into a SCSI connector.

Putting It All Together

Today, most new PCs ship with a CD-ROM drive. CD-ROM disks provide tremendous storage capacity (over 600Mb). As such, CD-ROM disks are ideal for storing multimedia programs, electronic books, or other large references. The computer can read, but cannot change the contents of the CD-ROM disk. In the future, most notebook computers will also ship with CD-ROMs. In addition, many computers will use CD-ROM burners (recorders) to create their own CD-ROM disks.

Glossary

CD-burner	A hardware device that lets users create their own CD-ROM disks.
CD-R	An abbreviation for compact disk recordable.
CD-ROM	An abbreviation for compact disk read-only memory. A CD-ROM disk is a storage mechanism whose contents the computer can read but not change. A CD-ROM disk can store tremendous amounts of data, over 600Mb.
single-speed drive	A CD-ROM drive that transfers data at 150,000 bytes per second (150 Kbs).

Lesson 28: Understanding SCSI Devices

As the number of users adding CD-ROM drives, a tape drive, as well as additional hard drives has increased, so too has the popularity of *SCSI* (pronounced scuzzy) devices. This lesson examines SCSI adapters and SCSI devices in detail. As you will learn, SCSI adapters make it easy for you to connect a wide variety of devices to your computer.

Installing a SCSI Adapter

Like other ports in your PC (such as a *parallel* or *serial port*), a SCSI adapter is a port that resides on a card that you install into an expansion slot within your PC's system unit.

A SCSI adapter normally uses a 50-pin connector. Figure 28.1 illustrates the two most common SCSI adapter types.

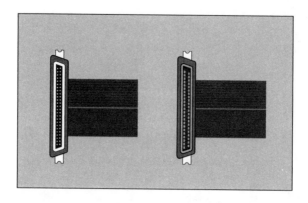

FIGURE 28.1 The two common SCSI adapter types.

Using a SCSI cable, you connect a device to the SCSI adapter. What makes SCSI connections unique, however, is that you can connect one SCSI device to another to create a chain of SCSI-based devices as discussed next.

Understanding SCSI-Device Chains

As shown in Figure 28.2, you can connect up to seven SCSI devices to one another to produce a *device chain*. In the case of Figure 28.2, the SCSI chain consists of an external hard disk, tape drive, and a CD-ROM drive.

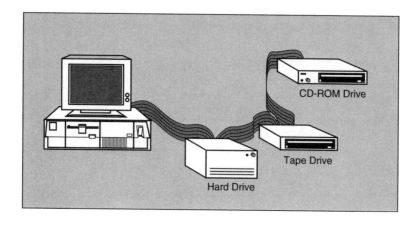

FIGURE 28.2 You can connect up to seven devices to a SCSI adapter.

Terminating the SCSI Chain

When you connect SCSI-based devices together to create a SCSI chain, you need a way to tell the SCSI adapter where the chain ends. To indicate the last device in the SCSI chain, you use a special connector, called a SCSI *terminator*. As shown in Figure 28.3, you plug the SCSI terminator into the last device in the SCSI chain.

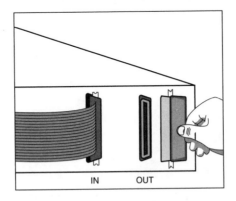

IN   OUT

FIGURE 28.3 You must terminate the end of a SCSI chain.

To add another device to the chain, you unplug the SCSI terminator, plug in the new device, and then use the terminator to terminate the new device.

NOTE   Some devices have built-in terminators you can turn on or off by setting a switch within the device. For more specifics on terminating a device using internal switches, refer to the documentation that accompanied the device.

Understanding SCSI Addresses

Each device in the SCSI device chain must have a unique SCSI address. SCSI devices use the address values 0 through 7. Normally, the SCSI adapter card will use address 7. When you connect a device to the SCSI chain, you must ensure that the device uses a unique SCSI address. Most devices have a switch that lets you quickly select the address value you desire.

The SCSI adapter uses the SCSI address to prioritize device importance. The higher the address, the higher the device priority. For example, if you have a SCSI-based disk whose performance is very important, you would want to assign the device a high priority address such as 6.

NOTE

SCSI Adapters and Notebook Computers

If you are using a notebook computer that contains a PCMCIA slot (discussed in Lesson 29), you can purchase a PCMCIA-based SCSI adapter and connect a SCSI device chain to your notebook as shown in Figure 28.4

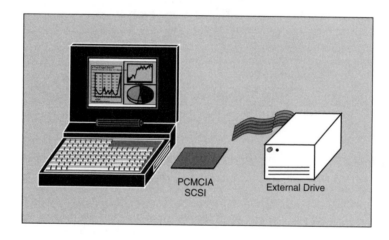

PCMCIA
SCSI

External Drive

FIGURE 28.4 Using a PCMCIA-based SCSI adapter.

If your notebook does not support PCMCIA, you can purchase a hardware device that converts the notebook's parallel port into a SCSI connector. The problem with such parallel-port based SCSI adapters, however, is that they are normally much slower than a standard SCSI device.

SCSI Buyer's Guide

Use the following list as a guideline as you shop for a SCSI adapter:

❖ Is the SCSI adapter compatible with your PC and other devices?

❖ Does the SCSI adapter come with device drivers for your operating system?

❖ Are there performance benchmarks available for the SCSI adapter? Some SCSI adapters are slower than others.

❖ Is the SCSI adapter software or hardware controllable? Many users find software controllable SCSI adapters easier to install.

Putting It All Together

A SCSI adapter is a hardware card into which you connect up to seven hardware devices to build a SCSI device chain. Each device in the SCSI chain must have a unique address, that you assign. SCSI addresses range from 0 through 7. You must indicate the last device in SCSI chain by terminating the device using a switch or terminator connector.

Glossary

device chain

The process of connecting one device to a SCSI adaptor, a second device to that device and so on, creating a chain of devices. You can connect up to 7 devices to a SCSI adaptor.

SCSI

An abbreviation for small computer systems interconnect. A SCSI adapter makes it easy for users to connect up to seven devices to their PC, using a SCSI chain.

SCSI address

A value from 0 through 7 that uniquely identifies a device within the SCSI chain.

SCSI terminator

A special hardware connector that indicates the end of a SCSI-device chain.

Lesson 29:
Understanding
PCMCIA Cards

If you use a notebook computer, you may be limited on the number of hardware upgrades you can perform. In short, if you are using an older notebook, you hardware upgrades may be limited to increasing your hard disk size or to installing a faster modem. If you are using a newer notebook, you may be able to upgrade your notebook using PCMCIA cards.

In short, a *PCMCIA* card is a small credit card like cartridge that you insert into a slot in your notebook computer. Each PCMCIA card contains the electronics for a specific device. For example, one PCMCIA card may contain the electronics for a modem, while a second PCMCIA card provides a SCSI interface. If you are shopping for a notebook computer, you will want to purchase one that supports PCMCIA cards.

Using PCMCIA Cards

A PCMCIA card is a small credit-card-size cartridge that you insert into a slot on your notebook computer. Depending on your notebook type, your computer may support multiple PCMCIA cards.

Some notebook computers only have one PCMCIA slot into which you can insert cards as you need them. For example, assume that you have fast 28.8Kb modem on a PCMCIA card. When you need to use the modem, you simply insert the modem's PCMCIA card into the slot. Likewise, assume you have a PCMCIA card that contains a SCSI connector. If you later need to use a SCSI-based device, you can pop up the PCMCIA modem and replace it with the SCSI card.

Understanding PCMCIA Type I, II, and III Cards

When PCMCIA cards were first released, the cards (called *type I cards*) were larger than the cards available today. As the technology improved, hardware developers were able to design thinner cards. Today, you can purchase type I, II, and III PCMCIA cards. Before you buy a card, you need to verify that the card is compatible with your computer.

If you are using a newer notebook computer, it probably supports all three PCMCIA card types. The advantage of type II and III cards is that you can often insert two cards into the same notebook slot at one time. Thus, if your notebook computer requires modem and network access at the same time, you can insert both PCMCIA cards into the notebook slot. Because the older type I cards are thicker, you can only insert one type I card into a slot at any time.

The Future of PCMCIA

Today, PCMCIA cards provide notebook computer users with a way to upgrade their computer. Because of their simplicity of use, however, in the future you may find that desktop and tower-based computers provide support for PCMCIA cards. As discussed, you can purchase PCMCIA cards that contain memory, a modem, a network connector, a sound card, and even a SCSI interface. In the future, PCMCIA cards will continue to evolve to support TV connections, interfaces to fiber optic video-based communication, and much more. As their size and cost continue to decrease, PCMCIA cards will eventually lead to throw-away hardware. In other words, if you need a faster modem, you will simply pop out and discard your existing modem, so you can replace it with a newer faster one—all in less than one minute. PCMCIA truly provides users with *plug-and-play hardware*. When a user needs a specific device, they simply plug in the corresponding PCMCIA card and use (play) it.

PCMCIA Buyer's Guide

Use the following list as a guideline when you shop for PCMCIA cards or when you shop for a notebook computer:

❖ Does your notebook computer support PCMCIA cards?

❖ What PCMCIA card type does your notebook computer support?

❖ How many PCMCIA cards can you use at one time?

Putting It All Together

PCMCIA cards provide notebook computer users with an easy way to upgrade their computer. Each PCMCIA card contains the electronics for a specific device. When the user needs the device, they simply insert the corresponding PCMCIA card. Depending on the notebook computer type as well as the PCMCIA card type, the number of PCMCIA cards the user can use at one time will differ.

Glossary

PCMCIA

An abbreviation for Personal Computer Memory Card Interface Association—the group that defines the standards for PCMCIA cards.

plug-and-play hardware

Hardware cards that contain a chip that identifies the device to the computer. In this way, the operating system can determine the hardware card's type and then install the correct software.

Lesson 30: Understanding the Internet

Each day, newspapers, magazines, and even television shows discuss the *Internet*—today's information highway. Although estimates place the number of new Internet users at 1 million users a month, most people still have little idea of what the Internet is, what it can do for them, and at what cost. This lesson introduces the Internet. In the lessons that follow, you will learn how to use the Internet. For more information on the Internet, turn to the MIS: Press books *Welcome to... the Internet*, second edition, by Tom Badgett, 1995, and *Internet in Plain English*, by Bryan Pfaffenberger, 1995.

The Internet—a Huge Network of Computer Networks

In Lesson 26 you learned that a network consists of two or more computers connected to share resources such as disks, printers, or information stored in files. The Internet is a huge collection of computer networks (over 30,000 networks) that span the globe throughout 130 countries. Figure 30.1 illustrates a collection of networks.

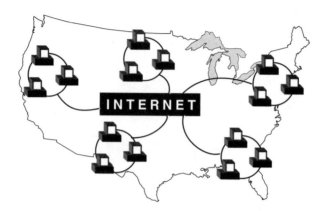

FIGURE 30.1 The Internet is a collection of computer networks.

When we think of computer networks, we normally think of computers connected by one or more cables. Because the Internet spans the globe, the computers it connects may use cables, phone wires, or even satellite transmissions. Using the Internet, users can exchange electronic-mail messages, share files, research specific topics, or even just chat with other users on-line.

Where the Internet Came from

Throughout the 1970s and 80s, the Internet was used exclusively by government institutions, researchers, and educators to exchange electronic-mail messages and research reports. Using the Internet, a researcher in Los Angeles can ask questions of an expert in Japan.

Over time, word of the Internet's power spread across the academic community. Soon, most colleges and universities connected their computers to the Internet. For years, the only way users could normally access the Internet was if the user was a student or faculty members at a school whose computers were connected to the Internet.

Who Pays for the Internet?

The Internet is unique in that, for the most part, it pays for itself. For example, assume that, as shown in Figure 30.2, Adams and Smith Colleges are connected to the Internet. Also, assume that Johnson College wants to connect.

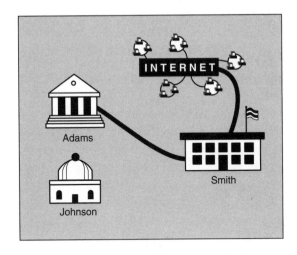

FIGURE 30.2 Two colleges connected to the Internet.

In this case, Johnson College, which wants to connect to the Internet, must pay the cost to establish a connection to the closest college. Depending on the distances involved, Johnson College might pay for a cable connection or possibly a satellite link. Once Johnson College's connection to the Internet exists, computers within the Johnson College network will have access to Internet. By placing the connection costs on the new member, the Internet essentially pays for itself. Figure 30.3 illustrates Johnson College's connection to the Internet.

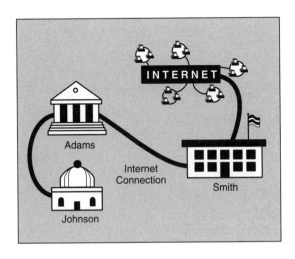

FIGURE 30.3 Johnson College connected to the Internet.

Why the Internet's Growth is Exploding

For many years, the Internet grew one university or research laboratory at a time, in the manner just discussed. In 1994, however, the Internet's growth exploded due to the fact that it could now be used for commercial purposes. As such, today on the Internet you can still research topics in an academic environment. In addition, you can also use the Internet to order pizza from Pizza Hut or to shop at a small on-line boutique or using a large on-line catalog.

Current estimates place the Internet's growth at over 30,000 new users each day! As shown in Figure 30.4, the Internet now consists of over 30,000 computer networks that reside in over 130 countries.

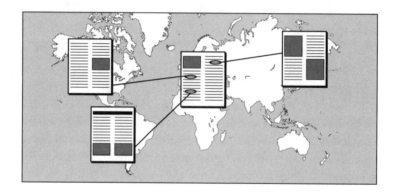

FIGURE 30.4 The Internet's presence spans the globe.

Understanding the Internet's Worldwide Presence

After you connect to the Internet, you can send e-mail messages to users around the world. Likewise, if a computer in Japan or Australia contains a file you need in order to complete your research, you can access that computer across the Internet. Best of all, as you traverse the globe using the Internet in this way, you do so for free! In other words, when you're out on the Internet, it doesn't cost you any more to access a computer across the world than it does to access a university computer across town!

Putting It All Together

The Internet is today's information highway. The Internet consists of over 30,000 interconnected computer networks (each of which can consist of multiple computers). The Internet is now available in over 130 countries. In Lesson 31 you will learn how you connect to the Internet. Likewise, in Lesson 32, you will examine activities you can perform on the network.

Glossary

Internet

An acronym for inter-network. The Internet is network of computer networks, consisting of over 30,000 computer networks across 130 countries.

the Net

A nickname for the Internet.

surfing the net

Lingo for connecting to and traversing the Internet for data.

Lesson 31:
How You Connect
to the Internet

In Lesson 31, you learned that the Internet is today's information highway. Each day, tens of thousands of users connect to the Internet for the first time. This lesson examines how you can connect to the Internet using your PC, modem, and data communication software.

As you will learn, companies, called *Internet providers*, make it easy for you to access the Internet for a minimal monthly fee.

Understanding Internet Providers

As you learned in Lesson 31, large companies and universities connect (either by cable or satellite link) their computer networks to the Internet. As you might guess, connecting a computer network to the Internet in this way can be very expensive. That's where companies called Internet providers come in.

An *Internet provider* is a company that has paid to connect its computer to the Internet. Next, for a fee, the Internet provider lets you dial into its computer using your PC and a modem. Once you dial into the provider's computer, you can access the Internet from your PC using the provider's connection. Figure 31.1 illustrates how an Internet provider lets you access the Internet.

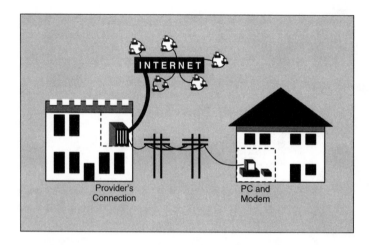

FIGURE 31.1 For a fee, you can access the Internet via an Internet provider.

What You Need to Start

As discussed, you access the Internet using your PC, a modem, and data-communication software. Admittedly, you can access the Internet using any modem. However, the faster your modem, the more you will enjoy the Internet. In short, if you plan to use the Internet on a regular basis, you will want to use, at a minimum, a 14.4Kb modem. If you plan to make extensive use of the Internet and the *World Wide Web* discussed in Lesson 33, you should purchase a 28.8Kb modem.

Depending on whether you use a standard or *SLIP-based Internet account*, as discussed next, the amount of software you will need to access the Internet will differ.

Standard Versus SLIP-Based Internet Accounts

When you shop for an Internet provider, you need to find out if the provider supports standard or SLIP-based Internet access. Most providers will offer both. Standard Internet access is text based. As shown in Figure 31.2, when you log into a text-based Internet account, you will normally encounter a menu of options.

FIGURE 31.2 A menu of text-based options for a standard Internet account.

The standard (text-based) Internet accounts make the Internet appear very much like a large bulletin board system (BBS). To perform different operations on the Internet, you select specific menu options. In addition, most standard Internet accounts may let you access a command prompt (normally a UNIX-based prompt). From the command prompt, you can issue Internet commands such as MAIL, FTP, TELNET, and GOPHER. For more information on Internet commands, turn to the MIS: Press books *Welcome to... the Internet*, second edition, by Tom Badgett (1995) and *Internet in Plain English* by Bryan Pfaffenberger (1994).

A standard Internet account is normally the provider's least expensive way for you to access the Internet.

If you use Windows, you will find that a *SLIP-based Internet* account makes the best use of your time. A SLIP-based account lets you access the Internet using Windows-based programs. A provider will charge you slightly more money for a SLIP-based account. However, because you are using the easy-to-use Windows-based programs, your time on the Internet will be more productive.

To use the SLIP-based connection from within Windows, you will need Windows-based Internet programs. If you examine Internet books in your bookstore, you will find that several books bundle Windows-based software with the books for free!

NOTE

Many providers offer a *PPP-based connection* that is similar to a SLIP account (you can access the PPP account from within Windows). However, the PPP account may be slightly faster than the SLIP account. As such, if you can get a SLIP or PPP account for the same cost, choose the PPP-based account if your software will support it.

How Much Providers Charge

Over the past year, a large number of providers have emerged. Because of competition among providers, most providers will offer several different pricing structures. For example, some may offer unlimited use for a fixed amount. Others may charge you an hourly rate. If you are like most users, you will probably find that you can spend considerably more time on the net than you would guess. As such, you are probably best served by the flat fee for unlimited access.

Most Internet providers will offer a local access telephone number that you dial to access their computer. Others, however, may offer an 800 number that gives you access. Although you won't have to pay long-distances fees to access the provider, the provider will charge you a higher hourly rate.

Accessing the Internet from Prodigy, CompuServe, or America Online

If you currently use an on-line service, you may already have access to the Internet. As such, you may not need to establish an Internet account with a provider. Some on-line services may not provide access to all the Internet capabilities you desire. Ask your on-line service to send you information on its Internet capabilities and the steps you must perform to access them. Also, ask your on-line service to specify any additional costs.

Provider Buyer's Guide

Use the following list as your buyer's guide as you shop for an Internet provider:

❖ Are you already using an on-line service? Does that service provide Internet access?

❖ Does the provider offer a local access telephone number?

❖ Does the provider offer standard and SLIP-based accounts?

❖ Can you get Windows-based software for the SLIP account?

❖ What are the provider's rates?

Putting It Together

To access the Internet from your PC, you need an account with an Internet provider (or an on-line service). In short, for a monthly fee, the Internet provider lets you dial into its Internet connection using your PC and a modem. There are two types of Internet accounts. *Standard Internet* access is inexpensive text-based access. Using a standard Internet account, you can access the Internet using menu options and Internet commands. A more expensive *SLIP* (or *PPP*) *account* lets you access the Internet from within Windows. Using Windows-based programs, you can point and click your way across the Internet. Lastly, if you currently use an on-line service such as Prodigy, CompuServe, or America Online, you may already have limited Internet access. Ask your service provider for more information on its Internet capabilities.

Glossary

Internet provider	A company that, for a fee, lets you access their Internet connection using your PC and modem.
PPP	An abbreviation for point-to-point protocol. A PPP-based Internet account lets you access the Internet from within Windows.
SLIP	An abbreviation for serial line Internet protocol. SLIP-based Internet accounts let you access the Internet from within Windows.
Standard Internet account	A text- or menu-based Internet account.

Lesson 32: Things You Can Do on the Internet

Lesson 30 introduced the Internet, today's information highway. In Lesson 31, you learned how to access the Internet using an Internet provider. In this lesson, you will get a quick overview of the things you can do on the Internet. For more specifics on how you perform these operations, turn to the MIS: Press book, *Welcome to the Internet*, second edition, by Tom Badgett (1995).

Send and Receive Electronic Mail

The most common operation performed across the Internet involves *electronic mail* (or *e-mail*). As discussed in Lesson 35, e-mail lets you send memos, letters, reports, or even binary files (such as programs or spreadsheets) to one or more users. Figure 32.1 illustrates a screen from an e-mail program. To send a mail message to another user, you must specify the user's e-mail address and the message subject. Then, you simply type your note and send the message.

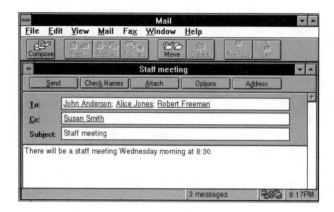

FIGURE 32.1 Sending an e-mail message to a user.

The user to whom you send a message does not have to be logged into the Internet for your message to arrive. Instead, the next time the user logs into the Internet, they are notified of their new mail.

Using e-mail software you can send messages to users worldwide. Table 32.1, for example, lists several famous users you will find on the Internet. To send mail message to these users, simply use their e-mail address.

TABLE 32.1 FAMOUS USERS ON THE INTERNET.

PERSON	E-MAIL ADDRESS
Bill Clinton	president@whitehouse.gov
Tom Clancy	tomclancy@aol.com
Newt Gingrich	georgia6@hr.house.gov
Al Gore	vice.president@whitehouse.gov
Rush Limbaugh	70277.2502#compuserve.com

File Transfer Operations

Across the Internet, there are more than 2 million documents—with more than 75,000 new documents added to the Internet each day. To help you access these documents, the Internet provides special computers called *ftp sites*, from which you can *download* (copy) the files the site contains. *ftp* is an abbreviation for *file transfer protocol*. A *protocol* is simply a set of rules that govern specific operations. In this case, ftp defines the rules that programs must follow to copy files to or from an ftp Internet site. Regardless of the information you need, you will very likely find related information at an ftp site. Your challenge, however, becomes locating the site that contains the information. If you examine Internet books in the bookstore, you will find that many of the books list the files you will find at different ftp sites.

Figure 32.2 illustrates a Windows-based ftp program. Using the ftp program, you specify the site that contains the files you desire. Next, you simply click your mouse on the files you want and then direct the ftp program to retrieve the files back to your PC!

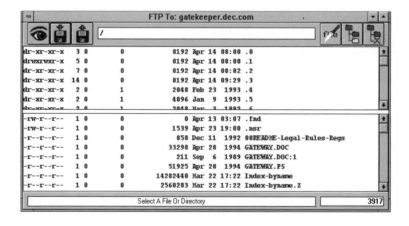

FIGURE 32.2 A Windows-based ftp program.

Chatting with Other Users

At any given moment, tens of thousands of users are connected to the Internet. Using an on-line chat program similar to that shown in Figure 32.3, you can chat with other users.

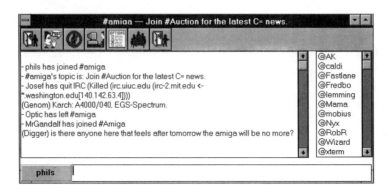

FIGURE 32.3 A Windows-based on-line chat program.

Using the chat program, you will find users discussing (chatting about) a wide range of topics. In short, you use the chat software to join the conversation you desire. Next, you simply start typing. Each time you press **Enter**, the other users in the conversation immediately see your message.

Exchanging Information Using Newsgroups

An Internet *newsgroup* is similar to a huge bulletin board that users across the Internet can read or post comments on. Across the Internet, there are almost 10,000 different newsgroups, each of which focuses on a specific topic. For example, you can find newsgroups that discuss computers, basketball, or just about anything else you might think of. Using newsgroup software similar to that shown in Figure 32.4, you select the newsgroup you desire. Next, you can browse through the latest postings or add your own comments. As you browse the Internet books in the bookstore, you will find books that list the newsgroups you can browse.

FIGURE 32.4 A Windows-based newsgroup program.

Exchanging Information Using Mailing Lists

A *mailing list* is a collection of e-mail addresses of users interested in a specific topic. Across the Internet, there are thousands of mailing lists. To start, you subscribe to (for free) a mailing list that focuses on a topic of interest to you. Other members of the list, in turn, will send you (and everyone else on the list) e-mail messages that contain information about the topic. For example, if you subscribe to a mailing list that focuses on basketball, users might send you e-mail messages that contain trade rumors, box scores, and so on.

As you browse the Internet books in the bookstore, you will find books that list the mailing lists to which you can subscribe. Should you tire of a mailing list, you simply cancel your subscription.

Traverse the World Wide Web

Lesson 33 discusses the World Wide Web in detail. As you will learn, the *Web* presents topics using a graphical format similar to that shown in Figure 32.5.

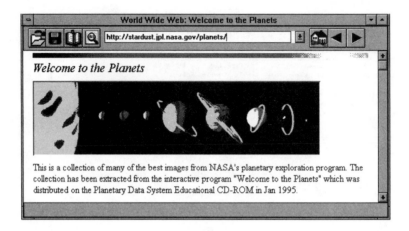

FIGURE 32.5 A World Wide Web site.

The World Wide Web consists of thousands of sites. Using Web browser software (*Mosaic* is the best-known browser) you select a site. As you read through a document, you will encounter bold or italic text that contains a link to a second document. If you click your mouse on the link, the browser will display the new document. What makes the Web unique, however, is that the second document might reside at a computer across the world.

Research Topics

As you have learned, the Internet consists of millions of documents worldwide. Assume, for example, that you are researching the basketball player, Michael Jordan. Your first challenge is to locate documents that discuss Jordan. Using Internet programs such as *Gopher* or *Archie*, you might first search for information on sports. Next, you can narrow down the list of sports sites to those that discuss basketball. Then, you can narrow down your list of basketball sites to those that discuss Jordan. Figure 32.6 illustrates a Windows-based Gopher program you can use to perform such search operations.

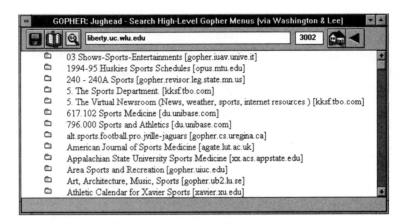

FIGURE 32.6 Searching the Internet using a Windows-based Gopher program.

Putting It All Together

Access the Internet there are more topics to research and discuss that you could ever possibly access. If you're looking for information, you'll find it on the Internet. As you first start out across the Internet, you will find the Internet large and intimidating. The best way to master the Internet is to take it one program at a time. For example, you should start with electronic mail. After you are comfortable with e-mail, you can move on to the World Wide Web. By approaching the Internet one program at a time, you will find the Internet much less frightening and much easier to master.

Glossary

Archie   A software program that helps users locate information on the Internet.

download   The process of copying a file from a remote computer.

FTP

An abbreviation for file transfer protocol, the software that controls most file transfers across the Internet.

Gopher

A menu-based program that helps user's locate information across the Internet.

mailing list

A collection of e-mail addresses that correspond to users who are interested in exchanging information about a specific topic.

Mosaic

A graphical software program that lets users access information across the World Wide Web.

newsgroup

An electronic bulletin board that users across the Internet can read or post messages to.

protocol

A set of rules that govern a specific operation, such as a file transfer.

Lesson 33: Understanding the World Wide Web

L
esson 30 introduced the Internet, today's information highway. As you have learned, the Internet contains over 2 million documents worldwide. One of the most difficult aspects of using the Internet is finding the information you need.

This lesson introduces the *World Wide Web* (WWW) which makes it easy for users to traverse through related documents. As you will learn, the Web lets you graphically display *hyperlink* (or *hypertext*) documents that may contain text and graphics. *Hyperlinked* documents are so named because they contain electronic links to other documents. By clicking your mouse on a hyperlink, you can quickly display the related document's contents.

Understanding Hyperlinked Documents

As stated, hyperlinked documents may contain one or more links to other documents as shown in Figure 33.1.

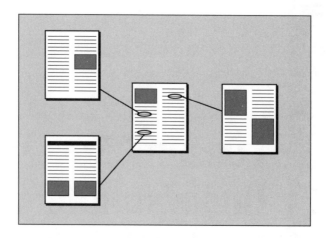

FIGURE 33.1 A hyperlinked document contains links to other documents.

To view a hyperlinked document, you use a special software program called a *Web browser*. When the browser displays the document, it will normally underline the linked text or display the text using a unique color. If you click your mouse on the hyperlink, the browser will immediately display the linked document.

What makes the World Wide Web unique is that linked documents don't need to reside on the same computer. In fact, a linked document might reside across the world, as shown in Figure 33.2.

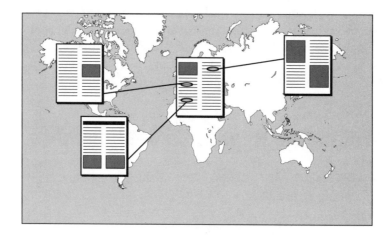

FIGURE 33.2 Linked documents can be dispersed around the world.

As you traverse hyperlinked documents, your browser—behind the scenes—may pull in documents from Japan, Australia, or other locations around the world.

What You Need to Get Started

To access the World Wide Web, you will use your PC, modem, and special software called the Web browser. If you examine Internet books at your bookstore, you will find that several books bundle a Web browser with the book, for free! The best-known browser is named *Mosaic*. As such, you will find that many books bundle an enhanced version of Mosaic.

Next, you will need a SLIP- or PPP-based Internet account as discussed in Lesson 32. The Web browsers normally run from within Windows, which requires a SLIP- or PPP-based connection.

NOTE If you are connected to an on-line service such as Prodigy, CompuServe, or America Online, you may be able to access the World Wide Web directly from the service. For more information on Web access, contact your service.

Traversing the Web

Across the Internet, hyperlinked documents are stored at computer locations called *Web sites*. Each Web site has a unique name. Table 33.1 lists the names of some interesting Web sites.

TABLE 33.1 INTERESTING WEB SITES ACROSS THE INTERNET.

http://www.nasa.gov	NASA Homepage
http://www.pc.ibm.com	IBM Homepage
http://www.rocketsci.com	Rock Web Homepage
http://www.Chili.rt66.com/cyspacemalls	On-line Shopping
http://narc.nasa.gov/fbi/	FBI Homepage

Using your Web browser software, you specify the name of the Web site you desire. The browser, in turn, will connect you to the site, displaying the site's introductory screen (or *homepage*). Figure 33.3, for example, illustrates the White House homepage.

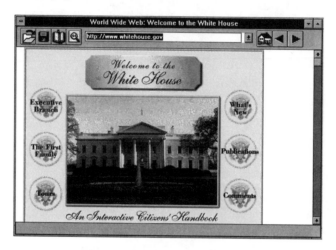

FIGURE 33.3 The White House homepage.

As you use your Web browser to read a document, you can click your mouse on hyperlinks that appear within the document to move to a related document. For example, in the case of the White House homepage, you can click your mouse on a link to the Executive Branch homepage. Your browser, in turn, will display the homepage shown in Figure 33.4.

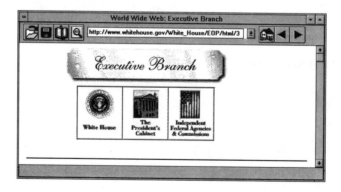

FIGURE 33.4 The Executive Branch homepage.

310

Because the Web presents information graphically, it is very easy for users to traverse Web documents to find the information they desire. Second, by using hyperlinks to connect related documents, the Web places the user one mouse click away from a document that discusses related topics. In short, the Web provides the first step in organizing the Internet's vast amount of information.

The Web's Future

Over the next year, the number of hyperlinked documents and web sites will explode. In the future, users will think of the Internet in terms of the Web. As you have seen, Web documents make extensive use of graphic images. As modem and PC speeds continue to increase, future Web documents will make extensive use of audio clips (voice and music) as well as video clips.

Putting It All Together

The World Wide Web consists of hyperlinked documents at over 20,000 sites across the Internet. Using special Web browser software, you can display documents on your screen, moving from one document to another, by clicking your mouse on hyperlinks that appear within the document text. Because Web documents can be quite large and can contain graphics images that the browser must download across the Net, you will want to use a fast modem when you access the Web. At a minimum, you will want a 14.4Kb modem, and ideally, a modem that supports 28.8Kb.

Glossary

homepage	The primary document at a World Wide Web site.
hyperlink document	A document that contains links to other documents that reside across the World Wide Web.
Web browser	Special software that lets a user display and traverse hyperlinked documents across the Web.

311

World Wide Web

A collection of hundreds of thousands of hyper-linked documents dispersed across the Internet. The Web gets its name from the interconnected documents that let users move quickly from one document to another.

Lesson 34: Understanding On-Line Services

Each day, tens of thousands of users use their PC and modem to dial into an on-line service such as Prodigy, CompuServe, or America Online. This lesson introduces on-line services and how you can use them. As you will find, the services provide more features than you can possibly access each day. For example, you will learn how to get the latest news, weather reports, stock prices, make your own airline reservations, shop on-line for software, clothes, flowers, or even fast food, and how you send mail or chat on-line with other users.

Which Service is Right for You?

Today, CompuServe, Prodigy, and America Online are the largest on-line services. In the near future, Microsoft will offer its own on-line service. The competition among on-line services is fierce. For this reason, most on-line services will let you try their service for a month, for free! The best way to choose an on-line service is to take each service for a test drive. Table 34.1 lists phone numbers you can call to get more information on each service.

TABLE 34.1 PHONE NUMBERS FOR POPULAR ON-LINE SERVICES.

America Online	800-827-6364
CompuServe	800-848-8199
Delphi	800-695-4005
GEnie	800-638-9636
Prodigy	800-776-3449

Each on-line service offers "basic services" that you get for your monthly fee. Other options, such as Internet access, may cost you more. Before you subscribe to an on-line service, make sure you know which services are free and which cost extra.

How You Connect to an On-Line Service

As you know, you use your PC and modem to dial into an on-line service. To get you started, each of the on-line services will provide you with software that you install and then use to dial into the service. Each service will offer you a local phone number you can call to connect to the service. In this way, you don't incur long-distance phone costs.

Things You Can Do On-Line

Depending on you interests, you'll find that the on-line services provide items of interest on sports, business, entertainment, computer games, as well as up-to-the-minute news and weather reports. In addition, you can use the on-line services to shop, make airline reservations, and more. The following sections briefly describe activities you do on-line.

Getting Up-to-the-Minute News

Throughout the day, many users don't have a chance to get away from their desk long enough to keep up with the day's current events. Each of the on-line services provides a current source of news. For example, Figure 34.1 illustrates CompuServe's news source.

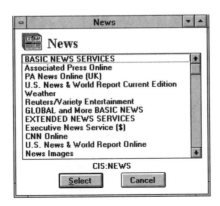

FIGURE 34.1 Getting up-to-the-minute news on-line.

Getting the Latest Stock Prices

If you are tracking different stock investments, you can use the on-line services to obtain the latest stock prices. For example, Figure 34.2 illustrates a company's stock prices within the Prodigy on-line service.

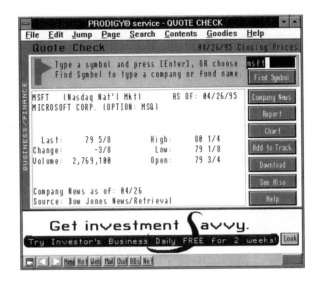

FIGURE 34.2 Getting up-to-the-minute stock prices.

Shopping On-Line

Whether you need to purchase new tennis shoes or flowers, you can probably do so on-line. Figure 34.3, for example, illustrates on-line shopping via America Online.

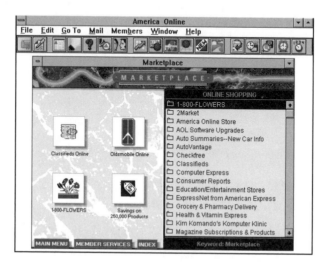

FIGURE 34.3 On-line shopping via America Online.

Sending and Receiving Electronic Mail

Lesson 35 discusses electronic mail (e-mail) in detail. In short, e-mail lets you send a message or file to another user. In the case of the on-line services, that user can reside across town or across the world. In addition to letting you send mail to users connected to the same on-line service, you can send mail messages to users who are connected to the Internet or even a different on-line service. In other words, a user who is connected to Prodigy can send a mail message to a user connected to CompuServe.

On-Line Chats

At any given moment, thousands of users connect to on-line services simply to chat on-line with other users. To chat with other users, a user joins a conversation and starts typing. Each time the user types a line of text and presses **Enter**, the other users in the conversation immediately see the user's message. Users can join conversations on a wide variety of topics (just about everything you can think of). Figure 34.4, for example, illustrates an example of an on-line chat within the Prodigy on-line service.

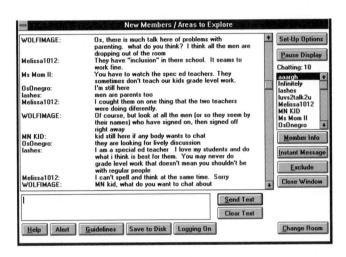

FIGURE 34.4 On-line chats let users converse on a wide variety of topics.

On-Line Service Buyer's Guide

Use the following list a guideline as you shop for an on-line service:

- ❖ What services do you want to use?
- ❖ Are the services you desire covered by basic costs or will you incur additional costs?
- ❖ Does the service charge for incoming or outgoing electronic mail?
- ❖ Does the service offer access to the Internet, and if so, what is the cost?
- ❖ Does the service offer access to the World Wide Web, and if so, what is the cost?
- ❖ What is the service's basic monthly charges?
- ❖ Does the service have a local access phone number?

317

Putting It All Together

Over the past few years, connecting to on-line services has become one of the most popular activities users perform with their computer. On-line services are an entertaining and sometimes addicting way for you to use your PC. The services give you access to huge amounts of information. In addition, the services make it easy for you to communicate with other users. If you have never connected to an on-line service, you should take advantage of a service's free trial period and take an on-line service for a test drive.

Glossary

on-line service

A service, that, for a cost, users can dial into using their PC and modem to access a wide variety of services, such as the ability to send and receive e-mail, access up-to-the-minute news, weather, and stock prices, and much more.

Lesson 35: Understanding Electronic Mail

With the continued use of local area networks within offices and the explosive growth of the Internet and other on-line services such as Prodigy, CompuServe, and America Online, users now make extensive use of *electronic mail* (*e-mail*). In short, e-mail lets users send electronic messages to other users across a network. Such messages might contain a brief reminder, memo, question, or a document such as a company's budget plan. This lesson introduces you to electronic mail. Although different e-mail programs may behave differently, the steps they perform are quite similar. In short, you use e-mail software to specify the users you want to receive the message, the message subject, and then you type the message itself. When you are through typing, the e-mail software will send the message to each user you previously specified.

Sending a Mail Message

As you have learned, a network is a collection of computers connected to exchange information and to share resources (such as disks and printers). E-mail provides one way for users to exchange information. As you can see in Figure 35.1, you can send an e-mail message to one or more users.

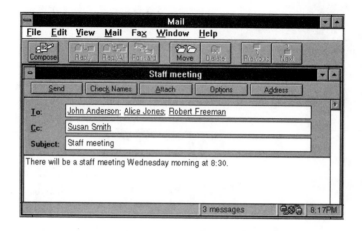

Figure 35.1 E-mail software lets you send messages to one or more users in one step.

Each user within a network has a unique name called the user's *e-mail address*. To send a message to a user, you must know the user's e-mail address. Next, most e-mail programs have a Send option. When you select the **Send** option, the program will normally ask you to specify the e-mail address of each user to whom you are sending the message. After you specify the e-mail addresses, the program will normally ask you to type in the message subject. Figure 35.2, for example, illustrates the Send dialog box that Microsoft Mail displays when a user prepares to send a message.

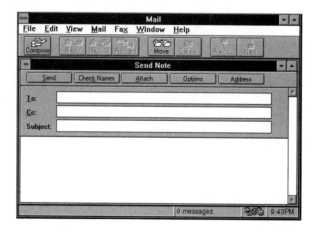

FIGURE 35.2 The Microsoft Mail Send dialog box.

Within the Send dialog box's To field, the users specifies the e-mail address of the user to whom they are sending the message. In this case, the Send dialog box also lets the user specify addresses of users to whom you want to "Courtesy Copy" (Cc) the message. Within the Subject field, the user will type a one-line statement that describes the message contents. For example, the Subject field might contain text such as **Reminder of Sales Meeting** or **1996 Budget Report**. When your message recipient receives your message, their e-mail program will very likely display the message subject. By reading only the message subject, the message recipient can quickly determine the message contents.

Lastly, in the case of Microsoft Mail, the user will type their message text and then click their mouse on the **Send** button. Figure 35.3 illustrates an e-mail message that is ready to be sent.

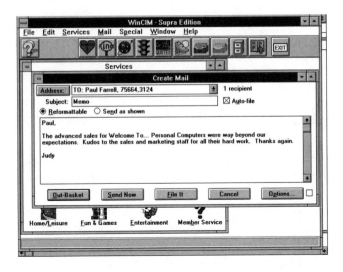

FIGURE 35.3 An e-mail message ready for sending.

Receiving an E-Mail Message

Normally, when a user sends you an e-mail message, your system will display a dialog box informing you of your new mail. Using your e-mail program, you can read the new message. Figure 35.4, for example, illustrates the Read dialog box within Microsoft Mail, within which you read your mail messages.

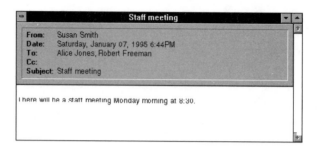

FIGURE 35.4 Reading a mail message within Microsoft Mail.

Using your e-mail software, you can save a message to a file on disk, print the message, forward the message to another user, or delete messages you no longer require.

You don't have to be logged onto your computer for a user to send you an e-mail message. Instead, the e-mail software will store your message in a file. When you later log onto the network, the e-mail software will notify you that you have new mail.

Mail, the Internet, and On-Line Services

As you have learned, e-mail software lets you send mail messages to other users within your local area network. Depending on your e-mail software, you may be able to send a mail message to users who are connected to the Internet as well as to other on-line services such as Prodigy, CompuServe, and America Online. If you are connected to one of these on-line services, you can send and receive mail messages to and from users who are connected to the same, or a different service, as well as to users who are connected to the Internet.

Putting It All Together

Electronic mail (or e-mail) is the exchange of electronic messages between users whose computers are connected by a network. The messages users send using e-mail can be short memos, letters, or even long documents. To send an electronic mail message to another user, you must know that user's e-mail address. Each user in the network must have a unique e-mail address that is assigned by their network administrator.

Glossary

e-mail

An abbreviation for electronic mail. Using e-mail, network users can quickly exchange memos and other documents with one another.

Lesson 36: Troubleshooting Your System

In Lesson 4 you learned several ways you can troubleshoot your system if it fails to start. In this lesson you will examine several common problems users experience, their causes, and their solutions. Fold the corner of this page to mark this chapter. It probably won't take long before you encounter one or more of these problems.

Hardware Problems

If your monitor or system unit does not work, follow the troubleshooting steps presented in Lesson 4. This section looks at other possible hardware problems that you may experience.

Printer Does Not Print

First make sure your printer is plugged in, turned on, and the printer's On-line light is on. If not, press the *On-line* button to place the printer on-line. If the printer still does not print, check the printer cable to insure it connects securely to the printer and to the printer port at the back of the system unit. If the system unit has multiple printer ports, you may need to experiment with each. If you cannot get your printer to print, your printer port, cable, or printer may be the problem. If you are using a serial printer, read the following section on setting the serial port speed. If the error persists, end your current program and then turn off and on (*cycle*) your computer and printer power.

The Printer Prints Unrecognizable Characters

As discussed in Lesson 10, you must be sure the device you attach to a serial port and the serial port agree on their communication speed and settings. If you are using a serial printer, review the printer documentation to determine the printer's communication settings. Use the DOS MODE command to assign these settings to the serial port. For more information on the MODE command, refer to a DOS book or the DOS user's manual that accompanied your computer. If the error persists, end your current program and then turn off and on (cycle) your computer and printer power.

Printer Does Not Print Within Windows

If your printer does not print from within Windows, first exit Windows to DOS and determine if you can use the DOS PRINT command to print a file (use the file AUTOEXEC.BAT as a sample file). If your printer prints, select the Windows Control Panel Printer icon. First, make sure the printer driver is installed and selected. For more information on adding or selecting a printer driver within Windows, refer to Windows on-line help or a book on Windows.

Printer Prints Incorrectly From Windows

If your printer does not print correctly from within Windows—perhaps it mis-aligns pages—Windows may not be using the correct printer driver for your printer. To begin, select the Control Panel Printer icon and insure you have the correct driver selected. If you are using the correct driver, contact your printer manufacturer and ask if they have a newer version of their printer driver.

A Program Ignores Your Mouse

As discussed in Lesson 9, not all software programs support the use of a mouse. If you are using a program that claims to support a mouse, but a mouse pointer does not appear, make sure you have installed the mouse device driver software that should have accompanied your mouse on floppy disk. In most cases you install the mouse driver by placing a DEVICE entry for the mouse driver in your DOS CONFIG.SYS file, or by invoking the command MOUSE.COM from within AUTOEXEC.BAT. For more information on CONFIG.SYS and AUTOEXEC.BAT, refer to a DOS book or the DOS user's manual that accompanied your system.

If other programs use your mouse, yet one does not, you may need to run a special setup program for your application and tell it you have a mouse. If your mouse pointer does not appear within Windows, use the Windows Setup program to install a device driver for the mouse.

A Program's Output Does Not Appear in Color

In most cases, this is a software problem, not hardware. If your other programs display colors correctly, refer to the program's documentation to determine if the software has a set up program that lets you specify your video adapter and monitor type, or a color selection menu. If you can't find the answer in the documentation, call the product's technical support line.

Multimedia Video Color is Strange

If you are using a multimedia program whose video appear as fuzzy colors, you are very likely using your video display in 16-color mode and the video requires 256 colors. In such cases, change you video display settings to support 256 colors. If you change the video settings the video color remains fuzzy, contact your video card manufacturer and ask them if they have a new video driver.

Multimedia Video is Choppy

If you are using a multimedia program whose video appears choppy, your system is having trouble keeping up with the video's frame rate. The problem may be your CD-ROM drive speed, video card speed, CPU speed, or a combination of these. In such cases, check the program's hardware requirements closely and then, if necessary, contact the company's technical support staff.

Modem Does Not Work

The steps in troubleshooting for your modem could easily fill a chapter of a book. Here's a few of the most common steps. Make sure the phone cable connecting the modem to the wall jack—and is often labeled—*Line* is inserted securely into the correct modem plug (one plug connects the modem to the wall jack, and another connects the modem to your phone). Test the wall jack with a telephone to ensure that the jack is working.

If you are using an external modem, make sure the modem has power and is on. Next, make sure the cable that connects the modem to the serial port is in place. Depending on your modem software, you may have to use the DOS MODE command to set the serial port's speed and data communication settings. If your modem is attached to a serial port other than COM1, make sure you inform the data communication software.

If you are using an internal modem, the modem's interrupt request (IRQ) may be conflicting with another device (normally your mouse), which may require you to change switches on the board. If you suspect an IRQ conflict may be the problem, have your retailer or an experienced user help you change the board's address.

Lastly, if your modem successfully calls the other computer, but only garbled letters appear on your screen, the data communication settings you are using do not match the ones in use by the other computer. Contact a user at the remote computer to verify the data communication settings. Use your data communication software to assign the correct settings to your modem.

Your Mouse Stops When Your Modem Starts

If, when you use your modem, your mouse quits working, or vice versa, you have an IRQ conflict between your mouse and modem. In such cases, have an experienced user help you open your system unit and change the IRQ setting for either device. Use the MSD command (discussed in this lesson) to determine available IRQs.

Your Modem Hangs Up Intermittently

If your modem hangs up randomly and your phone supports call waiting, incoming phone calls may be disconnecting your modem. In such cases, simply disable call waiting prior to each modem call by dialing *70 at the start of the phone number your modem is dialing. For example, to disable call waiting before you call 555-1212, you would dial *70,,555-1212. The two commas direct the modem to delay briefly after dialing *70 and before dialing the phone number.

How Devices Conflict

Hardware devices such as a modem or a mouse must communicate with your computer's CPU. To do so, each device has a unique wire that connects the wire to the CPU. When the device needs to notify your computer of a specific event, the device sends a signal down the wire, called the interrupt request (IRQ) line. Normally, when you purchase different hardware devices, the device uses a specific IRQ line. Unfortunately, the IRQ line used for modems often conflicts with that used for a mouse. Should such conflicts occur, you cannot use your mouse and modem at the same time. To resolve the conflict, you can normally use a DIP switch or jumper to select a different IRQ line for one of the conflicting devices. To determine the available IRQ lines, use the MSD command discussed next.

Troubleshooting Using Microsoft's MSD Command

When you are having trouble using a specific hardware device, there are many third-party diagnostic programs that may help you determine the cause of the error. If you are using Microsoft Windows or DOS 6, you can use the MSD command to display specifics about your hardware. *MSD* is an abbreviation for *Microsoft Diagnostic software*. When you start MSD, your screen displays a menu of available options similar to that shown in Figure 36.1.

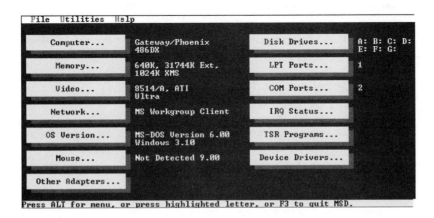

FIGURE 36.1 MSD's main menu of hardware options.

From MSD's main menu, should you type **Q** to display your computer's IRQ settings, you can determine the available IRQs using the screen shown in Figure 36.2. Normally, you can select the IRQ settings marked as Reserved. In addition, note that the system reserves an IRQ for the second printer (LPT2) and a second serial port (COM2). If you aren't using these devices, you can use their IRQs for a new device.

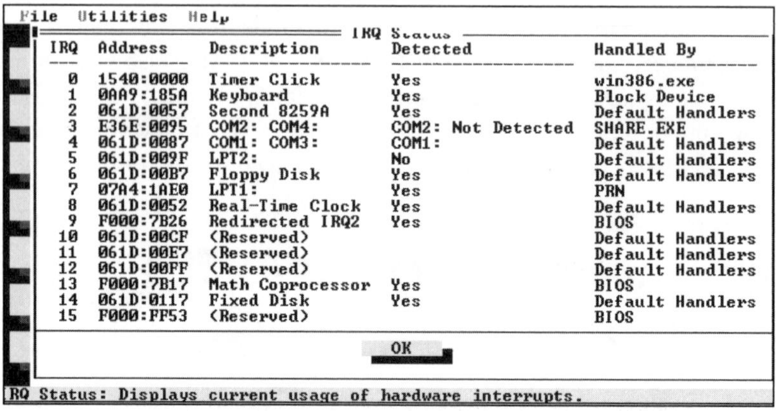

```
File  Utilities  Help
                                ── IRQ Status ──
 IRQ  Address     Description        Detected           Handled By
 ───  ───────     ───────────        ────────           ──────────
  0   1540:0000   Timer Click        Yes                win386.exe
  1   0AA9:185A   Keyboard           Yes                Block Device
  2   061D:0057   Second 8259A       Yes                Default Handlers
  3   E36E:0095   COM2: COM4:        COM2: Not Detected SHARE.EXE
  4   061D:0087   COM1: COM3:        COM1:              Default Handlers
  5   061D:009F   LPT2:              No                 Default Handlers
  6   061D:00B7   Floppy Disk        Yes                Default Handlers
  7   07A4:1AE0   LPT1:              Yes                PRN
  8   061D:0052   Real-Time Clock    Yes                Default Handlers
  9   F000:7B26   Redirected IRQ2    Yes                BIOS
 10   061D:00CF   <Reserved>                            Default Handlers
 11   061D:00E7   <Reserved>                            Default Handlers
 12   061D:00FF   <Reserved>                            Default Handlers
 13   F000:7B17   Math Coprocessor   Yes                BIOS
 14   061D:0117   Fixed Disk         Yes                Default Handlers
 15   F000:FF53   <Reserved>                            BIOS

                           ┌─────┐
                           │ OK  │
                           └─────┘

IRQ Status: Displays current usage of hardware interrupts.
```

FIGURE 36.2 Displaying IRQ setting using MSD.

DOS Error Messages

This section discusses common DOS error messages, their typical causes as well as their solutions.

Bad Command or File Name

DOS displays the following message when it can't locate a command that matches the one you just typed at the DOS prompt.

```
C:\> CHKDSK  <Enter>
Bad command or file name
```

If this error occurs, double check your spelling to ensure you spelled the command correctly. If the command is spelled correctly, check your current disk drive and directory, and if necessary, change to the directory containing the command.

NOTE

The DOS PATH command lets you specify several directories that you want DOS to automatically search for your commands, which makes your commands easier to execute.

For more information on PATH, refer to a DOS book or the DOS user is manual that accompanied your computer.

File Not Found

DOS displays this error message when it successfully executes your command, but could not find the file whose name you included in the command line. For example, the DOS TYPE command displays a file's contents on your screen. If you invoke TYPE with a filename that does not exist, DOS displays the File Not Found message.

```
C:\> TYPE FILENAME.EXT  <Enter>
File not found
```

Should this message appear, make sure you are spelling the filename correctly. Also make sure you are in the directory that contains the file.

Invalid Drive Specification

In Lesson 8 you learned each of your disks has a unique single letter name such as A, B, and C. DOS displays this error message when the disk drive letter you specify in a command does not exist. In most cases, this error message occurs because you have mistyped a drive letter.

```
C:\> DIR E:  <Enter>
Invalid drive specification
```

If DOS displays this error message the first time you type to reference your hard disk (drive C), you probably don't have a disk partition defined for the hard disk yet. For more information on partitioning your disk, refer to the FDISK command in a DOS book or the DOS user's manual that accompanied your computer.

Abort, Retry, Fail?

DOS displays this error message when it encounters a condition for which it cannot continue without your intervention. Such conditions may occur when your printer is out of paper, or when a floppy disk drive does not contain a disk.

```
C:\> DIR A:   <Enter>
Not ready error reading drive A
```

When DOS displays this message, DOS is asking you how you want it to continue. The two most common responses are A for Abort, or R for Retry.

If you type **A** to select Abort, DOS ends the program that is performing the operation responsible for generating the error, redisplaying its prompt. If you can correct the problem, perhaps by adding paper to the printer or by inserting a floppy disk into a drive, typing **R** for Retry directs DOS to repeat the operation that just caused the error, letting the program continue as if the error never occurred.

General Failure Error Reading Drive N:

DOS displays this message when the disk in the drive specified has not yet been formatted for use by DOS, or the drive cannot read the disk it contains. If you are using 360Kb or 720Kb disk drives, make sure the disk you are trying to access is not a 1.2Mb or 1.44Mb disk. If you are sure the disk size matches your drive, the disk was probably never formatted. DOS typically displays the Abort, Retry, Fail? message when this error occurs. Type **A** to select Abort.

Non-System Disk or Disk Error
Replace and Strike Any Key When Ready

DOS displays this error message when you try to start DOS from a disk that does not contain the special operating system files that DOS needs to boot. This error is most common when you leave a floppy disk in drive A and turn on your computer to start DOS. If drive A contains a floppy, remove the disk and press any key to start DOS from your hard disk. If DOS cannot boot from your hard disk, you may need to reinstall DOS.

Putting It All Together

Successfully troubleshooting your computer problems takes experience, patience, and sometimes a lot of luck! This lesson has presented steps you can follow to troubleshoot several common problems. For more information on DOS error messages, refer to a DOS book or the DOS user's manual that accompanied your computer.

Glossary

disk partitioning	The process of dividing a single physical hard disk into one or more logical drives.
IRQ	An abbreviation for interrupt request. An electronic signal from a device to the CPU that tells the CPU the device needs servicing.
power cycling	The process of turning off and on your computer's power.
troubleshooting	The process of determining the cause of a hardware or software error.

Lesson 37: Installing New Software

When you purchase software, the program and its related files are on one or more floppy disks or possibly a CD-ROM. If you are using floppy disks, make sure the program's floppy disk size matches the floppy disk drives on your computer. Should you need different size floppies, the software company that developed the program normally exchanges the disks. In some cases you must pay a small fee to cover the cost of shipping the new disks.

To help you *install* (sometimes called *load*) the software from floppy disk onto your hard disk, most software packages provide an *installation program* that determines your *system configuration* (printer, monitor type, disk sizes, and so on) and then copies only those files you need to your hard disk. Depending on the software program, the questions the installation program asks you differ slightly. However, the steps you should follow to install different software programs are essentially the same.

This lesson examines the steps you should perform before, during, and after the installation of a software program.

Before the Installation

Users are always excited and in a hurry to install new software on their computer. Be aware, however, that most software programs have license agreement notices, either on the outer package or on the envelope that encloses the disks containing the software. The *license agreement* is a legal document that specifies your "user rights" with the software, such as the number of computers on which you can install the software. You imply your acceptance of the licensing agreement by opening the package. Although you should find most licensing agreements fully acceptable, you need to know that the agreements exist.

NOTE If you use a computer in an office that has two or more computers, most license agreements require that you purchase a copy of the software for each computer in the office. You cannot, for example, buy one copy of a word processor and install the software on each system. Recently, large fines have been levied against companies that have violated their software agreements. Before you install software onto multiple computers, first check with the corresponding software company about their licensing requirements.

Hopefully, before you purchase the software, you made sure the software is fully compatible with your computer. If the software specifies its disk space requirements, use the DOS DIR command or the Windows File Manager to determine how much free space your disk contains. If your disk does not have enough available space, do not begin the installation until you make space available by deleting unnecessary files, or by moving files from your hard disk to floppy.

Because they must load special software, many installation programs ask you to identify your monitor type (see Lesson 6) and your printer type (such as HP-Laser Jet), the printer port (LPT1 or COM1), and possibly your keyboard type (see Lesson 5). Before you begin the installation, write down each of your hardware types.

Find the installation instructions in the documentation that accompanies the software. Read through the instructions one time before beginning the installation. You might even make notes in the margin, noting the responses you should select at different stages.

NOTE If you have not recently backed up the information on your hard disk to floppy, you should consider doing so now. Although such occurrences are rare, it is possible for a software installation to fail, possibly overwriting other information on your disk, or even leaving your disk in an unusable state. Backing up your disk before installing software is similar to buying insurance. Hopefully you won't need the backups, but if you do, they are there.

During the Installation

If your new software is on two or more floppy disks, one of the disks should be labeled *Setup*, *Install*, or *Disk 1*. Place that disk in your floppy disk drive A and issue the following DIR command:

```
C> DIR A: <Enter>
```

Examine the list of files for a file named READ.ME, README.DOC, or README.WRI (a file in the Windows Write format). If such a file (or one similarly named) exists, print and read the file's contents. The file typically contains notes or instructions not contained in the installation instructions or the manual.

To help you organize the information you store on your disk, most installation programs create a unique storage location for the software called a *directory*. Lesson 14 covers directories in detail. In general, a directory is a list of files you can best visualize as a filing cabinet drawer. If you have several software programs, one directory may contain your word processor, and another your spreadsheet. Many installation programs ask you the directory name you desire (in Windows, the name can contain eight characters). The installation program may display a default directory name. If a default name is present, select it. Otherwise, you need to choose a meaningful name that best describes the software, such as WINDOWS, DOS, WORD, or DBASE.

You start most installation programs by typing either the command name **SETUP** or **INSTALL**. Following the installation instructions provided with the software, begin the installation.

As you perform the installation, watch the prompts carefully and the instructions that appear on your screen. If you don't understand a specific prompt, refer to the installation instructions. In addition, many installation programs now include on-line help you can access by pressing **F1** or possibly F3.

Installing Software from Within Windows

If you use Windows, you must normally install your Windows-based programs while Windows is running. Normally, you use the Program Manager File menu **Run** option. When you select this option, Windows displays the Run dialog box as shown in Figure 37.1.

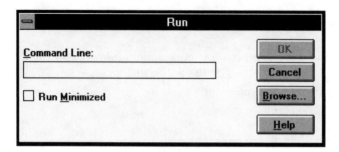

FIGURE 37.1 The Windows Run dialog box.

Type in the name of the desired installation program (normally preceded by a drive letter such as A: or B:). When you press **Enter**, Windows runs the corresponding installation program. Most Windows-based installation programs use either the name *Setup* or *Install*. To install a program from a floppy disk in drive A, for example, you would type **A:SETUP** at the Run dialog box's Command Line prompt.

After the Installation

Although you probably are in a hurry to get started with your new program, you should take time to complete and mail the registration card that accompanied your software. The registration card normally qualifies you to receive technical support, as well as notification about product updates. Also, place the original software disks in a safe location.

Next, spend time reading the Getting Started section of the software manual. The manual tells you how to start the program. If the software program provides an on-line tutorial, run the tutorial.

Putting It All Together

When you buy a new software program, the program comes on one or more floppy disks. To use the software, you want to install it onto your hard disk. Most software packages provide an installation program. Although installation programs differ, the steps you should follow to install different software programs are essentially the same. After you install one or two programs, you'll realize just how easy it is.

Glossary

installation program

A program that helps you install software from floppy disks onto your hard disk.

license agreement

A written agreement provided by a software developer that defines the user's rights to the software. Use of the software implies the user's acceptance of the agreement's terms.

system configuration

The software and hardware settings specific to a PC.

Lesson 38:
PC Do's and Don'ts

If you take care of your PC and don't mistreat it, it will last many years and you will greatly reduce your possibility of losing information. This lesson presents several things you should do, and some you should *not* do as you work with your PC. Pay attention to each. This information may prevent you from accidentally damaging your equipment.

Things You Should Do

This section describes different steps you should perform to protect your computer and disks.

Do Always Read the Manual

Most users have the bad habit of unpacking and installing new hardware or software without first reading the manual. In most cases, spending a few minutes reading the manual can save you hours of frustration later. If you find the manual too difficult to read, find a book on getting started with the product.

Do Run a Tutorial if Available

Many newer software packages provide a tutorial program that teaches you how to use the software's most important features. Such tutorial programs provide one of the fastest ways to get started. Figure 38.1, for example, illustrates the tutorial program provided with Microsoft Windows.

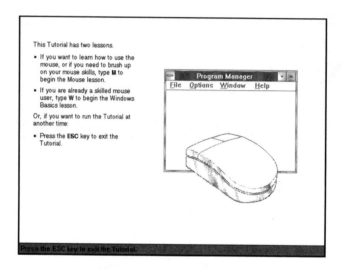

FIGURE 38.1 The Windows on-line tutorial.

Do Your Homework Before Calling a Company's Technical Support Line

Most hardware and software companies provide technical support numbers that you can call for help. You can save considerable time and assist the technical support staff by making a few notes before you call. Write down your program name, version number, serial number, as well as your DOS version number. If the program is displaying an error message, write down the error message so you can read it to the technical support representative. Your disk space and memory usage. Lastly, print copies of the DOS files AUTOEXEC.BAT and CONFIG.SYS and have them available.

Before you call technical support, issue the following commands. Make sure that your printer is turned on because the commands send their output to the printer:

```
C:\> CHKDSK > PRN  <Enter>
C:\> MEM > PRN  <Enter>
C:\> PRINT \AUTOEXEC.BAT  <Enter>
C:\> PRINT \CONFIG.SYS  <Enter>
```

In addition, you may want to invoke the DOS MSD command and use the File menu **Print Report** option to print a detailed summary of your system settings that you can fax to the technical support representative. Companies provide technical support to help you use their product. If you are having problems, don't hesitate to call them. Also, keep in mind that the more information you provide the technical support personnel, the faster they can solve your problem.

Do Organize Your Disks Using Directories

As you learned in Lesson 14, a *directory* is a list of related files, similar to the paper files you store in the drawer of a filing cabinet. As you store files on your disk, organize the files using directories. If you use a word processor, for example, you find that your disk quickly fills with different kinds of documents. Using directories, you can quickly organize these document files making them easier to locate in the future.

Do Save Your Work to Disk on a Regular Basis

As discussed in Lesson 8, disks let you save information from one session at the computer to the next. As you work with a word processor or spreadsheet, you should periodically save your document or worksheet to disk. It is very frustrating to spend several hours working on a document only to lose your work due to a power failure or computer malfunction. If you get in the habit of saving your work to disk every 15 minutes or so, you greatly reduce the amount of work you might lose due to a system error or a power outage.

Do Assign Meaningful File Names

As discussed in Lesson 13, you store information on disk as files. Each file must have a unique file name. A file's name should describe the file's contents. DOS file names consist of two parts: an eight-character base name, and a three-character extension. Use the three-character extension to describe the file's type such as LTR for letters, or DOC for a word processing document. Likewise, use the eight-character base name to give specifics about the file, such as who the letter is to.

Do Make Backup Copies of Your Files on a Regular Basis

As discussed in Lesson 22, the only way to protect your files is to make duplicate (or backup) copies. You should perform backup operations on a regular basis, ideally, each day. The more often you perform backups, the less work you stand to lose in the event of a disk failure or an errant command. After you complete your file backups, place the disks in a safe location, preferably at a location away from the computer. If your computer stores large amounts of information, you may find that a tape backup (see Lesson 22) provides a fast and convenient way to backup your disk. Lastly, if you are using DOS 6, the MSBACKUP command provides an easy to use menu-driven backup program.

Do Store Your Floppy Disks in a Safe Location

If you are using 5.25-inch floppy disks, always place the disk into its paper sleeve when the disk is not in use to protect the disk from dust and minor spills.

Next, place your floppy disks into a plastic disk container to reduce your chance of misplacing them, and to further protect them.

Lastly, do not expose the disks to unusual conditions such as excessive heat or cold, or to smoke or direct sunlight. If you treat your disks with care, they keep the information on them indefinitely.

Do Be Aware of Computer Viruses

As discussed in Lesson 40, a *virus* is a computer program maliciously written to destroy the information your disk contains or to make your computer unusable. If you only purchase your programs from reputable software companies, your chance of encountering a computer virus is very small. However, if you load programs from a bulletin board or from a disk given to you by another user, your risk of virus increases. If you use a modem to download files from bulletin boards or if you use shareware programs, you should buy virus detection software to protect your computer. If you are using DOS 6, the MSAV and VSAFE commands perform virus detection and removal.

Do Use a Surge Suppressor

As briefly discussed in Lesson 3, a surge suppressor protects your hardware from damaging surges of electrical power. You plug the surge suppressor into your wall outlet and then plug your hardware into the suppressor. The surge suppressor then filters the power. A surge suppressor does not prevent power losses.

If your computer has a modem connected to a phone line, you should purchase a surge suppressor that that filters spikes on the phone line as well.

Do Move Your Computer with Care

Whether you are moving your computer across country, across town, or across the room, you should do so with care. Before you move your computer, use a backup program to copy the contents of your hard disk to floppy. If your computer has a hard disk, use a disk utility program to park the disk's read/write head in a safe location. If you have an unused floppy disk, place it into the floppy drive. Lastly, if you have your computer's original boxes, use the boxes to pack the computer.

Some hard drives automatically park their heads when you turn off your computer's power. Refer to the documentation that accompanied your disk for specifics.

NOTE

Do Keep Your Computer Clean and Dust-Free

Over time, even if you use it regularly, your computer gathers dust. Computer retailers sell cleaning solutions for your keyboard, screen, and system unit. Before you clean your computer, make sure you turn the computer off to reduce the chance of shock. In most cases you can use a window cleaner to clean your screen. However, do not spray the cleaner directly on the screen. Instead, spray the cleaner onto a cloth and use the cloth to clean the screen. You may find that rubbing alcohol and a Q-tip does a good job of cleaning your keyboard and system unit.

As a rule, do not try to clean inside your system unit. In most cases you may cause more harm by trying to clean your system unit than by letting a little dust

345

collect. If your system unit becomes very dusty, you can purchase a small blower from your computer retailer to blow out the dust.

Do Be Patient and Ask Questions

Learning to use the computer can be a frustrating experience when you feel that you have no one you can ask for help. Lesson 43 presents several sources of information you can turn to. Remember, even computer experts were once new to computers. Don't be afraid to ask questions—you can bet the experts did and still do.

Do Joint a PC User Group

PC user groups consist of members with a wide variety of computer expertise. As a new user, you will find that other members can provide you with a wealth of information. In addition, most user groups have monthly meetings at which software companies present new programs and hardware companies present new products. If you have problems with your PC, you will find user group members who may have encountered the same problems and better yet, members who know how to solve your them.

Do Let Your Kids Use Your System

When you first bring home your new expensive PC, you may have a tendency to protect the PC from your kids. Don't. Instead, simply review with your kids the Dos and Don'ts presented here. If you have younger children whose fingers may be sticky, you might want to consider buying a second keyboard, which should cost you less than $20.

NOTE

You need to keep track of what your kids are doing with the PC, particularly if they are venturing out on Internet or another on-line service. You may, for example, not be pleased when you find that your teenager is spending hours with your PC because he has found the Playboy World Wide Web site on the Internet.

Do Consider an UPS

An *UPS* or *uninterruptible power supply* is a hardware device that provides your PC with about 15 minutes of power should you experience a power failure. If

you use a PC for business, the extra 15 minutes of power provides you with sufficient time to save your work to disk, so you don't lose any work. In the past,
UPS were expensive, costing several hundred dollars. Recently, however, their
cost has dropped considerably, making their use very attractive.

Things You Should Not Do

This section examines several things you should avoid to protect your computer
and software.

Do Not Cover the Computer's Air Vents

If you look at your computer's monitor, you find vents that let the monitor get
rid of the hot air its electrical circuits produce. Make sure you do not block these
vents by placing papers or other objects on top of the monitor. If the monitor
cannot get rid of its heat, you may damage the monitor and even possibly create
a fire hazard. In a similar way, make sure you don't block the system unit fan by
placing your computer too close to a wall. Many printers also have air vents.
Make sure that you do not place your printouts on top of the vents. Figure 38.2,
for example, illustrates computer, printer, and monitor air vents.

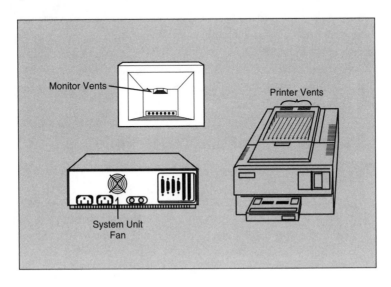

FIGURE 38.2 Do not cover your computer, monitor, or printer air vents.

Do Not Leave Your Monitor on for Long Periods if It Is Not in Use

Your monitor displays information by illuminating different screen picture elements. If the monitor's image remains unchanged for a long period (typically several days), the image may actually become burned into the screen display. If this occurs, you may need to replace your monitor.

To reduce the chance of *screen burn-in*, you can buy a *memory-resident* screen saving program. If your screen is not used for a period of time, the screen saver blanks your screen or displays a screen image that constantly changes. The first time you press a key, the screen saver restores the screen's previous contents.

Do Not Use Your Original Floppy Disk

The only time you should use the original floppy disks that accompany a software package is when you install the software on your hard disk. After that, place the original disks in a safe location. If your computer is floppy disk based, make working copies of all your original disks.

Do Not Move Your Computer While Its Power is On

Even if you only want to move the computer a few inches on your desk, make sure you first turn the computer's power off. When the computer's power is on, your hard disk spins inside the drive at 3600 RPMs. Even the slightest bump can cause the drive's read/write head to collide with the disk, destroying the information the disk contains. When the computer's power is off, the disk does not spin, reducing the chance of a disk crash.

Do Not Open the System Unit Cover While the Unit Is Plugged In

As discussed in Lesson 17, your system unit contains a 150- to 200-watt power supply. If you work inside your system unit while the unit is plugged in, you not only risk damaging the computer's electronic components, you risk electric shock.

Do Not Turn Off Your Computer While a Program is Running

As discussed in Lesson 15, each time you end a program, DOS redisplays its prompt and waits for you to type in the next command. As a habit, turn off your computer only when DOS is displaying its prompt. Do not turn off your computer while a program is running. Many programs do not save the information with which you were working to disk until you exit them. If you turn off the computer before the program ends, you may lose the information with which you were working.

Do Not Eat or Drink Next to Your Computer

It only takes one spilled soda to short out your computer's keyboard or to destroy the information of one or more floppy disks. Keep food and drinks away from your PC, and never set them on top of the monitor, not even for a minute.

Do Not Smoke Next Your Computer or Disks

As you have learned, your computer's hard and floppy disks must be treated with care. A leading cause of disk crashes is a smoky or dusty work environment. Do not smoke next to your computer. To read the information stored on a disk, the disk drive uses a small read/write head that floats just above the surface of the disk. Should the read/write head come in contact with the disk, a disk crash occurs and the information the disk contains is probably destroyed. If smoke particles gather in your disk drive, they may cause the read/write head to come in contact with the disk, destroying the information the disk contains.

Do Not Leave Power Cords or Cables Near Walkways

After you set up a computer, take time to make sure the cables connecting the PC are in a safe location where no one can trip over them, or where they may be damaged by someone walking past.

Do Not Load Software that You Do Not Own onto Your Computer

Loading and using software programs that you do not own is software *piracy* and is against the law. Put simply, if you don't own a software program, don't use it. If you own a business, make sure your employees don't load software software onto a company PC. Remember, if you are working in a network environment, you may need to sign special software license agreements before your software can be used by more than one computer.

Putting It All Together

If you treat your PC well, your PC will last a long time. Follow the rules presented in this lesson to protect your PC, your disks, and yourself.

Glossary

air vents	Holes in the computer's monitor and most printers which allow potentially harmful hot air to escape.
memory-resident screen saver	A program which saves your screen, avoiding the potential of burning an unchanged image into the screen.
screen burn-in	The process of permanently damaging a monitor's phosphors so that it displays the same image forever.
software piracy	Loading and using and/or duplicating software which you don't own.
virus	A software program written intentionally to disrupt and/or destroy the information contained on your disk, often rendering your computer unusable.

Lesson 39: Putting Together Your Purchase

Many of the lessons in this book have presented buyer's guides that you should follow as you shop for your computer and software. To help you organize these guides, this lesson groups all of the buyer's guides into one list. Don't be afraid to take this list with you while you shop. If your salesperson can answer the questions it contains, you can feel comfortable with his or her ability to help you.

This book discusses many different hardware devices and software programs. You don't need to buy them all at once. In fact, you probably only want to buy one software program now, on which you can strictly concentrate. When you feel comfortable with that software, you can shop for others.

Computer Buyer's Guide

❖ Do you have a computer at work or school with which you need to be compatible?

❖ What software programs do you need?
  – Word processor
  – Spreadsheet

- Database
- Desktop
- Desktop Publishing
- Games
- Others

❖ What is the hardware warranty?

❖ What is the technical support policy?

❖ What training is available?

❖ What capabilities do you need today?

❖ What capabilities do you want in the future?

Software Buyer's Guide

As you have seen, the number of software programs is almost limitless. As discussed in Lesson 1, your software costs can quickly exceed the cost of your computer. Take the time to research a software program before you buy it. As was the case for purchasing hardware, check several computer magazines to compare the software cost. Use the following checklist guide to help you with your software purchases:

❖ List the capabilities the software must perform.

❖ Is the software compatible with your existing computer, monitor, and printer?

❖ Does the software require additional hardware such as more memory or a mouse?

❖ Does your computer support multimedia software? (See Lesson 23.)

❖ Is the software compatible with your version of DOS or Windows? (See Lesson 12.)

❖ What size floppy disk do you need for the software? (See Lesson 8.)

❖ Does the manufacturer provide technical support?

❖ Does the retailer provide training? Are books about the software available?

❖ What is the policy on returns? Most companies only allow returns for defective disks.

Keyboard Buyer's Guide

In some cases, you may not have a choice over the keyboard you purchase (a laptop computer does not let you select a different keyboard). If you can select your keyboard, use the following checklist as a guide.

❖ Do you have a keyboard at work or elsewhere whose key positions you are already familiar with? It's very frustrating when the Shift or Ctrl keys aren't where you expect them to be.

❖ Are the keys responsive? Many keyboards feel spongy and may decrease your speed.

❖ Does the key layout meet your needs? Depending on how you use the keyboard, you may want to separate numeric and cursor movement keys.

❖ Does the keyboard reduce strain on your wrists? Would a keyboard pad help reduce wrist strain?

Video Buyer's Guide

As you have seen, there are many video adapters and monitors to choose from. Most newer computers come with the VGA and a compatible monitor. Be aware that some companies sell you the VGA card and a high-resolution monochrome monitor. If you want color, make sure you buy a color monitor.

If you are using programs that display graphics, better resolution improves the image appearance. If you are using programs that run in text mode, you may find that a better adapter and monitor can reduce your eye strain. Use the following list as your guide when you buy your video adapter and monitor:

❖ Do you need graphics capabilities? If so, what resolution?

❖ Do you have—or plan to buy—software that requires a specific adapter type?

❖ Do you need color?

❖ What is the monitor's dot pitch?

❖ Is the monitor non-interlaced?

❖ What is the monitor's refresh rate?

❖ Does the adapter card use a local video bus?

❖ Does your computer support local bus video?

❖ What size monitor do you require?

❖ Will the monitor selected work with the adapter card?

❖ How many hours a day do you expect to spend in front of the monitor?

❖ How much video memory do you require? In other words, how many colors do you need to display at high resolutions?

Printer Buyer's Guide

As the cost of laser and ink jet printers decrease, your choice of printers becomes more difficult. As before, compare the printer prices you are given with those listed in computer magazine advertisements. Use the following list as a guideline when you shop for your printer:

❖ How many pages do you expect the printer to print each day? Is printer speed important?

❖ Where will the printer be located? Is noise a factor?

❖ What will you use the printer for? Do you need letter quality or graphics capabilities?

❖ How much will the printer cost to maintain? Are toner or ink cartridges too costly?

❖ Does the printer provide the fonts you need? If not, are font cartridges or soft fonts available?

❖ Is the printer compatible with your software or does it need special device driver software?

❖ What is the warranty and where can you get the printer serviced?

❖ Do you have an available port to which you can attach the printer? Do you have the necessary cable?

❖ Do you need to print multipart forms? If so, you need an impact printer.

❖ Do you need to print 132 column documents?

❖ Do you need to print labels?

❖ Do you need to print transparencies?

❖ Do you need color printouts?

❖ What is the cost per page?

❖ What printer speed do you require?

❖ Does the printer support PostScript?

❖ How much memory does your printer require? How much data will you send to the printer at one time?

❖ Do you want to share the printer with two or more users?

❖ Do you have a local area network to which you can directly connect the printer?

Disk Drive Buyer's Guide

If you are purchasing a floppy disk drive, you must first decide if you want a 5.25-inch drive or a 3.5-inch drive. Ideally, your system will have two floppy disk drives, one of each type. As a rule, you want to buy the floppy disk drive with the highest capacity. For example, if you buy a 1.2 Mb 5.25-inch drive, the drive can read 1.2 Mb floppy disk as well as 360 Kb floppies. If you are adding a disk drive to your system, make sure your existing disk controller supports the drive.

If you are purchasing a hard disk, you need to determine how big a disk you need. To begin, make a list of all the programs you plan to load on your hard disk, and each program's disk storage requirements. Next, estimate the amount of data such as letters, reports, worksheets, and possibly temporary files you need to store. Add the amount of space you need for data to the amount of space your programs use. Multiply the result by three (a growth factor). The final result is the smallest hard disk size you should consider.

As you shop for disk drives, use the following list as a guideline:

❖ Can you afford to buy both a 5.25-inch and 3.5-inch floppy drive? Having both is very convenient. Make sure you purchase a 1.2 Mb 5.25-inch drive and a 1.44 Mb 3.5-inch drive.

❖ Do you already have a large collection of 5.25-inch or 3.5-inch disks?

❖ Is the disk drive compatible with your existing disk drive controller?

❖ If you are purchasing a hard disk, what is the disk's average access time? The faster the disk's average access time, the faster the disk's performance.

❖ How much disk space do you need?

❖ Is the disk compatible with your computer's BIOS (see Lesson 42)?

❖ What is the disk manufacturer's warranty and technical support policy?

❖ Does the disk require a special device driver?

❖ If you are adding a disk, what are the installation costs?

❖ Can you purchase a dual floppy drive that contains both a 3.5- and 5.25-inch floppy drive?

❖ Do you have an existing SCSI adapter to which you can connect a new drive? If not, what is the cost of the SCSI adapter?

❖ What is the hard drive's cost per byte (or megabyte)?

Mouse Buyer's Guide

Because of its popularity, many retailers include a mouse when you purchase a new computer. If you are considering purchasing a mouse, use the following checklist as your guide:

❖ Does your software support a mouse? How many mouse buttons does the software support?

❖ What is the cost difference between a bus and serial mouse?

❖ Do you have an unused serial port? (See Lesson 10.)

❖ Do you have an unused expansion slot to hold a bus mouse adapter card?

❖ Do you need a mouse pad? The pad improves the performance and feel of most mice.

❖ Would a trackball better suit your needs?

❖ Did you get the necessary mouse device driver software?

❖ Take time to demo one or more mice with your retailer to get a feel for the mouse's responsiveness.

Computer Port Buyer's Guide

If you are planning to purchase a new printer, keep in mind that a parallel printer receives information faster than a serial printer. Also, remember you must have an available port of the same type (serial or parallel) to which you attach the printer.

❖ If you are planning to buy a bus mouse or an internal modem, make sure you have an available expansion slot to hold the hardware board.

❖ When you buy a cable for a new device, pay attention to the port's sex to which you must attach the cable to ensure you purchase the correct cable type.

❖ Lastly, if you are buying a second serial or parallel card, tell your retailer you have an existing port and ask the retailer to change the board's switch settings as required.

Microprocessor Buyer's Guide

Every IBM PC and PC clone uses a microprocessor such as the 8088, 286, 386, 486, or Pentium. Before you buy any computer, make sure you know the microprocessor type and speed.

Due to their slow performance, very few PCs with the original 8088 are sold today. In most cases, the least expensive computer retailers offer is an IBM PC AT compatible using the 386. Cost-wise, the 386-based system is very attractive. However, be aware that the 386 will be very, very slow compared to newer processors. As a result, you should strongly consider a 486- or Pentium-based computer instead of the 386.

If you are considering a 486-based computer, you can reduce your costs by purchasing a computer with a slower clock speed, or a 486SX does not include a math coprocessor. Although the system may run slower, it fully supports existing software and should support future software. If you are considering a Pentium-based computer, systems with several different clock speeds are available.

Use the following list as a guide as you shop for a computer:

❖ What is the system cost?

❖ What is the clock speed? Remember, the higher the clock speed, the faster the computer.

❖ Do you require a math coprocessor?

❖ What is the bus size? The larger the bus size, the better the performance.

❖ Does the system run your existing software?

❖ What software won't the system run?

❖ Is your current processor upgradeable?

❖ Is upgrading your processor cost effective?

Also, see the Memory Buyer's Guide in Lesson 16.

Operating System Buyer's Guide

Most users won't change from using DOS to a different operating system such as OS/2 or UNIX without a significant amount of research on the benefits and disadvantages of making such a change. As such, the following list provides guidelines you should keep in mind when you consider upgrading to a new version of DOS.

❖ Is the new version fully compatible with your existing hardware and software?

❖ Does the new version have additional hardware requirements (such as more memory)?

❖ What capabilities does the new version provide? How many of those capabilities will you use?

Although some new versions may not appear to provide considerable new features, they may fix errors that exist in your current version, or they may improve the operating system's performance.

Memory Buyer's Guide

Upgrading your computer's memory capabilities may not be as easy as you might guess. Most users should let their retailer perform the upgrade for them. Use the following list as a guideline as you begin shopping for memory:

❖ Will your programs use the additional memory? If you can't use it, don't add it.

❖ Does your computer need extended or expanded memory? The 286, 386, 486, and Pentium can use both. Extended memory, however, provides better performance.

❖ How much memory does your software require? Does the software require a specific memory type: extended or expanded?

❖ Do you plan to use existing memory? If so, what is its speed?

❖ Do you have space for memory on the motherboard or do you need a memory board?

❖ Do you need SIMMs or SIPPs?

❖ How much will the memory installation cost?

❖ What is the warranty? Where can you get service?

Laptop Buyer's Guide

Over the next few years, laptop computers may become the fastest selling class of personal computers. Use this list as a guide when you shop for a laptop.

❖ When do you plan to use the laptop? Is a long battery life necessary?

❖ What programs do you plan to run on the laptop? How much disk space will you need?

❖ What is the CPU type and speed? (See Lesson 11.)

❖ How much RAM does the laptop have? Can it hold more?

❖ Does the laptop have a built-in modem?

❖ Can you attach a standard keyboard and monitor to the laptop?

❖ Does the laptop have a serial and parallel port?

❖ Is the battery pack replaceable? If so, how much do replacements cost?

❖ What is the warranty? Where can you get the laptop serviced?

❖ What is the technical support policy?

❖ What software comes with the laptop?

❖ What is the screen display type and resolution? Does it display color?

Modem Buyer's Guide

If you are considering buying a modem, use the following list as your guidelines:

❖ What services or bulletin boards do you plan on accessing with your modem? Do these services have membership dues or long distance costs?

❖ What is the highest baud rate your modem can support?

❖ Does your modem support data compression?

❖ Can your modem send and receive faxes?

❖ Do you have an available serial port to which you can connect an external modem?

❖ Do you have an available expansion slot into which you can insert an internal modem?

❖ Do you have more than one computer to which you might want to attach the modem? Remember, external modems easily connect to a serial port.

❖ Does the modem price include a data communications program? Do you need fax capabilities?

External Storage Device Buyer's Guide

As you shop for an external storage device, use the following as a guideline:

❖ How much information do you need to store?

❖ Is speed or storage capacity a priority?

❖ Does the drive require a SCSI adapter?

❖ Is your SCSI adapter compatible with the drive?

❖ Do you need to use the external storage media to ship files?

Tape Backup Buyer's Guide

As you shop for a tape backup unit, use the following as a guideline:

❖ How much data do you need to back up?

❖ Do you need to back up multiple computers?

❖ Do you prefer an internal or external tape backup unit?

❖ What software comes with the unit? Does the software perform data compression?

❖ Does the software let you select specific files for backing up?

❖ How does the tape backup unit connect to the system?

Scanner Buyer's Guide

If you are looking to buy a scanner, use the following as a guideline:

❖ Will an inexpensive hand held scanner produce the quality image you require?

❖ How many images will you scan per week?

❖ Will you scan black and white, color images, or both?

❖ What is the scanner's resolution? The higher the resolution, the sharper the resulting image.

❖ What software accompanies the scanner? Will you get an image editor and OCR software?

SCSI Buyer's Guide

Use the following list as a guideline as you shop for a SCSI adapter:

❖ Is the SCSI adapter compatible with your PC and other devices?

❖ Does the SCSI adapter come with device drivers for your operating system?

❖ Are there performance benchmarks available for the SCSI adapter? Some SCSI adapters are slower than others.

❖ Is the SCSI adapter software or hardware controllable? Many users find software controllable SCSI adapters easier to install.

PCMCIA Buyer's Guide

Use the following list as a guideline when you shop for PCMCIA cards or when you shop for a notebook computer:

- Does your notebook computer support PCMCIA cards?
- What PCMCIA card type does your notebook computer support?
- How many PCMCIA cards can you use at one time?

Internet Provider Buyer's Guide

Use the following list as your buyer's guide as you shop for an Internet provider:

- Are you already using an on-line service? Does that service provide Internet access?
- Does the provider offer a local access telephone number?
- Does the provider offer standard and SLIP-based accounts?
- Can you get Windows-based software for the SLIP account?
- What are the provider's rates?

On-Line Service Buyer's Guide

Use the following list a guideline as you shop for an on-line service:

- What services do you want to use?
- Are the services you desire covered by basic costs or will you incur additional costs?
- Does the service charge for incoming or outgoing electronic mail?
- Does the service offer access to the Internet, and if so, what is the cost?
- Does the service offer access to the World Wide Web, and if so, what is the cost?
- What is the service's basic monthly charges?
- Does the service have a local access phone number?

Putting It All Together

As you shop, you eventually narrow your choices down to a few different PCs or software packages. Go to a library and look up reviews on the products that appear in recent computer magazines. When you think you've made your choices, talk them over with members of a local user group. If they feel you made wise choices, you probably have.

Lesson 40: Protecting Your Investment

A PC is an expensive investment of your time and money. In Lesson 38 you read several things you should do and should not do as you work with your computer. This lesson looks at ways you can protect your hardware and software from theft, fire, or damage from other sources. Should such a catastrophe occur, this lesson discusses ways you can reduce your loss.

Insuring Your PC

One of the first things you should do when you plan to buy a PC is to contact your insurance company to determine what coverage your home owner's insurance provides for not only your PC, but also any software you buy. Also, if you travel with a laptop computer, find out if your insurance covers the computer in your car, a plane, or a hotel room.

Many insurance companies may not consider your computer as personal property, covered by your home owner's insurance, if you use the computer for any business purpose.

NOTE

As you unpack your PC, make copies of your invoices, and record the serial number for your system unit, printer, keyboard, monitor, as well as other devices. Next, make copies of each software invoice and record the serial numbers listed on the original disks. Take photographs of your system and place these items in a fireproof container or safe deposit box with your other important records. Should you ever need to make an insurance claim, or identify stolen property, you have the exact records you need.

NOTE

Although your insurance company may reimburse you for the cost of your software, they probably won't cover losses for time you have spent working with the software. For example, if you have paid a data entry person $2,500 to type customer information into a database, and your computer is stolen, you probably cannot claim the lost data. Likewise, if you have been paying a programmer to develop a large custom software package, and damage to the disk or computer results in a loss of the program, you probably won't be successful in making an insurance claim on the development costs. Your only protection against lost data is duplicate (or backup) copies of the information. Backups are discussed later in this lesson. Computer magazines often advertise several companies that specialize in computer insurance. If you are using your PC for business purposes, these companies may be able to provide you with the protection you need.

Insurance Checklist

Each time you purchase hardware or a software package, record the following information. You may later need the information to file an insurance claim, or to justify tax deductions.

- ❖ Product name:
- ❖ Company name:
- ❖ Company Address:
- ❖ Company Phone:
- ❖ Serial number:
- ❖ Cost (including shipping and tax):
- ❖ Notes:

Protecting Your Hardware

Lesson 38 covers the Dos and Don'ts of working with your computer. In general, if you don't mistreat your PC, it lasts for years. As discussed in Lesson 3, you should plug your computer into a surge suppressor that protects its electronic circuits from damage by surges of power traveling down power lines. Such surges can be caused by lightning, or a failed electric company junction box. Surge suppressors aren't just for computers. If you have a stereo system or TV, you should consider plugging them into a surge suppressor for protection as well.

Protecting Your Disk

After you install a software program on your hard disk, place the original disk in a safe location. If you are using a floppy disk-based computer that does not have a hard disk, never work with the original floppy disks. Instead, make working copies of your disk and place the originals in a safe location.

Figure 40.1 illustrates floppy disk storage cases. You should buy such a case and place it next to your computer. Whenever you are done using a floppy disk, place the disk back into its protective paper sleeve and then store the disk in the disk holder. Using the disk holder not only helps you organize your disks, it reduces their chance of damage from a spill, or from objects set on top of them.

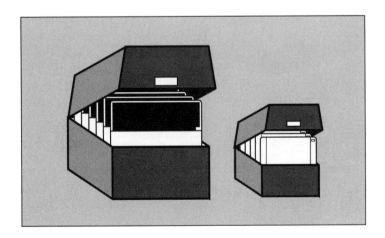

FIGURE 40.1 Floppy disk storage cases.

Disk Recovery Software

As you work with your computer, you may accidentally issue a command that erases one or more files from your disk, or overwrites key information on the disk. There are several software programs you can buy that may be able to "unerase" a file, recovering the information your disk contains. Such programs are *disk utilities*. Table 40.1 lists several disk utility programs.

TABLE 40.1 DISK UTILITY SOFTWARE.

Disk Utility	Where to Purchase
DOS 6 or later	Computer retailer
PC Tools	Computer retailer
Norton Utilities	Computer retailer

Virus Protection

A *computer virus* is a program someone has intentionally written to destroy the information on your disk, or to prevent you from using your computer. Although computer viruses regularly make the news, you are much more likely to lose information by issuing the wrong command yourself than by having your computer infected by a virus.

Because they are computer programs, you must run a virus before it can damage your disk. A virus gets on your computer's disk by either attaching itself to another program or by disguising itself as a harmless program such as a computer game. If you only buy your computer programs from reputable companies, you will probably never encounter a virus. If your computer has a modem and you use the modem to download programs (whose origin you do not know) from a bulletin board, you increase the possibility of encountering a virus. Likewise, the same holds true if you get a disk full of programs from another user.

When you run the program containing the virus, the virus may search your disk for, and attach itself to other programs (spreading itself). The virus may immediately make itself known, possibly erasing your disk or preventing you from using your computer, or the virus might wait for a special event, such as Friday the 13th.

There are several virus prevention programs you can buy that search your disk for known viruses. In some cases the software will tell you of the virus. In others, the software can destroy the virus. Table 40.2 lists several virus prevention programs.

TABLE 40.2 VIRUS PREVENTION SOFTWARE.

VIRUS PREVENTION PROGRAM	WHERE TO PURCHASE
DOS 6 or later	Computer retailer
Central Point Anti-Virus	Computer retailer
PC Tools	Computer retailer
Norton Anti Virus	Computer retailer
Virex-PC	Computer retailer

If you work in an office filled with computers, you may want to set aside one computer as a system for checking all disks that enter the office for viruses. If everyone in your office tests each floppy disk for viruses before they use the disk on their own system, you greatly reduce the chance of a computer viruses damaging your disk or files.

Backing Up Your Files

As discussed, the only way you can fully protect your computer work is to make duplicate (called backup) copies of your files. If your computer is stolen, damaged, or if you accidentally erase the information on your disk, you can use your backup copies. The more often you make backup copies, the less information you stand to lose. For example, if you have a data entry person typing in customer information, and you make backups each day, the most information you stand to lose is one day's work. However, if you only backup your files weekly, you can quickly lose a considerable amount of work.

In most cases, performing backups only requires 10 to 15 minutes each day. Backup disks are like an insurance policy. Hopefully, you won't need them, but if you do, thank goodness they are there.

Depending on the importance of your data, consider keeping your backup disks at a location away from your computer. Assume, for example, a doctor's office has its patient billing information on the computer, and the office is vandalized. If the backup disks are in the same room as the computer, both the data and the backup copies will be destroyed.

There are several software programs you can buy that make performing backups fast and easy. Table 40.3 lists several of these programs.

TABLE 40.3 BACKUP SOFTWARE PROGRAMS.

BACK UP SOFTWARE	WHERE TO PURCHASE
Central Point Software	Computer retailer
Fastback Plus	Computer retailer
Norton Backup	Computer retailer
PC Tools Deluxe	Computer retailer

As discussed in Lesson 22, a tape backup may increase the speed and ease of your backup operations. If you are purchasing a computer for a business, a tape backup unit is one of the best investments you can make.

In fact, many tape backup programs let you direct them to automatically run, unattended, at night. As such, the only burden you incur by performing regular backups is placing the tapes in a safe location after the backup completes.

Surge Suppressors and Uninterruptible Power Supplies

Never plug your computer directly into a wall outlet. Instead, plug your computer into a surge suppressor as shown in Figure 40.2. As discussed, surge suppressors protect your computer from spikes of electricity that can quickly destroy your computer's electronic circuits.

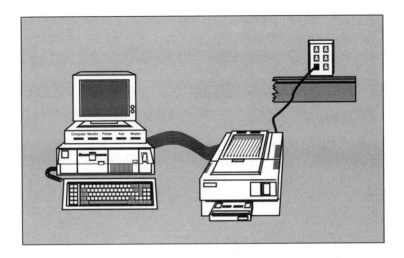

FIGURE 40.2 Protect your computer hardware with a surge suppressor.

Your computer is not the only device you should protect using a surge suppressor. If you have an expensive TV, VCR, or stereo system, you should plug them into a surge suppressor as well. If you travel with a laptop computer, you should purchase a small surge suppressor as shown in Figure 40.3 that fits into your briefcase.

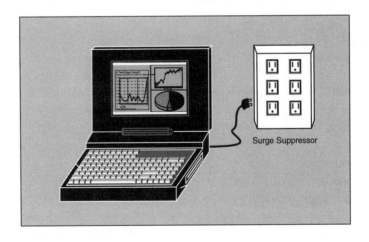

FIGURE 40.3 Travel with a small surge suppressor to protect your laptop.

Also, today, most PCs have modems that users connect to a telephone wall jack. If you are shopping for a surge suppressor, find one that will filter surges on telephone wires as well. As it happens, lightning that strikes telephone wires and travels into your modem port could seriously damage your computer.

Surge suppressors only protect your computer from spikes of electricity. A surge suppressor cannot protect your data from a loss of power. If you work with critical data for which you cannot afford a loss of data, you can protect your data using an uninterruptible power supply (UPS). Should a power loss occur, the UPS provides up to 15 minutes of power. In this way, you have sufficient time to save your work to disk. Unfortunately, comparatively inexpensive uninterruptible power supplies still cost several hundred dollars.

Putting It All Together

Your computer and the software you purchase represents a large investment. If you treat your system with care, it will last for years. In any case, you need to take steps to reduce your chance of loss should your computer be damaged or stolen. You can protect your computer's hardware with an insurance policy. The best way to protect the information on your computer is with duplicate copies.

Glossary

backups
: A set of disks containing duplicate copies of your files.

disk utility
: A software program that helps you recover erased or damaged files, or a damaged disk.

rider
: An insurance coverage that "rides with" an item from one location to another. You may need rider coverage to protect a laptop computer.

virus
: A software program intentionally written to disrupt your work, possibly by damaging your files or by rendering your computer unusable.

Lesson 41: Putting Your PC to Work

With the changing economy, there are many ways to put your PC to work to supplement or to generate additional income. As you will learn in this lesson, you can perform many of these tasks without having to be a PC expert. In addition, by putting your PC to work, you quickly learn more about your PC's capabilities and those of your software. As you begin, start slowly. Most PC-related tasks typically take two times as long to complete as you would estimate.

Word Processing

As you know, word processing is the generating of formatted reports, memos, and documents. If you live near a university, students are always in need of a good typist or word processor. To perform such operations you need a laser printer and a word processor that provides a spell-checker. In many cases, students simply want to get their documents started so you can provide the document to them on disk. In such cases, you need to ensure that your word processor is compatible with that of the student. In fact, after you complete one or two jobs, you may want to purchase additional word processors. To begin, you should probably use Word for Windows or WordPerfect. These two word processors are widely used, provide the capabilities you need, and should be compatible with the student's word processor. If you examine bulletin boards around the university, you should find advertisements for word processing. Use such adds as a guideline for your pricing.

In addition, many businesses generate more typing than can be completed during the day. In such cases, you may find that you can pick up documents in the late afternoon, type them at night on your word processor, and then return the hard copy and disks to the business the following day. Also, many word processors include grammar checking software that can flag grammar errors such as passive voice, long sentences, and noun/verb mismatches. Using such software, you can help your client produce a better document.

Mailing List Generation

Many businesses have lists of clients, old clients, and potential clients to which they would like to send mailings. A *mailing list* is a file containing names, addresses, and phone numbers. To create a mailing list, you can use a word processor or a database program. Many word processors support *mail merging* that lets you create customized letters from a mailing list. For example, assume that a doctor wants to send short letters to each patient. Using a mail merge operation, you can change a letter from beginning with *Dear Patient* to a more personal *Dear Jim* or *Dear Mary*. The mail merge operation automatically inserts names, addresses, pet names, and so on in the correct location within the letter. If you perform mail merge or mailing list operations, you normally charge an hourly rate. Your rate should be similar to what you would charge for word processing operations. For specifics on mail merge operations, refer to your word processor documentation.

Newsletter Creation

Many companies, schools, and even clubs generate newsletters on a regular basis. If you have a powerful word processor you can easily create such newsletters. By purchasing and including different clip art pieces within the newsletter, you can quickly improve the newsletter's appearance. Lastly, if you purchase a hand held scanner, you can include photos. Newsletter creation is much more time-consuming and difficult than standard word processing. As such, you need to adjust your rates accordingly. Figure 41.1 illustrates a sample newsletter created with a word processor.

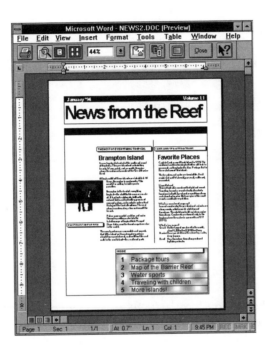

FIGURE 41.1 A sample newsletter.

Trend Analysis Reports

As you have learned, a spreadsheet program lets you generate graphs of different values, such as your monthly expenses. When you perform word processing operations for a business, you may be able to also help the business create spreadsheets that let them track their expenses, sales, and so on. Next, simply show the office manager how easily the spreadsheet graphs can be used to determine trends and you will find yourself creating a myriad of different spreadsheets. Figure 41.2 illustrates a graph created with a spreadsheet that quickly summarizes sales for several months.

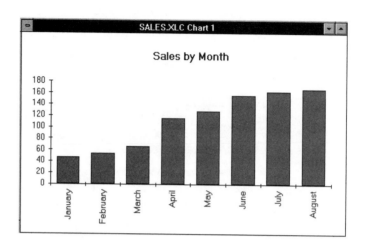

FIGURE 41.2 Using spreadsheet graphs for trend analysis.

PC Tutoring

By finishing this book, you have actually learned a considerable amount about the PC. As such, you can put your knowledge to work helping others set up their PC or learn about new software programs. If you have a word processor, for example, learn the steps to install the software, support different printers, and so on. Next, spend time learning how to perform advanced operations such as word processing mail merge operations. You can then begin teaching others to perform the same operations. Many PC stores provide classes and need teachers. As your skills increase, you can begin teaching such classes. As you do, you open up opportunities to teach office workers how to perform word processing, create mailing lists, and so on. If you are working with businesses, one of the first lessons you should present is how to perform backup operations.

As discussed in Lesson 30, most users have heard of the Internet, but don't know how to access it. As such, if you master connecting to and accessing the Internet, you may find considerable teaching and consulting opportunities.

Computer-Generated Art

Not everyone is artistic. However if you are, you may find many companies in need of custom logos, newsletter art, and so on. There are many PC drawing packages that you can use to generate such images. To perform such operations, you will want a large screen, a mouse, and a very high quality printer. If you are interested in performing such operations, use a PC drawing package to create a portfolio that illustrates your work. Figure 41.3 illustrates a sample of computer-generated art.

FIGURE 41.3 A sample of computer generated art.

Creating Home Pages

Lesson 33 introduced the Internet's World Wide Web. As you learned, computers around the Internet, called *Web site*s make extensive use of hyperlinked documents. Users create hyperlinked documents using a word processor to insert special symbols into the document that later direct the Web browser to display text using bold or italic characters or to display specific graphic images. The *HTML* (*hypertext markup language*) specifies which symbols the user should place with the document for specific tasks. For example, to display text in italics, the user inserts one set of HTML symbols. Similarly, to display text in bold characters, the user inserts a different set of HTML symbols. As it turns out, HTML is actually very easy to use. After you understand HTML, you can use it to create Web homepages for different companies.

Putting It All Together

The PC provides a myriad of work opportunities. This lesson has only presented a few. As you increase the number of software programs with which you are proficient, the number of business opportunities you create for yourself will also greatly increase.

Glossary

homepage	The primary document at a World Wide Web site.
HTML	An abbreviation for hypertext markup language —the text editing symbols you use to create a hypertext, Web document.
mail merge	The process of combining database entries with a word processing document to create a custom letter.

Lesson 42:
Commonly Asked
Questions

The previous lessons have introduced you to many different PC concepts. This lesson addresses many of the questions I have received from new users over the past ten years. Hopefully, the discussion presented here answers questions you have in mind.

Questions on DOS

The following questions relate to DOS, your computer's disk operating system.

What Version of DOS Do I Need?

In general, you normally want the latest version of DOS, just as you would want the latest version of any software package. When DOS first released in 1981, the version number was 1.0. DOS version numbers have two parts: a *major* and *minor version number*. In the case of DOS 1.0, 1 is the major version number and 0 is the minor. When the DOS developers release a new version of DOS, the developers change the version number based upon the significance of their changes to DOS. If the changes are few, the developers increase the minor version number. DOS 1.0, for example, might change to DOS 1.1. If the changes are significant, the developers change the major version number. DOS 5.0, for example, became 6.0. The next major release of DOS will be version 7.

If I Have Microsoft Windows, Why Do I Need DOS?

As discussed in Lesson 12, your PC must first run the operating system before it can run any other program. DOS is the PC operating system. Windows is a program you can run after DOS is loaded. Windows provides a *graphical* (picture-based) interface that makes your PC easier to use. If you are using the Windows 95, Windows NT, or OS/2 operating systems discussed in Lesson 12, you do not need DOS. As discussed, both Windows 95, Windows NT and OS/2 can run DOS and Windows-based programs.

What is COMMAND.COM?

As discussed in Lesson 15, when your computer successfully starts DOS, your screen displays the DOS prompt, similar to the prompt shown here:

```
C:\>
```

To execute a command, you type the command name at the DOS prompt and press **Enter**. COMMAND.COM is a special DOS command that DOS automatically runs each time it starts. COMMAND.COM in turn displays the DOS prompt and executes the commands you type. COMMAND.COM (often called the *command processor*) also contains the internal DOS commands such as CLS, DATE, and TIME.

What is AUTOEXEC.BAT?

After DOS runs COMMAND.COM during your system startup, DOS checks to see if your disk contains a file named AUTOEXEC.BAT that contains a list of command names you want DOS to execute automatically each time it starts. AUTOEXEC.BAT exists to help you customize your system. For example, if you work in a network environment, you may want DOS to run one or more network programs each time it starts. The commands you place in your AUTOEXEC.BAT file may be very different from those of another user. The point to remember is that DOS automatically executes these commands each time your system starts. AUTOEXEC.BAT is a file you can create and change yourself using an editor or your word processor. AUTOEXEC.BAT, therefore, is simply a file that contains one or more DOS commands, as shown here:

```
@ECHO OFF
CLS
SET PATH=C:\WINDOWS;C:\DOS
SMARTDRV 2048
SET PROMPT=$P$G
SET TEMP=C:\TEMP
```

What is CONFIG.SYS?

As you just learned, each time your system starts, DOS automatically executes the commands in the file AUTOEXEC.BAT. In a similar way, DOS examines your disk for a file named CONFIG.SYS. Unlike AUTOEXEC.BAT that contains the names of commands you want DOS to execute, the CONFIG.SYS file contains single-line entries that tell DOS how you want to configure memory, the number of files you want DOS to let you open at one time, and so on. The entries in the file CONFIG.SYS are not commands. Instead, each entry configures a different aspect of your system. The following entries illustrate a sample CONFIG.SYS file:

```
DEVICE=C:\WINDOWS\HIMEM.SYS
DOS=HIGH
BUFFERS=10
FILES=40
DEVICE=C:\DOS\ANSI.SYS
```

CONFIG.SYS is an ASCII file you can create using an editor, such as EDIT, provided with MS-DOS.

How Does MS-DOS Differ from PC-DOS?

Microsoft Corporation develops DOS. The letters *MS* stand for Microsoft. IBM licenses DOS from Microsoft for use on their IBM PC and PS/2 computers. IBM calls DOS *PC-DOS*. From a user perspective the two DOS versions are the same. A user running PC-DOS version 3.3 has the same capabilities as a user running MS-DOS version 3.3. Recently, Microsoft announced DOS 6.0. IBM, in turn, made a few modifications to the DOS utility programs and are calling their version *PC-DOS 6.1*. The differences between MS-DOS 6.0 and PC-DOS 6.1 are more political than operational.

When Should I Use Directories?

A directory is a list of related files. Visualize a directory as a filing cabinet drawer you use to organize related files. When you store information as files on your disk, you should group related files within directories. In general, each of your different application programs should have their own directory. Within your word processing directory for example, you might further organize your files by creating different directories for your memos, letters, and reports.

How Does a Low-level Disk Format Differ from the DOS FORMAT Command?

A *low-level format* is performed by the disk controller card to prepare your disk for use with the controller. The low-level format operation carefully examines the disk's entire surface. If parts of the surface are damaged and cannot store information, the low-level format operation marks the locations as unusable. In most cases, your computer retailer performs the low-level format operation for you, before you receive your computer. Low-level formatting only applies to hard disks.

The DOS FORMAT command prepares a disk for use by DOS. Before DOS can store and retrieve files from a disk, DOS requires the disk to contain several key pieces of information. The FORMAT command places this information on the disk. In the case of a floppy disk, FORMAT also examines and identifies damaged locations on the disk.

What is Booting DOS?

Booting DOS is the process of starting DOS so you can use your computer. A *cold boot* occurs when you turn on your computer to start DOS. A *warm boot* occurs when you restart DOS by pressing the **Ctrl-Alt-Del** keyboard combination.

As discussed, you should never boot your computer when a program is running. Doing so may damage your files, losing the information they contain.

What is the BIOS?

Many new users confuse DOS and BIOS. DOS is your computer's disk operating system. When you start your computer the computer loads DOS from disk. *BIOS*, which resides on one or more hardware chips, is an abbreviation for *basic input and output system*. Your computer's BIOS lets the computer communicate with input and output devices such as its screen, keyboard, and disk. Depending on the age and type of your computer, you may need to upgrade your computer's BIOS before you can run a specific program or add a new hardware device. If you must upgrade the BIOS, have your retailer or a very experienced user do so for you. As shown in Figure 42.1, DOS resides on disk, whereas the BIOS is on a computer chip.

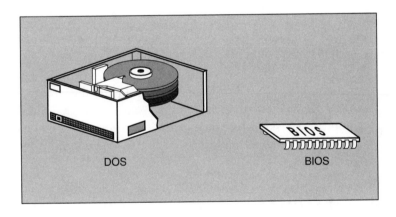

FIGURE 42.1 DOS is software, and the BIOS is on a chip.

What is Memory Management Software?

As you learned in Lesson 15, DOS and your DOS-based programs run within your computer's first 640Kb of memory. To help DOS make the best use of this memory region, you can use *memory management software*. Such software moves memory-resident programs, device drivers, and other information to free up memory for your program use. If you are using DOS 5 or DOS 6, you can use the DOS memory-management capabilities to increase the amount of memory. If you are not using DOS 5 or DOS 6, there are several third-party software programs that manage memory.

Disk-Related Questions

The following questions relate to floppy, hard, and RAM disks.

What is Disk Compression?

Regardless of their disk size, computer users have a habit of filling up almost any disk. To help users increase the size of their disks, many companies now offer *disk compression software*. In general, the compression software stores the disk's information in a unique format that consumes less disk space. Using disk compression software, for example, you can increase the size of a 40Mb to 80Mb and a 100Mb disk to 200Mb! Disk compression software programs let you instantly increase your disk's storage capacity without having to purchase a new disk. If you are using DOS 6, the DBLSPACE command lets you compress your disk.

NOTE

If you compress your disk, do not use third-party disk software, such as an UNDELETE program, until you are sure the program fully supports compressed disks. Most disk utility programs do not support compressed disks and may destroy the information your disk contains.

What is a RAM Disk?

In Lesson 16 you learned that *RAM* is the computer's fast electronic memory. Using special software called a device driver, DOS lets you use a portion of the computer's RAM to simulate a disk drive. Like a hard disk or floppy drive, the RAM drive has a unique drive letter such as E or F. Because the RAM drive is electronic and has no mechanical parts, it is much faster than even the fastest hard disk. However, because the information RAM holds is never magnetized onto a disk for long-term storage, the RAM drive's information is lost when you turn off your computer or restart DOS. Most users use RAM drives to store temporary files.

What is a Disk Crash?

As discussed in Lesson 8, a disk drive uses a device called its *read/write head* to read information from, and to write information to, the disk. As the hard disk spins within the drive at 3600 or more RPMs, the drive's read/write head floats just off the disk's surface. If you bump or jar the computer, the read/write head may actually make contact with the surface, grinding off the disk's special coating, and destroying the information the disk contains. In most cases, you must replace your disk drive following a drive crash.

What is Disk Parking?

When the computer is on, the disk's read/write head floats just off the disk's surface. When you turn the computer off, the disk quits spinning and the read/write head actually rests on the disk's surface. To reduce the chance of the head damaging a location containing information, should someone bump the computer, many drives move the head to a special *landing zone* that does not contain data. If your hard disk does not automatically park itself, you can purchase software that parks the disk's head. You should always park the head before you move the computer. Figure 42.2 illustrates the landing zone on a disk surface. As you can see, the landing zone is away from the information stored on your disk.

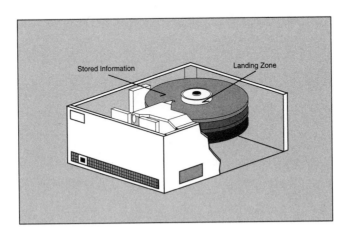

FIGURE 42.2 The disk landing zone.

How Can I Mail Floppy Disks?

Most office supply and computer retailers sell cardboard diskette mailers that protect your disks from damage when you mail them. Your disks' biggest threat when you mail them is damage from bending. Most mailers contain warnings not to bend the package and not to expose the package to electric or magnetic fields. Before you mail a diskette, make sure you have a backup copy of the disk's contents that you keep until the disk arrives safely at its destination.

Can I Replace My Existing Disk Drive With a New Higher Capacity Disk?

As discussed in Lesson 17, your floppy and hard disk drives connect to a hardware board called the *disk controller* that oversees all disk operations. Before you buy a new disk drive, you must insure the drive is compatible with your existing disk controller. If you have an older controller, you may need to upgrade both your disk and disk controller.

What is a Disk Partition?

When the IBM PC first released in 1981, hard disk drives were very expensive. For years, the largest affordable hard disks for PCs were 10Mb to 20Mb. As a result, the largest disk size DOS would support was 32Mb. As disk technology improved, hard disks larger than 32Mb became available. To let users with these larger disks use the entire disk's storage capacity, DOS lets the users divide the disk into several different sections called *partitions*. In general, each partition appears as a unique disk drive. Beginning with DOS 4, DOS increased its partition size from 32Mb to 512Mb. With DOS version 5, DOS again increased size, this time to 2 gigabytes! Today, most users only use one or two disk partitions. Using one partition simplifies your initial startup and installation. Using two partitions, however, may protect files by storing your files on two logical disks. Assuming your disk partitions create drives C and D, commands you issue on drive C will not affect files stored on drive D and vice versa.

Can the Airport X-Ray Machine Damage My Disks?

As a general rule, the x-ray machine itself cannot damage your disk. However, the motorized belt that moves suitcases under the x-ray can generate a magnetic flux that is capable of damaging your disk. If you ask for a "hand check" of your computer at the airport, the security personnel examine your computer (having you turn it on) as opposed to running the system through the x-ray machine.

What is a Peripheral?

A *peripheral* is any device other than the keyboard and screen that you attach to your computer, such as a printer, modem, mouse, or network.

What is a CD-ROM?

CD-ROM is an abbreviation for *compact disk/read-only memory*. A computer's CD-ROM disk looks very similar to a musical compact disc you would play using your stereo. A CD-ROM disk can store many times as much information as the typical hard disk. A single compact disc, for example, can hold an entire set of encyclopedias.

A CD-ROM disk requires a special disk drive similar to the one shown in Figure 42.3. As discussed in Lessons 23 and 27, a CD-ROM can store tremendous amounts of information, such as video and sound. Because of the success of multimedia, in the future most PCs will ship with CD-ROM drives. Today, their use is still limited because users cannot yet store information on the disk. Instead, users purchase CD-ROM disks that already contain the information they desire. In the future, users will be able to store tremendous amounts of information on a CD-type device.

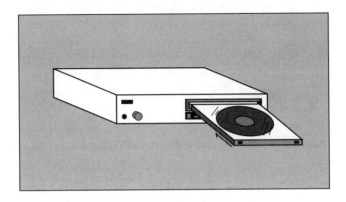

FIGURE 42.3 A CD-ROM drive.

How Does an UPS Differ from a Surge Suppressor?

One of the most frustrating events you can experience is a power outage that shuts off your computer before you save your work. One way to prevent such loss of data is by using an UPS.

UPS is an abbreviation for *uninterruptible power supply*. Like a surge suppressor, an UPS is a hardware device into which you plug your computer's hardware. Also, like a surge suppressor, an UPS protects your equipment from surges of power. Most importantly, however, the UPS provides a large battery that powers your computer should the power fail. In most cases, the UPS will provide you with about 15 minutes of power, which is more than enough time for you to save your current work and exit the program. An UPS typically costs $300 or more depending on its capabilities.

Application Software

The following questions relate to different application software programs, as discussed in Lesson 2.

What is Shareware?

As discussed, software programs are very expensive and their cost can quickly add up and surpass your hardware cost. *Shareware* is software that developers let you try, and if you like it, pay a small fee. Many computer magazines advertise shareware programs. A shareware word processor, for example, might cost you $10. Although a shareware program doesn't provide you with all the capabilities you would find in an expensive application program, it meets most of your needs, at a nominal cost. If you purchase shareware programs from a reputable shareware dealer, you greatly reduce your chance of encountering a computer virus, as discussed in Lesson 40. Never install shareware programs on your disk without first examining the disk that contains the program for computer viruses.

What is WYSIWYG?

WYSIWYG is an abbreviation for *what-you-see-is-what-you-get*. When you use a WYSIWYG word processor, for example, the document you print matches the document you see on the screen. In other words, the document you see on the screen is the document you get when you print. Figure 42.4, for example, illustrates a graphics image within a word processing document. When you print this document, the hard copy appears just as it does on your screen.

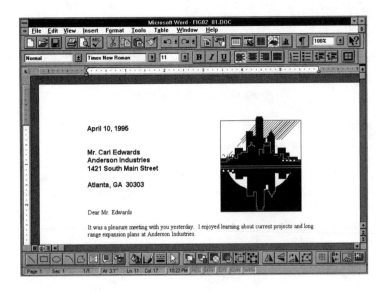

FIGURE 42.4 A WYSIWYG word processor.

What is a Shell?

As discussed, when DOS starts, DOS displays its command prompt. To execute commands, you type the command's name at the DOS prompt and press **Enter**. To make the computer easier to use, many users run a special program called a *shell* which lets them select their commonly used commands from a menu, as opposed to requiring the user to memorize long or difficult commands. Figure 42.5 illustrates the shell interface provided with DOS 6.

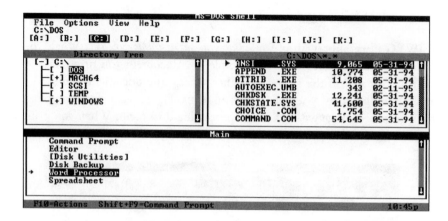

FIGURE 42.5 The DOS Shell interface.

What is Memory Resident Software?

As discussed in Lesson 16, when you run a program, DOS loads the program into your computer's memory so the computer can run it. After the program ends, DOS loads the next program into memory, overwriting the old program. A *memory resident program*, (sometimes called a *terminate and stay resident program* or *TSR*) on the other hand, stays in memory the entire time you use your computer. Memory resident programs provide your computer with additional capabilities such as access to a network or the ability to use a mouse.

What is Integrated Software?

Most users buy a word processor, spreadsheet, and possibly a database program. *Integrated software* is a program that either provides each of these capabilities or helps you use these programs together. In other words, integrated software tries to make your programs easier to use.

What are On-line Services?

An *on-line service* is a company that provides you with the ability to use your computer and a modem to dial into the company's computer to access resources such as up-to-the-minute news, stock market and weather information, or shop in on-line stores. The largest on-line services include Prodigy, CompuServe, and America Online. To access an on-line service, you will normally pay a monthly fee. Depending on the services that you access, your monthly fee may vary. Recently, many on-line services provide access to the Internet.

What is the Internet?

As discussed in Lesson 30, the *Internet* is a collection of computer networks, connected together to exchange information and to share files. The Internet spans 150 countries worldwide and consists of over 20,000 computer networks. Across the Internet, there are over 2 million documents. Using Internet-based programs, you can search for and find the information you need, regardless of your desired topic. To access the Internet, you normally join an on-line service or use a special company called an *Internet provider*.

What is the World Wide Web?

Across the Internet, there are over 2 million documents. Your biggest challenge in using the Internet is finding the information you need. The *World Wide Web* is a collection of documents that contain special links from one document to another. For example, you might be reading a document on travel that resides on a computer in Los Angelos. Within that document, you may encounter a link called Traveling to Japan. When you click your mouse on the document, your Web software will display the related document. That document might reside on the same computer, a computer across town, or even a computer in Japan. To access World Wide Web, you use your computer, modem, and special software called a *Web browser*.

Putting It All Together

This lesson presented answers to several commonly asked PC questions. As you work with your PC, don't be afraid to ask questions. As you will find, the more you learn about your computer the more you will want to know.

Glossary

AUTOEXEC.BAT	A file containing a list of command names you want DOS to execute automatically each time it starts.
BIOS	An abbreviation for basic input and output system, BIOS lets the computer communicate with input and output devices such as its screen, keyboard, and disk.
booting	The process of starting up your computer.
CD-ROM	Compact disk-read-only memory, with the capability to store many times as much information as the typical hard disk.
cold boot	The process of turning on your PC's power and starting the operating system.
COMMAND.COM	Also known as the command processor, this special DOS command is automatically run each time DOS starts. It also contains internal DOS commands such as CLS, DATE, and TIME.
CONFIG.SYS	A file containing single line entries that tell DOS how you want to configure memory, as well as the number of files you want DOS to let you open at one time.
disk compression	Software that enables users to increase the size of their disks by compressing the information in a unique format that consumes less disk space.
disk crash	A destruction of the information on your disk, usually occurring when the computer's read/write head comes in contact with another surface, and therefore grinds off its protective coating.
disk parking	The process of moving your a hard disk's read/write heads over a safe location on the disk so you can move the PC without the risk of a disk head crash.

disk partition	A section of a hard disk that corresponds to a drive letter such as C and D. Each hard disk can be divided into several different sections, allowing users to utilize the entire disk's storage capacity, and to divide their disk into two or more logical drives.
graphical interface	Picture-based screen within Windows that allows the user to see and manipulate graphic objects that correspond to programs and documents.
integrated software	Software that provides multiple capabilities such as word processing, database, and spreadsheet operations.
Internet provider	A company, who, for a free will let you dial into their Internet connection using your PC and a modem.
landing zone	A special location on a hard disk upon which the drive's read/write heads actually come to rest when you park the drive.
major version number	The primary number used to identify the version of a software program, In the case of DOS 6.2, for example, the primary version number is 6.
memory management software	Software that moves memory-resident programs in order to free up memory for your program use.
memory resident software	A DOS-based program that when you run it remains present in your computer's memory. Many device drivers use memory resident software.
minor version number	The number used to identify the version of a software upgrade. In the case of DOS 6.2, for example, the minor version number is 2.
peripheral	Any device other than the keyboard and screen that you attach to your computer (such as a printer, modem, mouse, etc.).

shareware

Software that is a bit reduced in capabilities (compared to expensive commercial software) that developers often let you try at a very reduced fee.

TSR

An abbreviation for terminate-stay resident software—another name for memory resident software.

UPS

An abbreviation for uninterruptible power supply, it is a device into which you plug your computer's hardware. Should your office lose its power, the UPS provides power to your computer for up to 15 minutes.

warm boot

The process of restarting the operating system without cycling the PC's power. Normally by pressing the Ctrl-Alt-Del keyboard combination.

Web browser

A software program that lets you traverse hypertext documents on the World Wide Web.

Lesson 43: Where to Find Additional Information

The lessons in this book have introduced you to many of the key concepts you need to get started with a PC. It won't take long before you will want to buy new software and put your computer to other uses. As you prepare to do so, take advantage of the many sources of available information. In most cases, these sources can answer questions and provide hardware and software reviews that may save you time and money. This lesson discusses several such information sources.

User Groups

Almost every major city has a PC user group whose members regularly get together to exchange hardware and software knowledge. To locate a user group near you, just ask a local computer retailer.

User groups have members at all levels of expertise. If you have questions, a member probably has the answer or can point you in the right direction.

Most user groups have meetings once a month. The group may have a small annual fee that covers its operating costs. Depending on the group's size, hardware and software vendors may attend the meetings and show new products. Some user groups even publish newsletters that contain product reviews and tutorials.

In addition, members interested in specific products such as a word processor may form special interest groups that meet weekly.

Don't be intimidated by the thought of joining a user group. All of the groups' members were once new users too. They would love to have you join and will make you feel at home. For information on user groups in your area write to:

Association of PC User Groups
1730 M. Street, N.W., Suite 700
Washington, DC 20036

Computer Magazines

Throughout this book, I have recommended that you browse through computer magazines to compare hardware and software costs. If you go to a library, news-stand, or bookstore, you'll be amazed at the number of computer magazines on the shelves. In addition to containing pages of advertisements listing the latest hardware and software products, most magazines are filled with product reviews. If, for example, you are thinking of buying a new printer, you can find out which printer the experts feel is the best buy. Likewise, the software reviews tell you which programs are the most powerful, and which ones are the easiest to use. Such reviews take much of the guesswork out of your computer purchases. Many magazines also include tutorials, tips, tricks, and possible traps for the most popular software programs.

Before you subscribe to one or more magazines, read a few issues at the library or buy them from a bookstore. Make sure the articles are written at a level you not only understand, but that you find useful.

Computer Books

Most users don't read software manuals, because in general, the manuals are hard to read. As an alternative, users turn to computer books. Almost every popular software program has books to help the first-time user get started, books to make subjects simple, books you can use to teach yourself about a topic, as well as books on advanced concepts. Because a book can devote many pages to a concept, books are usually much easier to read and understand than the product manual.

Before you head to the bookstore to buy a book, write down a few questions or problems you want the book to solve. If several books on the same topic exist, check each book's table of contents and index to determine which book best answers your questions and which book is easiest to use.

Video Training

As you read through computer magazines, you will see advertisements for training videos on popular software programs. In many cases the videos cost under $50. If you consider that a book may cost you $25 and takes you considerably longer to read than the two hour video, the videos become an attractive learning alternative. Most computer magazines should list one or more sources for training videos.

Local Retailers

Your computer retailer can often answer many of your questions about hardware, and possibly about popular software packages. Be aware, however, that the best product may just happen to be the one they have on the shelf. If you have a specific product in mind, ask your retailer if you can demo the software on a computer in the store.

Many retailers offer classes on DOS and other popular programs. Such classes provide you with a quick way to get started. If you purchase a computer at a local computer store, the retailer may include one or more classes with the purchase of your computer. Before you finalize your sale, inquire about available classes.

Continuing Education Classes

Most colleges and universities offer a variety of computer classes through their continuing education programs. The classes normally meet one or two times a week for several weeks. The advantage such classes provide is that you can learn about a concept in class, go home and try it and then return to the following class with your questions. Continuing education classes provide a great way to learn without the stress of time-consuming, graded course work.

Bulletin Boards

As discussed in Lesson 2, computer bulletin boards provide users whose computers have modems with a way of exchanging information and posting questions. For information about bulletin boards in your area, contact your retailer or local user group. For more information on bulletin boards, see the MIS:Press book, *Using Computer Bulletin Boards*, 2e, by John Hedtke.

Internet and the World Wide Web

There are over 2 millions documents on the Internet that cover just about every topic that you can imagine. If you have a specific question, you can probably find answers on the net. In addition, by joining a mailing list or a newsgroup, you can stay abreast with the latest news about your topic of interest. For more information on the Internet, refer to the MIS: Press books, *Welcome to... The Internet*, 2e, by Tom Badgett, and *Internet in Plain English*, by Bryan Pfaffenberger.

In addition, you may be able to find answers using online services such as Prodigy, CompuServe, or America Online.

Putting It All Together

If you are having trouble with your computer's hardware, or difficulty running a specific program, or you just don't know how to get started, relax. There are many sources you can turn to for help. Remember, every computer user was once a new user. Don't be afraid to ask questions. You'll be surprised how many users are willing to help.

Glossary

active-matrix display	A monitor that uses small microprocessors to manage (control) pixels in a small region (a matrix of pixels) on the screen—improving the monitor's picture quality.
air vents	Holes in the computer's monitor and most printers that allow potentially harmful hot air to escape.
analog signal	A wave-like signal. Normally, sound is represented as an analog wave. The computer, however, must store a digital representation of the sound.
application software	A computer program that performs a specific task such as word processing.
Archie	A software program that helps users locate information on the Internet.
ASCII file	A file that contains only characters and digits. A word processing document, for example, contains hidden formatting characters and as such, is not an ASCII file.
AUTOEXEC.BAT	A file containing a list of command names you want DOS to execute automatically each time it starts.

automated backup | An operation that automatically backs up specific files at a predefined time without user intervention.

backups | A set of disks containing duplicate copies of your files.

baud rate | The number of bits (binary digits) the computer sends per second. The higher the baud rate, the greater the amount of information exchanged per second.

BIOS | An abbreviation for *basic input and output system*, BIOS lets the computer communicate with input and output devices such as its screen, keyboard, and disk.

booting | The process of starting up your computer.

bursting | The process of tearing off the proper tractor-feed from a sheet of paper.

bus | A collection of wires over which the computer sends information.

bus mouse | A mouse that connects to your PC using an expansion slot card that plugs into your PCs bus as opposed to using a serial port.

byte | A unit of information that corresponds to a character of the information.

CAD | An abbreviation for *computer-aided design*. CAD software helps engineers and drafters create and change complex designs using a computer screen and mouse.

card | Another term for interface card.

cascade | The process of connecting one device to a SCSI adapter and then connecting a second device to that device and a third device to the second. A SCSI card lets you connect up to seven devices.

CD-burner | A hardware device that lets users create their own CD-ROM disks.

CD-R | An abbreviation for *compact disk recordable*.

CD-ROM	An abbreviation for *compact disk read-only memory*. A CD-ROM disk is a storage mechanism whose contents the computer can read but not change. A CD-ROM disk can store tremendous amounts of data, over 600Mb.
conventional memory	PC memory from 0 to 640Kb.
CPU	An abbreviation for *central processing unit*. The computer's microprocessor.
clicking	The process of aiming the mouse pointer at a screen object, pressing, and releasing the mouse select button.
clip art	Pictures and other graphic images you can place unchanged in a report, newsletter, or other document.
clone or compatible	A computer that can freely exchange software (and possibly hardware parts) with another computer.
CMOS	An abbreviation for *complementary metal oxide semiconductor*. Many computers use a battery-powered CMOS memory to remember the system configuration and date and time.
CMYK	An abbreviation for *cyan, yellow, magenta, and black* —the four colors used to print color images.
cold boot	The process of turning on your PC's power and starting the operating system.
COMMAND.COM	Also known as the command processor, this special DOS command is automatically run each time DOS starts. It also contains internal DOS commands such as CLS, DATE, and TIME.
command line	The information typed at the DOS prompt to execute a command. The command contains a command name and possibly other information such as a file name.
CONFIG.SYS	A file containing single line entries that tell DOS how you want to configure memory, as well as the number of files you want DOS to let you open at one time.

CPS   An abbreviation for *characters per second*, a unit of measure used to describe printer speed.

CRT   An abbreviation for *cathode ray tube*, a term often used for the screen display.

cursor movement keys   The set of keys that let you move the cursor up, down, right, or left throughout your document.

cylinder   For the purpose of this book, a cylinder is a track on a hard disk.

database   An organized collection of information.

data communication   A set of values, such as the amount of information
parameters   sent per message, that two computers must agree upon before they can successfully communicate.

data compression   Software and hardware techniques that reduce the amount of data needed to represent information. To reduce the amount of data sent across phone lines, the sending modem might compress data and the receiving modem would decompress it.

database software   A computer program that helps you store, sort, print, and retrieve information.

demodulating   The process of converting an analog signal to a digital signal the PC understands.

density   A measure of how much information a disk can store in a fixed area. As disk technology has improved, double-density and quad-density disks are able to fit twice as much and four times as much information in a fixed area as the PC's original floppy disk.

desktop publishing   The creation and printing of professional quality reports and newsletters using a personal computer.

device chain   The process of connecting one device to a SCSI adaptor, a second device to that device and so on, creating a chain of devices. You can connect up to 7 devices to a SCSI adaptor.

device driver	Special software that lets the operating system (DOS) or Windows use a hardware device such as a mouse.
dialog box	A framed region on your screen that allows an exchange of information between the user and the program, providing messages regarding specific actions, or requesting further information from the user.
digital signal	A signal represented using ones and zeros.
directory	A list of related files. Directories help organize your disk by grouping related files, just as you might place related files in the same filing cabinet drawer.
disk cartridge	A floppy disk-like cartridge (but larger) with the storage capacity of a hard disk
disk compression software	Software that enables users to increase the size of their disks by compressing the information in a unique format that consumes less disk space.
disk controller	A circuit board that oversees and controls disk operations.
disk crash	A destruction of the information on your disk, usually occurring when the computer's read/write head comes in contact with another surface, and therefore grinds off its protective coating.
disk formatting	The process of preparing a disk for use for a specific operating system, such as DOS.
disk parking	The process of moving your a hard disk's read/write heads over a safe location on the disk so you can move the PC without the risk of a disk head crash.
disk partition	A section of a hard disk that corresponds to a drive letter such as C and D. Each hard disk can be divided into several different sections, allowing users to utilize the entire disk's storage capacity, and to divide their disk into two or more logical drives.
disk partitioning	The process of dividing a single physical hard disk into one or more logical drives.

disk utility	A software program that helps you recover erased or damaged files, or a damaged disk.
docking station	A hardware chassis into which you can plug your notebook computer. A docking station may provide a screen, keyboard, CD-ROM, and sound card which in turn the notebook's processor can access.
DOS	An abbreviation for *disk operating system*. DOS is the most commonly used PC operating system.
DOS prompt	The message DOS displays when it is ready for you to type your next command. The DOS prompt typically contains the current disk drive letter and possibly the current directory, such as:
	`C:\>`
dot pitch	The distance, in millimeters between a monitor's successive red, green, or blue phosphors.
double-clicking	The process of aiming the mouse pointer at a screen object and quickly pressing and releasing the mouse select button twice. Many programs require you to double-click the mouse on an object to select it.
download	The process of copying a file from a remote computer.
DPI	An abbreviation for *dots per inch*, a unit of measure used to describe printer resolution.
dual-floppy drive	A floppy disk drive that combines a 3.5-inch and 5.25-inch floppy drive into a single unit that consumes only a single drive bay.
e-mail	An abbreviation for *electronic mail*. Using e-mail, network users can quickly exchange memos and other documents with one another.
ergonomic keyboard	A keyboard specifically designed to reduce physical strain on your hands and wrists.
executable program	Any computer program—such as your word processor, spreadsheet, or even Microsoft Windows.

expanded memory	A memory expansion technique that combines hardware and software to let 8088-based PCs access more than 1Mb of memory. Although it was initially developed for the 8088, all PCs can use expanded memory.
expansion slots	Slots within your computer's chassis into which you can insert a card such as a modem.
extended memory	Memory above 1Mb in 286, 386, or 486 machines.
extended warranty	A warranty sold to you by a computer store that extends the basic warranty provided with your computer.
external command	A larger DOS command whose instructions DOS stores in a file on disk. Before DOS can execute an external command, DOS must load the command from disk into memory.
external hard drive	A hard drive you can connect and disconnect from your computer.
external modem	A modem that resides outside of the PC that typically connects to a serial port.
external tape backup unit	A device which you can move from one computer to another to back up multiple systems.
facsimile machine	A copy-machine-like device that copies a page and transmits the contents across phone lines to a receiving fax machine which in turn prints the page.
field	An entry within a database record, such as an employee's name.
file	A named collection of information stored on a disk.
file compression	The use of special software to reduce the amount of storage space a file requires. Using file compression, backup software may be able to store 200Mb of data onto a 120Mb tape.
file extension	The three character portion of a filename that describes the file's type, such as MEM for a memo, DOC for a document, or RPT for a report.

File Manager	A special program provided with Windows that helps you manage files on your disk by copying, renaming, moving, printing, or even deleting the files.
formatting	The process of preparing a magnetic tape for use.
FTP	An abbreviation for *file transfer protocol*, the software that controls most file transfers across the Internet.
function key	A key labeled F1 through F15 to which a software program can associate a specific function such as printing or spell checking the current document.
Gb	An abbreviation for *gigabyte*. One Gb is approximately one billion bytes.
Gopher	A menu-based program that helps user's locate information across the Internet.
graphical interface	The picture-based screen within Windows that allows the user to see and manipulate graphic objects that correspond to programs and documents.
graphics mode	A video display mode in which the monitor can display both text and pictures.
grayscale image	A black and white representation of a color image whereby different colors are represented using different shades of grey.
hackers	Computer users who intentionally and often maliciously try to break into a computer system.
hard copy	A paper printout from a computer.
hardware	The computer's physical parts, such as the system unit, keyboard, monitor, as well as the cables that connect them.
hi-res mouse	A mouse capable of responding to precise movements. Hi-res mice are useful for creating detailed computer aided drawings.
homepage	The primary document at a World Wide Web site.

HTML	An abbreviation for *hypertext markup language*—the text editing symbols you use to create a hypertext, Web document.
hyperlink document	A document that contains links to other documents that reside across the World Wide Web.
Hz	An abbreviation for *hertz* that is the number of cycles per second. Microprocessor clock speeds are measured in hertz. The more hertz, the faster the clock.
icon	A graphic image that represents an object such as a program or printer.
installation program	A program that helps you install software from floppy disks onto your hard disk.
integrated software	Software that provides multiple capabilities such as word processing, database, and spreadsheet operations.
interface card	The hardware board containing a device port that you place inside your system unit that lets you attach a device to your computer.
interlaced monitor	A video monitor that displays images by refreshing every other line of the monitor's display with each vertical refresh operation.
internal command	A small command whose instructions DOS keeps in memory at all times.
internal modem	A modem whose electronics reside on a hardware card you insert into your PC.
Internet	An acronym for *inter-network*. The Internet is network of computer networks, consisting of over 30,000 computer networks across 130 countries.
internet provider	A company, who, for a fee, will let you dial into their Internet connection using your PC and a modem.
interrupt request	A signal from a device such as a sound card to the CPU that notifies the CPU that the device needs to be serviced. Each device must have a unique interrupt request line.

407

IP switches	Small switches found on a hardware device or interface card.
IRQ	An abbreviation for *interrupt request*. An electronic signal from a device to the CPU that tells the CPU the device needs servicing.
joystick	A small hand-held device a user can use to interact with many game programs.
Kb	An abbreviation for *kilobyte*. One Kb is 1,024 bytes.
Kb	With respect to modems and data communications, Kb is an abbreviation for *kilobaud*. A 14.4Kb modem, for example, transfers 14,746 (14.4 x 1024) bits per second.
keyboard combination	Two or more keys depressed at the same time. For example, to press the Ctrl-C keyboard combination, you would hold down the Ctrl key and type C.
keyboard pad	A small sponge-like pad that you place in front of your keyboard to elevate your wrists and reduce wrist strain.
LAN	An abbreviation for a *local area network*, typically a network whose computers are all contained within the same, or adjacent buildings.
landing zone	A special location on a hard disk upon which the drive's read/write heads actually come to rest when you park the drive.
laptop computer	A computer with battery power, that you can unfold and work with on your lap. A laptop computer may weigh from 10- to 20-pounds.
LCD	An abbreviation for *liquid crystal display*. Many laptop computers use an LCD monitor due to compact electronics.
license agreement	A written agreement provided by a software developer that defines the user's rights to the software. Use of the software implies the user's acceptance of the agreements terms.

local bus video	A video card that communicates directly with the CPU using the fast (local) bus normally used by the CPU to access the computer's electronic memory.
mailing list	A collection of e-mail addresses that correspond to users who are interested in exchanging information about a specific topic.
mail merge	The process of combining database entries with a word processing document to create a custom letter.
major version number	The primary number used to identify the version of a software program. In the case of DOS 6.2, for example, the primary version number is 6.
math coprocessor	A specialized microprocessor that can improve your system performance for programs that perform complex math operations.
maximizing	The process of enlarging a program window to full screen.
Mb	An abbreviation for *megabyte*. One Mb is approximately one million bytes.
mechanical mouse	A traditional mouse that moves the mouse pointer by spinning a rubber trackball.
memory address	A value that identifies a location in your PC's memory. Devices use unique memory locations to communicate with the CPU.
memory board	A hardware expansion slot card that contains RAM chips. Many older (286- and 386-based) systems use memory cards. Newer systems use SIMMs.
memory effect	A physical characteristic of rechargeable batteries that causes them to lose storage capacity if they are recharged while they still have a charge.
memory management software	Software that moves memory-resident programs in order to free up memory for your program use.
memory-resident screen saver	A program which saves your screen, avoiding the potential of burning an unchanged image into the screen.

memory resident software	A DOS-based program that remains present in your computer's memory. Many device drivers use memory resident software.
menu	A list from which the user can select a specific option using their keyboard or mouse.
MHz	An abbreviation for *megahertz* or millions of cycles per second.
micro-processor	The computer's electronic brain that oversees every operation the computer performs.
MIDI	An acronym for *musical instrument device interface* that lets you connect electronic instruments to your personal computer.
minimizing	The process of hiding the program's window, or setting it aside by returning it back to an icon.
minor version number	The number used to identify the version of a software upgrade. In the case of DOS 6.2, for example, the minor version number is 2.
modulating	The process of converting a digital signal into an analog signal for transmission over phone lines.
Mosaic	A graphical software program that lets users access information across the World Wide Web.
motherboard	Your computer's primary electronic card that houses the CPU and random access memory (RAM).
mouse select button	The mouse button you click (or double-click) to perform an operation within Windows.
mouse trackball	The small ball underneath the mouse that detects (tracks) the mouse movement across the surface of your desk.
mouse trails	The use of multiple graphic mouse pointers that appear to chase the mouse pointer across the screen. Mouse trails highlight the mouse pointer's movement across the screen.

mouse trap	A small plastic holder in which you can place your mouse when it is not in use. Most mouse traps connect to your monitor.
MPC	An abbreviation for *Multimedia Product Council*, whose logo helps you determine compatible multimedia hardware and software.
multimedia	The combination of text, sound, and video to present information in a meaningful way.
multipart form	A form that consists of two or more pages that contain the same information. Using an impact printer, you can print data to each page.
multiprocessor	A computer that uses more than one CPU.
multi-sync monitor	A monitor capable of recognizing multiple electronic signals such as those used by a VGA or EGA.
multitasking	The ability to run two or more programs at the same time.
network administrator	The individual responsible for setting up and maintaining a computer network. The network administrator is a privileged user who has complete access to files across the network.
newsgroup	An electronic bulletin board that users across the Internet can read or post messages to.
notebook computer	A small laptop computer that, when closed, is about the size of a notebook. Notebook computers may weigh from 6- to 10-pounds.
numeric keypad	The set of number keys at the far right of the keyboard that resembles a 10-key adding machine.
on-line service	A service, that, for a cost, users can dial into using their PC and modem to access a wide variety of services, such as the ability to send and receive e-mail, access up-to-the-minute news, weather, and stock prices, and much more.

operating system

A special software program your computer runs when it first starts. The operating system, in turn, lets you use devices such as your printer, store information on disk, and run other programs.

optical character recognition (OCR)

Software that lets you scan a page of text and then extract the text to a word processing file.

optical mouse

A mouse that uses a special reflective pad that moves the mouse pointer by optically (based on light reflections on the pad) tracking its movement.

overstriking

A keystroke that replaces or overwrites the character that immediately follows the cursor.

parallel device

A device that communicates with the computer by sending or receiving 8-bits of data (a byte) over 8 wires. A parallel ribbon cable, for example, contains 25 wires.

passive-matrix display

A monitor that uses a single microprocessor to manage all the pixels on the entire screen. Passive matrix displays have lower picture quality than their more expensive active matrix counterparts.

PC

A personal computer.

PCMCIA card

A credit card sized electronic card that contains the electronics for a specific device such as a modem or network card. PCMCIA cards provide a way to expand a notebook PC's hardware.

peripheral

Any device other than the keyboard and screen that you attach to your computer (such as a printer, modem, mouse, etc.).

photo CD

A CD-ROM disk that contains photographic images in an electronic format that a user can integrate into a document.

photo editing

The use of computer software to edit an image stored in an electronic format on disk. Photo editing might include color correction, image elimination, or image combination.

pica	A standard typewriter character size that compounds to ten characters per inch.
PIM	An abbreviation for personal information management. PIM software lets you organize the essential information you use to manage your appointments, schedules, and so on.
pixel	A picture element or dot that the monitor can turn on or off, or display in a unique color, which, when combined with other pixels, creates a graphics image.
plug-and-play hardware	Hardware cards that contain a chip that identifies the device to the computer. In this way, the operating system can determine the hardware card's type and then install the correct software.
point	A unit of measure used to describe the size of a font. A point is equal to 1/72 of an inch.
point and shoot	Another term for positioning and then clicking the mouse select button.
port	A connector on the back of your system unit to which you attach a printer, monitor, or other hardware device.
portable computer	A computer whose system unit, screen display, and keyboard you can easily move from one location to another. A portable computer may weigh from 20 to 25 pounds, and is not battery-powered.
POST	An abbreviation for *power-on self-test*, the built-in diagnostic test that the system unit runs each time you turn on your computer.
PostScript	A printer programming language.
power cycling	The process of turning off and on your computer's power.
PPM	An abbreviation for *pages per minute*, a unit of measure used to describe laser printer speed.

PPP	An abbreviation for *point-to-point protocol*. A PPP-based Internet account lets you access the Internet from within Windows.
preformatted tape	A magnetic tape that is already formatted for immediate use by your tape drive.
printer driver	Software that allows an application program to use your printer.
protected mode	A special mode of operation for which the processor protects (prevents) one program from interfering with another. Windows 95 supports protected mode processing while DOS does not.
protocol	A set of rules that govern a specific operation, such as a file transfer.
QWERTY	A keyboard layout for which the top row of letters begin with the letters Q through Y.
RAM	An abbreviation for *random access memory*, the computer's electronic memory.
refresh rate	The speed at which a monitor updates (refreshes) the red, green, and blue phosphors that create a screen image. The faster the refresh rate, the less monitors flicker.
resolution	The number of pixels the monitor can use to display an image. The higher the resolution, the sharper the image quality.
RGB	An abbreviation for the colors *Red*, *Green*, and *Blue*. The MCGA and CGA create additional colors by combining different combinations of red, green, and blue.
ribbon cable	A thin (flat) cable that contains several wires. A parallel ribbon cable, for example, contains 25 wires.
rider	An insurance coverage that "rides with" an item from one location to another. You may need rider coverage to protect a laptop computer.

root directory	A special directory with which all disks start and from which each directory you create grows. The root directory is so named because your other directories grow from root much like branches of a tree.
ROM	An abbreviation for *read-only memory*, the computer's pre-programmed memory.
scanner	A hardware device which allows you to quickly make electronic copies of photographs and text.
screen burn-in	The process of permanently damaging a monitor's phosphors so that it displays the same image forever.
SCSI	An abbreviation for *small computer system interconnect*. The SCSI standard provides a way for users to connect different hardware devices, such as a disk drive or CD-ROM, to their PC.
SCSI address	A value from 0 through 7 that uniquely identifies a device within the SCSI chain.
SCSI terminator	A special hardware connector that indicates the end of a SCSI-device chain.
serial device	A device that communicates with the computer one bit at a time over a single wire. Most mouse devices, for example, are serial devices.
serial mouse	A mouse that connects to the PC using a serial port such as COM1.
server	A network computer to which users can connect to receive special services such as file sharing or resource sharing.
shareware	Software that is a bit reduced in capabilities (compared to expensive commercial software) that developers often let you try at a very reduced fee.
shells	A special program from within which the user runs other programs. Shell programs are often menu driven and easy to use.

SIMMs

An abbreviation for *single inline memory module*—a small hardware module that contains multiple RAM chips.

single-speed drive

A CD-ROM drive that transfers data at 150,000 bytes per second (150 Kbs).

SLIP

An abbreviation for *serial line Internet protocol*. SLIP-based Internet accounts let you access the Internet from within Windows.

software

Computer programs written to perform specific tasks, such as a word processor or spreadsheet.

software piracy

Loading and using and/or duplicating software which you don't own.

software suite

A collection of two or more key software programs such as a word processor, spreadsheet, and a database bundled together and sold as a single product.

sound board

A hardware board that lets your computer play high quality sounds.

spreadsheet

A computer program that automates an accountant's worksheet letting you track budgets, or other values, and perform "What If" forecasting.

Standard Internet account

A text- or menu-based Internet account.

subdirectory

A directory that appears within another directory.

surfing the net

Lingo for connecting to and traversing the Internet for data.

surge suppressor

A hardware device that sits between your wall plug and computer equipment that protects the equipment from damaging electrical bursts.

synthesizer

An electronic device that produces (synthesizes) sounds. Sound cards for example can produce sounds that mimic a piano, guitar, and so on.

system configuration

The software and hardware settings specific to a PC.

system disk

A disk containing the operating system software.

standard cable	A cable that wraps (bundles) its wires into a single cable.
telecommunications	The process of exchanging information between computers over telephone lines.
text mode	A video display mode in which the monitor displays letters, numbers, and punctuation symbols.
the Net	A nickname for the Internet.
toggle key	A key, that when pressed, turns a function such as CapsLock or NumLock on or off based on the function's current setting.
toner	The powder-like ink used by a laser printer or copy machine.
toolbar	A row of icons that appears near the top of the program's window. Each icon corresponds to a specific operation.
transfer rate	The speed, in megabytes per second, at which a disk can transfer information to or from the computer's memory.
troubleshooting	The process of determining the cause of a hardware or software error.
TSR	An abbreviation for *terminate-stay resident software*—another name for memory resident software.
upper memory	The 384Kb memory region between 640Kb and 1Mb.
UPS	An abbreviation for *uninterruptible power supply*, it is a device into which you plug your computer's hardware. Should your office lose its power, the UPS provides power to your computer for up to 15 minutes.
VDT	An abbreviation for *video display terminal*, a term often used for the screen display.
video adapter	An electronic circuit board within the system unit to which you attach the monitor that controls the text and graphics capabilities.

virus

A software program written intentionally to disrupt and/or destroy the information contained on your disk, often rendering your computer unusable.

WAN

An abbreviation for *wide area network*—a computer network whose computers may be dispersed across a city, state, country, or even the world.

warm boot

The process of restarting the operating system without cycling the PC's power. Normally by pressing the Ctrl-Alt-Del keyboard combination.

Web browser

Special software that lets a user display and traverse hyperlinked documents across the Web.

window

A framed region on your screen within which a program can run.

write-protected disk

A disk whose contents can be read by a disk drive, but cannot be changed or erased.

word processor

A computer program that helps you create, change, format, and print documents such as letters, memos or reports.

workgroup

Two or more users that collaborate on the same project.

work space

The area you set aside at which you will work with the computer or perform other work-related tasks.

workstation

A PC from which the user can log into the network. A workstation may have its own disk drives and printer, or it may not have either.

World Wide Web

A collection of hundreds of thousands of hyperlinked documents dispersed across the Internet. The Web gets its name from the interconnected documents that let users move quickly from one document to another.

Index